The Quintessential Cat

By R P Thrall
1876

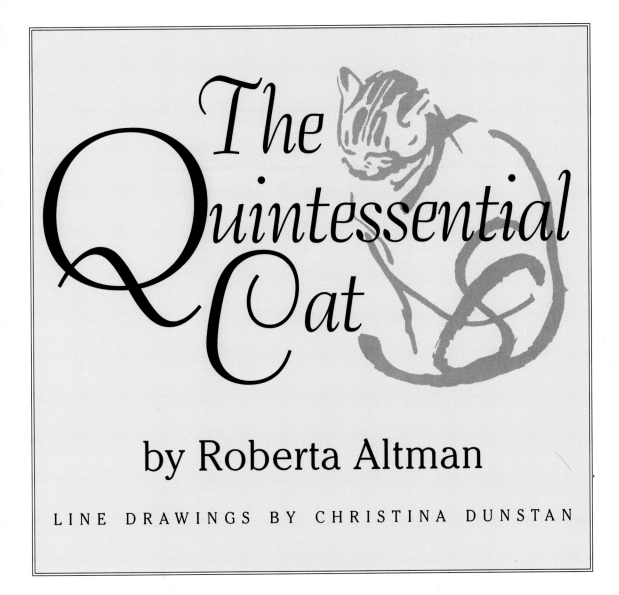

The Quintessential Cat

by Roberta Altman

LINE DRAWINGS BY CHRISTINA DUNSTAN

MACMILLAN • USA

MACMILLAN
A Prentice Hall Macmillan Company
15 Columbus Circle
New York, NY 10023

Library of Congress Cataloging-in-Publication Data

Altman, Roberta.
The quintessential cat / Roberta Altman.
p.   cm.
Includes bibliographical references and index.
ISBN 0-671-85008-3 :
1. Cats—Encyclopedias.   I. Title.
SF442.2.A38   1994
599.74′428—dc20   94-14095
CIP

Designed by Irving Perkins Associates

Manufactured in the United States of America

10 9 8 7 6 5 4 3 2 1

Minnie from the Outskirts of the Village, *painted in 1876 by R. P. Thrall.* (COURTESY OF THE SHELBURNE MUSEUM, SHELBURNE, VERMONT. PHOTOGRAPH BY KEN BURRIS.)

"The Naming of Cats" from *Old Possum's Book of Practical Cats,* © 1939 by T.S. Eliot and renewed 1967 by Esme Valerie Eliot. Reprinted by permission of Harcourt Brace & Company.

ACKNOWLEDGMENTS

So many people were purr-fectly wonderful in the help and encouragement they gave me along with their enthusiasm for *The Quintessential Cat.* Friends regaled me with their own cat tales—adventures their cats had had or adventures they'd "heard" about. Special thanks to Elena and artist Will Barnet; Marilyn Dipboye of Cat Collectors; researchers Bonny Rifkin and Jeffrey Golick, without whom the "Quint" in *The Quintessential Cat* would probably have had to be removed; Jim Pratfield and photographer Paul Coughlin of Petography, Inc., who took the flattering picture of Miel . . . and me; my agent, Joe Vallely who is surely one hillbilly cat; and Deirdre Mullane, my editor who never pawsed in her efforts to make this book the best darn cat book there ever was (and had some fun doing it).

For
Molly and Miel,
Dot and Spot,
Max and Charlie,
without whom this volume could not
have been written.

Miel was an excellent editor—if I wrote something
he didn't like, he simply ate it.

Contents

Foreword

The phrase "curiosity killed the cat" is as much a part of the language as "have a nice day," but Andy Rooney would say, "Why did curiosity kill the cat—why not the cat's owner?" This and many other questions about pets of the feline purrsuasion remain largely unanswered despite the growing number of books now available on this fascinating subject. Although I readily admit to having little curiosity about the infamous curious cat, I did harbor a few question marks pertaining to my favorite pets, despite my prodigious knowledge on the subject. I have owned and bred cats for some thirty-odd years and I still pick up a new fact or two from time to time . . . but now my cup runneth over! Here is a collection of cat facts, stories, pictures, legends and more to delight every cat fancier. Ms. Altman has gathered a fascinating array of "cat-mobilia" organized in an easy A-to-Z format for rapid reference or hours of delightful reading. Here you will find descriptions of various breeds, origins of old legends, facts on famous cats, cats in poetry, cats in literature, cats in cartoons, and cats in movies. There are fifty-seven million homes in America that include at least one cat, indicating a growing need for more and more information on these fabulous felines, and this book is the purr-fect place to start.

ALISON STEELE

Cat Drawing *by Saul Steinberg, pen and ink on paper, 1964.* (COURTESY OF WILLIAMS COLLEGE MUSEUM OF ART, BEQUEST OF LAWRENCE H. BLOEDEL, CLASS OF 1923.)

Alison Steele, in addition to being a passionate cat lover, is known as "The Nightbird," the dean of America's female Radio Disc Jockeys. She is currently on WXRK New York, the home of Howard Stern, from two until six A.M. She's been seen on local and national television, appears in many commercials, and contributes articles to a variety of publications on both music and cats. She is also the owner of the cat boutique, Just Cats, in New York City.

Introduction

I first realized that a cat encyclopedia was needed when I looked up "Garfield" (and if you don't know who he is put this book right back on the shelf) in several dictionaries—including the unabridged Random House dictionary of the English language, which has over two thousand pages—and couldn't find him. James Garfield the president was listed but not Garfield the cat! Without making any judgment calls, I would say that more people are familiar with Garfield the cat than Garfield the president of the United States.

So I knew that this book definitely filled a gap. When one friend said, "Another cat book?" My first response was, "There can never be too many cat books." Then I explained that after looking through countless cat books on countless shelves, I could find none that was what my fantasy cat book would be. I wanted a cat book that would have it all—from proverbs, superstitions, and fables, to cats in movies, music, and literature, to cat breeds and behavior, and so on. It would be a book that I would have to have in *my* personal library, a book that you could pick up anytime, open to any page, and find interesting or amusing information on cats; a book that would elicit more than an occasional "Oh my goodness" and a call to a fellow cat lover to say, "Did you know that . . .?"

My last book was *The Cancer Dictionary*—not exactly what you'd call a light project. So working on *The Quintessential Cat* was even more of a delight. I found funny stories, heartwarming stories, and more than one story that brought tears rolling down my cheeks (a little embarrassing when sitting in the main room of the New York Public Library). For example, in the story about a cat who woke up a family when the house caught on fire, the cat saved the family but perished in the blaze. The reverse has occurred as well. During the devastating fires on the West Coast in the fall of 1993, the British film director Duncan Gibbons tried to rescue a stray cat near the house he was renting. Neither survived.

My own cats—Molly and Miel—have been a source of tremendous pleasure. They are not only a comfort but a constant source of amusement. Watching these two cats, each with its own unique personality, is endlessly fascinating. (You will come across them occasionally in these pages.) They do manage to get their way most of the time. And they know it.

Of Jeoffry, My Cat

For I will consider my Cat Jeoffry.
For he is the servant of the Living God duly and daily serving him.
For at the first glance of the glory of God in the East he worships in his way.
For is this done by wreathing his body seven times round with elegant quickness.
For then he leaps up to catch the musk, wch is the blessing of God upon his prayer.
For he rolls upon prank to work it in.
For having done duty and received blessing he begins to consider himself.
For this he performs in ten degrees.
For first he looks upon his fore-paws to see if they are clean.
For secondly he kicks up behind to clear away there.
For thirdly he works it upon stretch with the forepaws extended.
For fourthly he sharpens his paws by wood.
For fifthly he washes himself.
For sixthly he rolls upon wash.
For Seventhly he fleas himself, that he may not be interrupted upon the beat.
For Eighthly he rubs himself against a post.
For Ninthly he looks up for his instructions.
For Tenthly he goes in quest of food.
For having consider'd God and himself he will consider his neighbour.
For if he meets another cat he will kiss her in kindness.
For when he takes his prey he plays with it to give it a chance.
For one mouse in seven escapes by his dallying.
For when his day's work is done his business more properly begins.
For he keeps the Lord's watch in the night against the adversary.
For he counteracts the powers of darkness by his electrical skin & glaring eyes.
For he counteracts the Devil, who is death, by brisking about the life.
For in his morning orisons he loves the sun and the sun loves him.
For his is of the tribe of Tiger.
For the cherub Cat is a term of the Angel Tiger.
For he has the subtlety and hissing of a serpent, which in goodness he suppresses.
For he will not do destruction, if he is well-fed, neither will he spit without provocation.
For he purrs in thankfulness, when God tells him he's a good Cat.
For he is an instrument for the children to learn benevolence upon.
For every house is incompleat without him & a blessing is lacking in the spirit.
For the Lord commanded Moses concerning the cats at the departure of the Children of
    Israel from Egypt.
For every family had one cat at least in the bag.
For the English Cats are the best in Europe.
For he is the cleanest in the use of his fore-paws of any quadrupede.
For the dexterity of his defence is an instance of the love of God to him exceedingly.
For he is the quickest to his mark of any creature.
For he is tenacious of his point.
For he is a mixture of gravity and waggery.

For he knows that God is his Saviour.
For there is nothing sweeter than his peace when at rest.
For there is nothing brisker than his life when in motion.
For he is of the Lord's poor and so indeed is he called by benevolence perpetually—
    Poor Jeoffry! poor Jeoffry! the rat has bit thy throat.
For I bless the name of the Lord Jesus that Jeoffry is better.
For the divine spirit comes about his body to sustain it in compleat cat.
For his tongue is exceeding pure so that it has in purity what it wants in musick.
For he is docile and can learn certain things.
For he can set up with gravity which is patience upon approbation.
For he can fetch and carry, which is patience in employment.
For he can jump over a stick which is patience upon proof positive.
For he can spraggle upon waggle at the word of command.
For he can jump from an eminence into his master's bosom.
For he can catch the cork and toss it again.
For he is hated by the hypocrite and miser.
For the former is afraid of detection.
For the latter refuses the charge.
For he camels his back to bear the first notion of business.
For he is good to think on, if a man would express himself neatly.
For he made a great figure in Egypt for his signal services.
For he killed the Icneumon-rat very pernicious by land.
For his ears are so acute that they sting again.
For from this proceeds the passing quickness of his attention.
For by stroaking of him I have found out electricity.
For I perceived God's light about him both wax and fire.
For the Electrical fire is the spiritual substance, which God sends from heaven to sustain
    the bodies both of man and beast.
For God has blessed him in the variety of his movements.
For, tho he cannot fly, he is an excellent clamberer.
For his motions upon the face of the earth are more than any other quadrupede.
For he can tread to all the measures upon the musick.
For he can swim for life.
For he can creep.

CHRISTOPHER SMART, English poet (1722–1771)

𝒜byssinian ⌒ There are several theories as to the origin of the Abyssinian, one of the oldest known breeds of cat. Some believe Abys are descended from cats worshiped in Egypt more than four thousand years ago. Another theory is that the Abyssinian originated on the coast of the Indian Ocean and parts of Southeast Asia. And yet another theory has British soldiers taking Abys from North Africa, where they originated, to England during the late 1860s. The first Aby to reach England was named Zula and was imported by Mrs. Barrett-Lennard in 1868. By 1882 they were recognized as a separate breed in England. In the early twentieth century, authorities declared that Abys were the result of chance matings rather than planned breeding. They were then called "ticks," "British ticks," and "bunny cats."

Abys first came to the United States in the early 1900s. They resided in Oradell, New Jersey, with their owner, Jane Cathcart, and were shown in Boston in 1909. The next appearance of the Abyssinians in the United States was in the 1930s, when a great number were imported. The first reported litter born in America was in 1935.

An Abyssinian has a muscular body, arched neck, large ears, and almond-shaped eyes. It comes in a variety of shades of ivory, brown, and red. Because Abys tend to have small litters, they are one of the most expensive breeds of cats.

Abyssinians are extremely active, intelligent, busy, and friendly, are people-oriented, and make wonderful companions. This is Grand Champion Byblos Djibouti. (PHOTOGRAPH © 1993 CHANAN. PHOTOGRAPH COURTESY SUZANNE BOROWICZ, REGIONAL DIRECTOR FOR ACCA, BYBLOS ABYSSINIANS.)

PERSONALITY: Abyssinians are very alert and intelligent. They have small, sweet voices often referred to as "bell-like." They are lovable and loyal. They are one of the most popular breeds and make wonderful pets.

Actors and Others for Animals ～

This nonprofit organization was founded in 1971 by Diana and Richard Basehart in North Hollywood, California. The organization subsidizes the spaying and neutering of thousands of animals a year, as well as other surgeries for pets of the elderly, poor, and handicapped. It also runs a humane-education program to teach children about the care of pets. Among its celebrity supporters are Loretta Swit, Jo Anne Worley, Loni Anderson, Sally Struthers, Mariette Hartley, Hal Linden, Jack Klugman, Cindy Williams, Ricky Schroder, Bea Arthur, and Jack Jones. Contact Actors and Others for Animals at 5510 Cahuenga Blvd., CA 91601; 818/985-6263.

Adamson, Lydia ～

Like Lillian Jackson Braun, the pseudonymous mystery writer Lydia Adamson has composed a series of thrillers featuring an ailerophile amateur sleuth, in which cats play prominent roles in the setting up and unraveling of each suspenseful tale. In the books, the fortyish Alice Nestleton, would-be actress, cat-sitter, and part-time consultant to the NYPD, lives with her own two cats Bushy, a Maine coon cat, and Pancho, a somewhat more reticent stray. As Alice pursues her precarious careers, she often finds herself drawn into murder and mayhem, earning a reputation as the "Cat Woman" as she tracks down the suspects. In *A Cat in the Manger*, for example, Alice is cat-sitting eight lovely Himalayans on a beautiful Long Island estate when she stumbles across a corpse; in *A Cat in a Glass House*, the disappearance of a gorgeous red

tabby "kitchen cat" provides the missing clue to an intrigue involving Chinese cuisine, contraband smuggling, and eastern philosophy; and in *A Cat in Wolf's Clothing*, seventeen murder victims are all discovered to be cat-owners and a cat toy is left at each murder scene.

The complete Alice Nestleton cat capers are: *A Cat in the Manger, A Cat of a Different Color, A Cat in Wolf's Clothing, A Cat by Any Other Name, A Cat in the Wings, A Cat with a Fiddle,* and *A Cat with No Regrets.*

See also LILLIAN JACKSON BRAUN.

Advertising ～

Cats have been used more than any other animal for advertising and publicity in the media. They first appeared in magazine ads as long ago as the late nineteenth century, when they were used for a number of different products, including medicine and soap. Cats could also be found on old sheet music, product labels, posters, signs, magazine covers, children's

Cats have been a popular subject of greeting cards, as on this turn-of-the-century Valentine.

Cats have often been used by artists in advertising and the media. This lithograph by Edward Penfield appeared on the cover of Harper's. (COURTESY OF THE METROPOLITAN MUSEUM OF ART, MUSEUM ACCESSION, 1957.)

toys, bottles, and so on. Over the years cats have been used to endorse a large number of products, including household fluids, sewing thread, newspapers, magazines, cigars, cigarettes, alcohol, calendars, various foods, cat food (of course), and so on. In the late 1800s, advertising cards were frequently distributed by stores featuring cats endorsing some product. Many people would collect these colored, beautifully illustrated cards. At the turn of the century, advertising buttons became a popular way to promote products and many were given away.

In Japan, Satoru Tsuda came up with the idea of using trained cats in TV commercials. When he advertised for stray cats hundreds were dropped at his door. He chose four and spent long hours training them to do several tricks, including

standing on their hind legs, holding poses for the camera, and wearing "clothes" created just for them—outfits that cost over five hundred dollars each. And while many of his colleagues scoffed, his efforts paid off. The cats were an instant hit with advertisers, who put them in TV commercials, magazine ads, and billboards; and entrepreneurs put the cat pictures on calendars, diaries, pendants, brooches, and posters.

Tsuda's cats, posed as street toughs, wore black leather jackets and Samurai warrior headbands as they stood beside miniature motorbikes; they wore punk costumes and carried electric guitars and were photographed as a rock band; they posed as schoolgirls, teachers, policemen, and soldiers. The cats earned millions for Tsuda, who showed his appreciation by feeding them the very finest food and housing them in warm, comfortable, and elegant surroundings.

Following are just a few of the products that have been pushed by cats:

· The Great Atlantic and Pacific Tea Company used the back of a die-cut card to advertise its 135 stores in 1883. The front of the card featured two adorable cats, the female cat saying, "Don't Tommy, Don't" as Tommy tries to fondle her. The A & P eventually became a huge chain of supermarkets in the United States.

· Black Cat Whiskey was introduced in 1889. A black cat appeared on the label. Perhaps this black cat brought some bad luck, as the company went out of business in 1919 with the prohibition of alcohol in the United States.

· Starting in 1883, Clarks Thread used cats on advertising cards to promote their thread, probably because cats like to play with string and thread. Other thread companies did the same.

· A black cat appeared on the package of Snappy Snaps used for fastening dresses during World War I. It definitely made Snappy stand out from the other brands.

· In 1983 a poster was created by Brandt

Kittens love string, and advertisers, like the Corticelli Thread Company, love kittens. (COURTESY OF HISTORIC NORTHAMPTON, NORTHAMPTON, MASSACHUSETTS.)

Brands that showed three cats together, staring ut wide-eyed. The caption below read "We Don't Want You to Smoke." The poster was put out in cooperation with the American Lung Association. Finally, after years of promoting cigarettes and cigars by appearing on boxes, labels, packages, and ads, the popular pussycats were shown supporting the opposite point of view.

· Because mother cats so carefully transport their kittens, moving companies have often used the cat as a symbol.

· Perhaps the best-known cat in advertising did wonders for the product it represented. MORRIS, who was the official spokesman for 9-Lives cat food, starred in print and TV commercials. He also appears on every can of the company's cat food. According to Morris, "The cat that doesn't act finicky soon loses control of his owner." (Perish the thought!)

See also CHESSIE.

Aesop's Fables

~ Aesop, the Greek writer known for his fables, lived around 500 B.C. A number of his tales, which used animals to make moral or satirical points, involved cats—including *The Cat and the Fox, The Eagle and the Cat, Venus and the Cat, Cat and the Cock*, and *The Cat, the Cock and the Young Mouse*.

In *Belling the Cat* a council of mice hold a general council to decide the best way to outwit their common enemy, the cat. After much discussion, all agree that the best method would be putting a small bell on a ribbon and tying it around the cat's neck. In that way, the mice could always hear the cat approaching. "That is all very well," says one old mouse. "But who is to bell the cat?" Not surprisingly there are *no* volunteers, to which the old mouse says, "It is easy to propose impossible remedies."

Here are four of Aesop's most well known cat fables.

Cats are featured in a number of fables by Aesop, the master Greek storyteller of the sixth century B.C. This illustration from A Cat and a Cock *is by the twentieth-century American artist Alexander Calder.* (COURTESY OF THE METROPOLITAN MUSEUM OF ART, GIFT OF MONROE WHEELER, 1949.)

VENUS AND THE CAT

In ancient times there lived a beautiful cat who fell in love with a young man. Naturally, the young man did not return the cat's affections, so she besought Venus, the goddess of love and beauty, for help. The goddess, taking compassion on her plight, changed her into a fair damsel.

No sooner had the young man set eyes on the maiden than he became enamored of her beauty and in due time led her home as his bride. One evening a short time later, as the young couple were sitting in their chamber, the notion came to Venus to discover whether in changing the cat's form she had also changed her nature. So she set down a mouse before the beautiful damsel. The girl, reverting completely to her former character, started from her seat and pounced upon the mouse as if she would eat it on the spot, while her husband watched her in dismay.

The goddess, provoked by such clear evidence that the girl had revealed her true nature, turned her into a cat again.

APPLICATION: *What is bred in the bone will never be absent in the flesh.*

(continued)

5

The Hen and the Cat

All the barnyard knew that the hen was indisposed. So one day the cat decided to pay her a visit of condolence. Creeping up to her nest the cat in his most sympathetic voice said: "How are you, my dear friend? I was so sorry to hear of your illness. Isn't there something that I can bring you to cheer you up and to help you feel like yourself again?"

"Thank you," said the hen. "Please be good enough to leave me in peace, and I have no fear but I shall soon be well."

APPLICATION: *Uninvited guests are often most welcome when they are gone.*

The Cat and the Fox

A fox was boasting to a cat one day about how clever he was. "Why, I have a whole bag of tricks," he bragged. "For instance, I know of at least a hundred different ways of escaping my enemies, the dogs."

"How remarkable," said the cat. "As for me, I have only one trick, though I usually make it work. I wish you could teach me some of yours."

"Well, sometime when I have nothing else to do," said the fox, "I might teach you one or two of my easier ones."

Just at that moment they heard the yelping of a pack of hounds. They were coming straight toward the spot where the cat and the fox stood. Like a flash the cat scampered up a tree and disappeared in the foliage. "This is the trick I told you about," she called down to the fox. "It's my only one. Which trick are you going to use?"

The fox sat there trying to decide which of his many tricks he was going to employ. Nearer and nearer came the hounds. When it was quite too late, the fox decided to run for it. But even before he started the dogs were upon him, and that was the end of the fox, bagful of tricks and all!

APPLICATION: *One good plan that works is better than a hundred doubtful ones.*

(continued)

THE CAT AND THE MICE

A cat, grown feeble with age, and no longer able to hunt for mice as she was wont to do, sat in the sun and bethought herself how she might entice them within reach of her paws.

The idea came to her that if she would suspend herself by the hind legs from a peg in the closet wall, the mice, believing her to be dead, no longer would be afraid of her. So, at great pains and with the assistance of a torn pillow case she was able to carry out her plan.

But before the mice could approach within range of the innocent-looking paws a wise old gaffer-mouse whispered to his friends: "Keep your distance, my friends. Many a bag have I seen in my day, but never one with a cat's head at the bottom of it."

Then turning to the uncomfortable feline, he said: "Hang there, good madam, as long as you please, but I would not trust myself within reach of you though you were stuffed with straw."

APPLICATION: *He who is once deceived is doubly cautious.*

African folktales ∼ In addition to their prominence in ancient Egypt, cats appear in numerous African tales. According to one, when the rainy season was approaching a man asked a dog if he would help him build a house. The dog replied that he just didn't have the time; he had to run around, bark, hunt, chase, sleep in the shade, yawn, scratch, catch fleas, and wag his tail. The man then asked the cat for help. She also said she was too busy; she had to sleep, yawn, wash, wait by a mousehole, catch a mouse, growl at a bird, lie down, jump up, meow, and rub her tail against everything. But then the cat said, "All that can wait until tomorrow. I will help you build your house." And when the house was finished, the man told the cat she could stay inside by the fire. And he told the dog he would have to sleep outside under the moon and stars.

Another tale went like this: a woman went to a god and pleaded for a child. Each of her children had died at birth. The god agreed and told her the child would first cause her to be in debt but would eventually repay her. She gave birth to a son, and one day the son asked for some gold to buy salt. Instead he bought a dog. A month later he asked for some gold to go trading. Instead he bought a cat. And when he asked for some gold the next month to go trading, his mother gave it to him but told him it was the last gold she had. Instead of trading, he bought a pigeon. "This has turned out no better than before," his mother said. One day the pigeon called to the boy and told him that he, the pigeon, was the chief of a village and if he was returned, the boy would be handsomely rewarded. The boy agreed to return the pigeon to the village and was in turn rewarded with pots of gold and a magical ring that would grant him anything he desired. He asked that a village be created, and when it was, he made his mother the queen and he became the chief. However, it wasn't too long before the magical ring was stolen. The boy/chief sent his dog and cat to find it and bring it back. While the dog slept on the road, the cat retrieved the ring. On the way back the dog offered to carry the ring and dropped it in a river as he was swimming across, where it was promptly swallowed by a big fish. The cat jumped in, caught the fish, and told him that he would be eaten if he didn't return the ring. The fish complied. When they arrived back at the village, the cat told all, though the dog pleaded with him not to. The boy/chief then told the cat that whatever mat he slept on, he would lie upon it only if the cat lay upon it as well. And that whatever food he was eating, he would always put some in the cat's dish. The dog was banished to sleep in the smoldering embers of the dead fire when the chilly night arrived.

On a Cat, Ageing

He blinks upon the hearth-rug,
And yawns in deep content,
Accepting all the comforts
That Providence has sent.

Louder he purrs, and louder,
In one glad hymn of praise
For all the night's adventures,
For quiet, restful days.

Life will go on for ever,
With all that cat can wish:
Warmth and the glad procession
Of fish and milk and fish.

Only—the thought disturbs him—
He's noticed once or twice,
The times are somehow breeding
A nimbler race of mice.

SIR ALEXANDER GRAY

To a Cat

Cat! who hast pass'd thy grand climacteric,
  How many mice and rats hast in thy days
  Destroy'd?—How many tit bits stolen? Gaze
With those bright languid segments green, and prick
Those velvet ears—but pr'ythee do not stick
  Thy latent talons in me—and upraise
  Thy gentle mew—and tell me all thy frays
Of fish and mice, and rats and tender chick.
Nay, look not down, nor lick thy dainty wrists—
  For all the wheezy asthma,—and for all
thy tail's tip is nick'd off—and though the fists
  Of many a maid have given thee many a maul,
Still is that fur as soft as when the lists
  In youth thou enter'dst on glass-bottled wall.

JOHN KEATS, British poet (1795–1821)

Age ～ The age of a cat is a relative thing. The average cat lives about fifteen years (indoor cats generally live longer than outdoor cats, who are subject to many more hazards), although it has been reported that Puss, a cat in Great Britain owned by Mrs. T. Holway, celebrated his thirty-sixth birthday on November 28, 1939—and died the next day. There is more reliable information that Ma, a female tabby in Devon, England, owned by Alice St. George, lived to be thirty-four years old. A cat's first year is equal to fifteen human years; when a cat is two, its human age is twenty-five; and when a cat is fourteen, its human age is seventy-two. When a cat is in her teens and twenties, each year is equivalent to only about three human years. That is referring, of course, to the cat's age in only one of its nine lives.

Ailurophilia ⤳ a morbid or inordinate love of cats. Is that really possible?

> I suspect that many an ailurophobe hates cats only because he feels they are better people than he is—more honest, more secure, more loved, more whatever he is not.
>
> WINIFRED CARRIERE, American writer, twentieth century

> It is easy to understand why the rabble dislike cats. A cat is beautiful, it suggests ideas of luxury, cleanliness, voluptuous pleasures.
>
> CHARLES PIERCE BAUDELAIRE, French poet (1821–1867)

> The real objection to the great majority of cats is their insufferable air of superiority.
>
> P.G. WODEHOUSE, English writer and humorist (1881–1975)

Ailurophobia ⤳ Hard as it is to believe, someone with ailurophobia fears and/or hates cats. Usually, this condition is a result of a childhood trauma. A very young child may have been bitten or scratched as it "played" with a fluffy little kitten (greatly resembling a stuffed animal) or adult cat. Or as a baby, a parent may have made a big issue out of the threat to the child from the family cat. If the cat got close to the baby, the parent would shout at the cat, frightening the baby as well as the cat.

Some of the more well-known ailurophobes include Alexander the Great, Napoleon, Mussolini, Genghis Khan, and Hitler. According to one story, Napoleon once started screaming for help as he was about to go to bed. An aide rushed to his assistance and found the general half undressed and slashing his sword wildly at the wall tapestry, behind which a cat was hiding.

At the request of another ailurophobe, President Dwight David (Ike) Eisenhower, there were no cats at the White House when the general lived there between 1953 and 1961. He hated cats and told his staff to shoot any cat it spotted. (I don't think that policy would improve a president's ratings today.)

It is hard to imagine a composer of beautiful music disliking what many consider the world's most beautiful animal. But the nineteenth century German composer Johannes Brahms, who is considered one of the greatest composers of symphonic music and songs, was a true ailurophobe. His dislike of cats was so intense that he would shoot arrows at cats in the neighborhood.

Algonquin cat ⤳ The famous Algonquin Hotel near the theater district in Manhattan caters to many writers and literary types—as well as one cat. There has been an "Algonquin cat" since the early 1930s. Rusty, the first, was adopted from a Broadway show when it closed. Matilda, who now resides at the hotel, has run of the place. She rides the elevator and will even spend an occasional night with a guest. Matilda was adopted from a place called Just Strays and has been at the hotel about four years. She has had some of her own adventures. Matilda sometimes roams outside of the hotel. Several years ago Matilda

was mugged on West 44th Street. Someone made off with her collar.

American bobtail ～ Cat breeder Rose

Estes has been mating domestic and wild bob-cats since the late 1970s. The American bobcat has only recently been recognized as a breed. They have abbreviated tails and may have some typical Siamese markings. The American Bobtail is a big cat. The male can weigh in at twenty pounds.

PERSONALITY: The American bobtail is an intelligent, watchful, and playful cat.

American curl ～ This relatively new

shorthair cat was developed by Joe and Grace Ruga in Lakewood, California, when a black, longhair stray with unusual swept-back ears turned up at their house in 1981. Six years later the cat's descendants were entered in competition.

PERSONALITY: The American curl is curious, playful, and whimsical.

American Indian folktales ～

One Native American story tells that many years ago was born a beautiful boy who grew up to be kind and gentle and full of compassion. He was thought to be sent from God, and he was called the Magician. When a devastating plague befell the people, the Magician knew he would have to search the forest for the only known antidote—the silver-leafed plant. But Irmah the Serpent reigned in the forest, and no one had ever returned alive. The Magician's dog wanted to go along but the Magician said it was just too dangerous. But a little cat secretly followed the Magician and when they were deep in the forest he jumped on the Magician's shoulder and said he would protect him. The Magician expressed thanks and thought to himself, "How can this little cat protect me?" That night as he slept Irmah crept up to the Magician and was ready to strike when the little cat attacked him. She clawed and scratched and bit the great serpent until finally, at sunrise, she won. The Magician woke up to find the evil Irmah dead and the forest a safe place for everyone. The Magician asked the brave little cat how he could reward her. She asked only that she no longer be an outcast, and that she be allowed to enter the wigwams and be a friend of the people. And that is how the cat came to be the friend of the Native Americans.

In a tale told by the Hopi, a boy went out to hunt during the dead of winter a long time ago. He saw tracks in the snow that he'd never seen before and followed them, ending at a large rock. There the boy found a strange animal, tied it up, and brought it home. When he asked his father what the animal was, he was told that it was a cat and that cats eat mice and rabbits. The boy went out and caught a rabbit for the cat. For four days, he kept the cat in a niche in the wall of his house and fed it. And that is how the cat became tame and has lived in Hopi homes ever since.

American shorthair ～ It is believed

by some historians that the first American short-hair, originally called the domestic shorthair, came to this country on the *Mayflower* in 1620, working its way over as a mouser.

By 1900 these "domestic" cats were starting to attract some attention in cat circles. A cat imported from England in the early 1900s named Champion Belle of Bradford was the first domestic shorthair registered in the United States. In

Zunoqua of the Cat Village *by Emily Carr, 1931.*
(COURTESY OF VANCOUVER ART GALLERY, EMILY CARR TRUST)

1964, for the first time a silver tabby shorthair named Shawnee Sixth Son won the Cat Fancier Association's (CFA) Kitten of the Year award. That was followed in 1965 with the CFA designation Cat of the Year going to a silver tabby. That marked a significant turning point for this cat. In 1966 its name was officially changed to the American shorthair to give it more respectability, since the purebred shorthairs were commonly confused with mongrels or "alley cats."

American shorthairs come in a great variety of colors, including pure white, coal black, pale blue-gray, deep, rich red, coppery brown, clear silver, bluish ivory, very pale cream, off-white and silver, brown, or blue. There are over two dozen types of American shorthairs. The type is determined by its color and markings.

PERSONALITY: American shorthair cats are good natured, hearty (quite resistant to disease), and strongly built. Because of the independent nature of the American shorthair, they are good cats for people who cannot spend too much time at home with them.

A lovely solid red American shorthair, Satin Song Fireball, with her kittens. Solid reds do not have the white undercoat of the cameos. All reds and cameos show some faint tabby markings. (COURTESY OF ANNE BURKE, SATIN SONG CATTERY, DIAMOND BAR, CALIFORNIA.)

This American shorthair displays a beautiful cameo coat, with color only on the tips of the hair. (COURTESY ANNE BURKE, SATIN SONG CATTERY, DIAMOND BAR, CALIFORNIA.)

American wirehair ∼ This breed of cat is uniquely American. It grew out of a spontaneous mutation, appearing in a litter of kittens in a barn in Verona, New York, in 1966. The sixth kitten in the litter was red and white with sparse, wiry hair. Joan O'Shea, a cat breeder living nearby, heard about the kitten and paid the farmer fifty dollars for it. O'Shea named the cat Adam, and when he was fourteen months old she bred him with a neighbor's calico cat. Two of the kittens were normal and the other two were red and white with the same wired coats as their dad. And the rest, as they say, is history.

Today there is a great variety in the coats of wirehairs. The coat may be sparse, crimped, coiled, springy, resilient, coarse, and hard to the touch. American wirehairs come in a variety of colors—some solid and some bicolors such as black and white, blue and white, or red and white. They remain fairly rare.

PERSONALITY: The American wirehair is generally quiet, reserved, even-tempered, and affectionate, and resistant to disease. They take a great interest in their surroundings.

Amis, Kingsley ∼ (b. 1922) The English novelist and poet, born in 1922, who wrote *Lucky Jim*, *Take a Girl Like You*, and *The Old Devils* (for which he won Britain's prestigious Booker Prize), is a cat owner and lover. As a child he had pet dogs; when married, he had dogs and cats; and finally he had just cats. He is considering cutting a hole in his study door so that his white cat, Sarah Snow, can come in at will to sit on his

A classic Silver Tabby American shorthair with the loveliest green eyes. (PHOTOGRAPH BY ISABELLE FRANCAIS.)

lap as he works. He talks to Sarah Snow often, as he explains in his poem "Cat-English," part of which follows:

It may seem funny, but my cat
Is learning English. Think of That!
For years she did all right with "meow,"
But that won't satisfy her now,
And where before she'd squawk or squeak
She'll try with all her might to speak.
So when I came downstairs today
I was impressed to hear her say
"Hallo." Not like a person, true;
It might not sound quite right to you,
More of a simple squeak or squawk—
Still, that's what happens when cats talk:
Their mouths and tongues and things are fine
But different shapes from yours and mine;
They simply try their level best
And our good will must do the rest.
So when I pick up Sarah's dish
And ask who's for a spot of fish,
I have to listen carefully,
But I've no doubt she answers "Me!"

• • •

If you've a sympathetic ear
Cat-English comes through loud and clear;
Of course, the words are short and few,
The accents strange, and strident too,
And our side never gets a crack
At any kind of answer back

• • •

Kingsley considers keeping pets important. And he says he is "suspicious of a household that doesn't have a cat . . . I associate a person having a cat with them being gentler than other people."

Amory, Cleveland ～ (b. 1917) This
American humorist and humanitarian (cat-itarian?) is the founder and president of The Fund

for Animals. He also used his cat, Polar Bear, as the subject of a trilogy that is both touching and very humorous. The first book of the series, *The Cat Who Came for Christmas*, was published in 1987, and recounts how the author rescued a thin, dirty, and injured white cat on a snowy Christmas Eve, never intending to keep him. Well, he didn't really keep him. It would probably be more appropriate to say that the cat kept Amory, much to Amory's good fortune. After the cat had turned paws down on all of his well-thought out suggestions for names, such as Purrmudgeon, Santa Claus, Chairman Miow, Muwzza (the name of Mohammed's cat) and so on, Amory tells how he finally came up with the right one:

I plunged into thought. History had failed, humor had failed, the holiday season had failed. What was left? For some reason I started to think of what some of my very favorite animals were—perhaps I could get a name from among them. I was in no mood to include the cat, but I did include the dog, the horse, the donkey, the tiger, the dolphin, the otter, the beaver and the bear. There were many others but, suddenly, with the bear I stopped. Bear would be a good name for him, I thought—he looked like a little bear. And, since he was white, what about Polar Bear?

And so the little white cat rescued on Christmas Eve was called Polar Bear. The story of Amory and Polar Bear continues in *The Cat and the Curmudgeon*, published in 1990. Both books made it onto *The New York Times* best-seller list. And the last book, published in 1993, is *The Best Cat Ever*. Some say it is the most loving and humorous of all Amory's cat books.

Animal Medical Center ～ This
multilevel, nonprofit facility in New York City was founded in 1911. It serves cats, dogs, and other

pets from New York and from the rest of the country as well twenty-four hours a day! In 1972, the Donaldson-Atwood Clinic was added to the site. It is one of the best cancer facilities for pets in the United States. In the last decade, the center has expanded its services, adding an acupuncture service, CAT scans, and a pet-therapy program for inmates at Rikers Island. In 1981 it founded the Institute for Human/Companion Bonding. Under this program residents in hospitals and nursing homes, as well as people with illness or disabilities, receive regular visits from kittens or puppies who are brought by volunteers. (510 East 62nd Street, New York, New York 10021; 212/838-8100)

Arabic folktales ～ Judging from their presence in folktales, cats have long been popular in the Arab world. According to one tale, the king of the cats went to the holy city of Mecca. Upon his return, the king of the mice said that "etiquette" required a visit to the cat king to congratulate him. The other mice said, in so many words, "Are you crazy? He is our mortal enemy." But the king of the mice explained that the king of the cats was a changed cat as a result of his trip to the holy land; that he was now a Hadji (one who had made a pilgrimage), that he prayed from sunup to sundown and that his prayer beads never left his paws. So the king of the mice set out to visit the king of the cats at his palace. He watched from his mousehole as the king of the cats prayed—chanting, praising Allah, and occasionally spitting over his left then right shoulder to drive off the devil. But when he chanced to spot the king of the mice, he stopped praying, dropped his beads and pounced at the mouse, who escaped into the hole. On his return home he told his followers that the king of the cats may pray like a Hadji, but he still pounces like a cat!

In a second Arabic legend the cat is outwitted by the rodent. (It doesn't happen often!) A cat was resting in the courtyard while on the roof above him strode a rat. Seeing the rat, the generous and pious cat called out, "Ya Haffeed. O Allah our Protector, preserve him," whereas the rat snapped back, "Allah preserve nothing! Why are you suddenly interested in my well-being, cat?" Just then the cocky rat tripped on a waterspout and went tumbling to the ground, where he was quickly pounced upon by the cat. The cat said, "So, rat, you became blasphemous when I called on Allah the Protector. So now you see the swift and terrible retribution from Allah that you have wreaked upon yourself." The rat quickly became very contrite. He begged the cat not to kill him until he could atone by reciting the Fatiha one last time. And then he asked the cat to pray with him and say, "May the Merciful One bring this affair to a just conclusion." The cat, who was now impatiently looking forward to this unexpected meal, agreed. But as soon as he raised his paws in prayer, the rat escaped. The very disappointed cat wiped his eyes in sadness. And that is why, whenever you see a cat raising it paws to his face, you know he's recalling the delightful dinner that the clever rat tricked him out of having.

In a Persian legend, the cat does not let the rodent beat him out of a fine dinner. This cat resided in a mosque, which was his duty to keep mice-free. One day, the cat spotted a sleek, brown mouse creeping along the inside of the mosque wall. The cat waited in ambush for the mouse. And when the mouse turned the corner, the cat grabbed him and held him tightly in his jaws. The mouse asked for one last request before dying— that the cat say the name of one of the great prophets so that the soul of the mouse would be blessed on its journey into the hereafter. The cat thought for a moment, then said "Jerjis." It was the one name he could say while keeping his jaws tightly clenched.

See also MOHAMMED.

> Like a graceful vase, a cat, even when motionless, seems to flow.
>
> GEORGE WILL, American columnist, author,
> twentieth century

Aristocats, The ∼ Set in Paris in 1910, this animated feature film released by Walt Disney Studios in 1970 is about a mama cat (Duchess) and her three baby cats (Berlioz, Marie, and Toulouse), who are kidnapped and left in the country by a mean butler whose mistress was planning to leave her vast fortune to her cats. (The butler, understandably, was not happy about that.) The hero in this film is Jack O'Malley, an alley cat who is smitten with Duchess, and goes very much out of his way to save Duchess and her kittens. Among the voices used for the various cats are Eva Gabor for Duchess, Phil Harris for O'Malley, Dean Clark for Berlioz, Liz English for Marie, and Gary Dubin for Toulouse. *The Aristocats* was the last animated movie that Walt Disney authorized before his death. It was produced four years after he died. In 1971 a comic book adaptation of the film was published by Gold Key. The kittens starred in the *Aristokittens* which was also published by Gold Key. And yet another spinoff was *O'Malley and the Alley Cats*, also published by Gold Key.

> Sometimes ascending, debonair,
> An apple-tree or lofty pear,
> Lodg'd with convenience in the fork,
> She watch'd the gardener at his work.
>
> "The Retired Cat," WILLIAM COWPER, 1791

Artists ∼ Cats have been the subject of paintings, murals, sculptures, textiles, and other works of art from very early on. They appear in every form of art and every style, religious and secular, from paintings by the great masters like Leonardo da Vinci to such contemporary artists as Andy Warhol and WILL BARNET. It would be hard, if not impossible, to find an artist from the classical period to today who has not painted, drawn, silk screened, wood blocked, etched, sculpted, or photographed a cat at some point. It would not be surprising if the cat were the most frequently rendered animal in works of art. Today, of course, one can find cat art on calendars, notepaper, posters, address books, and diaries. Cats are "in." But, then again, they always have been in the world of art.

Paintings of cats were found on the walls of tombs in ancient EGYPT some four thousand years ago. Cats at that time were considered sacred and were worshiped. In temples, cat sculptures, long and lean, were left as offerings to the goddess Bastet, the patroness of love and joy, and entire shrines were devoted to cats. In Rome, a cat was placed at the feet of the great statue of the Goddess of Liberty. Cats were also emblazoned on the shields and flags carried by Roman soldiers as symbols of independence.

In the first century, a uniform code of laws was created by Hyel the Good, Prince of Wales, which included cat codes. At the beginning of the codes, a drawing of a cat appears in an original copy of the manuscript. One of the codes reads, "The worth of a kitten after it shall kill mice is four legal pence; and so it always remains." Occasionally a cat would be used as a sculptural decoration on medieval churches. They were frequently carved on the seats used in choir stalls and were sometimes shown performing human activities.

The fifteenth-century artist Antonello da Mes-

A charming mother and kitten, from Andy Warhol's 25 cats name Sam and one Blue Pussy. (ILLUSTRATION © 1987 BY THE ESTATE OF ANDY WARHOL. COURTESY RANDOM HOUSE, INC.)

sino painted St. Jerome with his cat. St. Jerome, who translated the Bible into Latin, was obviously a cat lover. An old children's poem reads:

> If I lost my little cat, I should be sad without it,
> I should ask St. Jerome what to do about it,
> I should ask St. Jerome, just because of that
> He's the only saint I know that kept a pussy-cat.

(And a very wise saint he obviously was!)

Since the cat later came to represent evil, artists such as Ghirlandaio, Luini, and Cellini painted cats at the feet of Judas. According to one art historian, evil associations are also seen in Albrecht Dürer's famous engraving *Adam and Eve* (1504). However, others argue that the German artist shows the good cat in the foreground ignoring the mouse—because before the fall there were no adversaries. Franz Floris also painted the Garden of Eden with Adam, Eve, and a contented cat. Hieronymous Bosch (1460–1516) included a cat stalking off with a rat in its mouth in *Garden of Earthly Delights*, and a terrified cat appears in his *Adoration of the Magi*. During the Renaissance, cats were looked upon more favorably, as in the work of Italian artist Federico Barocci (1535–1612). His painting *Madonna of the Cat* is linked with the symbolism of the Virgin.

The cat was held in the highest regard by Italian Renaissance artist LEONARDO DA VINCI (1452–1519), who believed "The smallest feline is a masterpiece." In his painting *Madonna and Child with*

a Cat, Jesus is clutching the kitten in an attempt to keep it from escaping. Leonardo seemed intrigued by the cat's suppleness and the many different positions the cat could take. His studies of the cat showed it in all different activities. Leonardo's drawings of cats are considered to be among the most beautiful ever made.

As centuries passed, the religious point of view of the Middle Ages was replaced by a more scientific and modern point of view. By the end of the sixteenth century the cat was being represented as the companion of people. Early seventeenth-century Flemish artist Jan Brueghel painting *Paradise* pictures two cats living peacefully with two of the local rats.

In the nineteenth century, the beautiful paintings of French Impressionist PIERRE-AUGUSTE RENOIR sometimes contained cats. His *Woman with a Cat*, painted in 1880, captures the closeness and intimacy shared by the woman and her pet, as she holds it cradled in her arms. The American Impressionist Mary Cassatt painted *Children Playing with a Cat* in 1908, depicting a baby on his mother's knee, reaching out for the cat, sleeping peacefully in a little girl's lap nearby.

French artists seemed to particularly admire the cat, and they were a frequent subject for THÉOPHILE GAUTIER, THÉOPHILE STEINLEN, and many others.

In the twentieth century, the American graphic artist Edward Penfield used cats in much of his work. Cats also appeared in paintings by Marc Chagall and drawings by Alexander Calder and even Andy Warhol. His *25 Cats Name* [*sic*] *Sam and One Blue Pussy*, printed in a limited

Girl Making a Garland *by the late fifteenth-century artist Hans Suess von Kulmbach.* (COURTESY THE METROPOLITAN MUSEUM OF ART, GIFT OF J. PIERPONT MORGAN, 1917.)

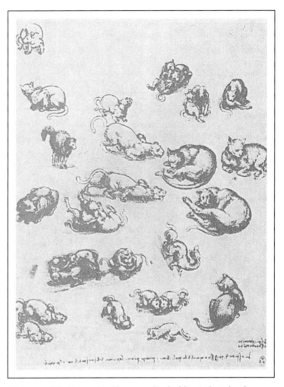

The great Italian artist Leonardo da Vinci sketched many studies of the cat.

edition in the mid-1950s, contains dozens of colorful, whimsical cats in different poses. All are named Sam with the exception of the last one, which is the "One Blue Pussy." (That cat is blue, naturally.)

In eastern art, cats began appearing in Chinese painting in the first century in the Sung Dynasty. During that time, cats were usually portrayed in paintings with aristocratic children. Generally, the paintings have a mood of playfulness. The traditional paintings were done on silk with many colors. In the eighteenth century, Chinese scholar-painters, skilled amateurs who painted for their own enjoyment, started depicting cats in their ink paintings.

The paintings by Korean artists resemble the

Paris Through the Window (Paris par la fenêtre), *painted in 1913 by the Russian-French artist Marc Chagall.* (COURTESY SOLOMON R. GUGGENHEIM MUSEUM, NEW YORK, GIFT OF SOLOMON R. GUGGENHEIM, 1937.)

style of the Chinese scholar painters. Pyon Sambyok, an artist with the government Arts Office was very skilled in painting animals, especially cats. He had the nickname "Koyang'i," which means cat.

In Japan, nineteenth-century artist Kuniyoshi became well known for his love and understanding of cats. He painted cats in virtually every setting imaginable. In his painting *The Cat Family at Home*, the cats are dressed as and behave like humans dining out at a restaurant. Kuniyoshi also painted realistic cats. In a later painting he shows cats at post offices along Tokaido road. The cats are doing cat things—napping, grooming, stretching, and meowing. There is even one cat with his head poking out from a basket. In a triptych, Kuniyoshi depicts scenes from the play *The Fifty-Three Stations*. The central panel illus-

trates the cat witch, with panels on each side emblazoned with dancing cats. On a more humorous note, Kuniyoshi spelled out the word *catfish* in his print *Catfish* using cats as Japanese letters.

The Japanese-born artist Tsugouhara Foujita (1886–1968), who did most of his work in France, gained an international reputation for his oil paintings, drawings, and watercolors of cats.

Information about the lives and works of numerous other artists can be found in this volume, including LESLEY ANNE IVORY, GOTTFRIED MIND, and LOUIS WAIN. It was of course very difficult to choose among the various works of cat art to represent here. I hope that you will find both some of your old favorites as well as some new works. (See the index for all works included in this book.)

In the middle of a world that has always been a bit mad, the cat walks with confidence.

ROSANNE AMBERSON, American writer, Twentieth century

Balinese ~ The Balinese cat is very much like a Siamese cat but with longer hair. It first appeared in the United States in the late 1940s or early 1950s. Although the cats were originally called "longhair Siamese," cat breeder Mary Smith proposed the name Balinese, remarking that her longhair Siamese were graceful and reminded her of dancers on the Island of Bali. Today, Balinese cats have hair that is much shorter and they resemble very closely the Siamese.

The coloring is the same as the Siamese—bluepoint, chocolate point, lilac point, and seal point. Other varieties include the frost tabby-point and the chocolate tabby-point.

PERSONALITY: Balinese are affectionate and highly intelligent. Like the Siamese they have loud, demanding voices but do not use them quite as consistently.

Barnet, Will ~ (b. 1911) Many of the paintings and graphics of this contemporary American artist, whose work appears in nu-merous distinguished museums including the Metropolitan Museum of Art in New York City, feature cats. His own cat, Madame Butterfly, has been immortalized in much of his work. Madame Butterfly is a calico cat but often appears in a color that complements the work as a whole. Also making frequent appearances in Will Barnet's paintings are his wife, Elena, as well as himself.

Elena Barnet tells an amusing story about Madame Butterfly, or "Fatso" as she frequently refers to her. Madame Butterfly was about ten years old when Hansi, a canary, also resided with them. Hansi, a "great singer," would be let out at breakfast time. Hansi would come to the table and partake of a small portion of scrambled eggs, one of his favorite dishes. Madame Butterfly was also present. One day, Madame Butterfly's whiskers got into attack position as she was sitting next to Elena and staring intently at Hansi. She cowed after a few harsh words from Elena. After awhile she made her way over to the trash can, very deliberately put her paw in, took out an envelope, and viciously tore it to threads. Hansi was fine and Madame Butterfly, I presume, saved face.

The artist Will Barnet includes cats in many of his paintings including this one, Woman Reading *(1970).* (COURTESY OF THE ARTIST.)

Bellay, Joachim du ～ (1522–1560)

This French writer of prose and poetry was one of the first to sing the praises of the cat. His cat Gris Argentin Petit Belaud, which means "silver-gray little Belaud," slept in his bed and ate at his table. When his cat died, he was grief-stricken and wrote a long memorial poem, composed of two hundred verses! Here is a very short excerpt:

> For three days now I have lost
> my well-being, my pleasure, all my love,
> my heart is almost breaking in me . . .

> Belaud who was, by chance,
> Nature's most beautiful work
> Thus made, as cats are made,
> Belaud whose beauty was such
> That he is worthy to be immortal.

See also WRITERS.

Bell, Book and Candle ～

The cat Pyewacket appeared in this 1958 movie produced by Phoenix/Columbia and based on a play of the same name that ran on Broadway. Pyewacket belonged to actress Kim Novak, who played the part of a witch. Pyewacket the cat was named after a famous cat owned by a witch in the mid-seventeenth century. Also starring in *Bell, Book and Candle* were James Stewart, Jack Lemmon, and Ernie Kovacs.

Bengal ～

The Bengal cat is a cross between the domestic Asian leopard cat and the American shorthair, bred in the late 1970s by Jean Mill of Covina, California, who wanted a domestic cat with the facial features, spotted pattern, and colors of the Asian leopard. Mill acquired eight fe-

A marble Bengal, Bet Sabe. The rare Bengal resembles the Asian leopard. (COURTESY NANCY TUBB, GLAMOURCATS.)

males that had been bred by a researcher at the University of California at Davis by crossing an Asian leopard cat with domestic shorthairs. Mill introduced male cats—one from a zoo in India and one from a Los Angeles shelter—and the Bengal came on the scene. Ten years later there were some two hundred Bengals in the United States. A large distinctive cat, the Bengal is quite a pricey kitten. It achieved championship status in the U.S. in 1991 and has recently been imported to England.

PERSONALITY: The Bengal's meow is a more wild-sounding scream than that of most pet cats—but they also tend to be very enthusiastic purrers. It is friendly, affectionate, curious, and intelligent.

Bentham, Jeremy ～ (1748–1832) This English philosopher was a loner whose chief companion was his adored cat, Langbourne. He honored his cat by bestowing titles on him. Langbourne eventually became Sir John Langbourne. His last title was The Reverend Sir John Langbourne, D.D. Bentham's basic idea of morality was that the best actions were those that brought happiness or pleasure to the greatest number of people; the bad actions brought pain.

Bill the Cat ～ Bill, a flea-bitten orange cat, appears in the comic strip *Outland,* drawn by Berkeley Breathed. He was introduced by the character Milo Bloom in the comic strip *Bloom County* (a precursor to *Outland*) in this way: "Never one to pass up a hot trend . . . we're introducing a new character. Meet Bill the Cat!" Bill had many adventures in Bloom County, including twice running for president on the National Radical Meadow Party ticket.

Binky ～ You may possibly not recognize the name Binky immediately, but you surely know the best-selling book of which she is the star: *All I Need to Know I Learned from My Cat.* Binky is a white and black cat who was adopted from a shelter by Suzy Becker. Carefully observing Binky, Suzy Becker determined which habits were needed to improve her own life—and put them in book form to share with others, making them accessible to ailurophiles and ailurophobes alike. Certainly anyone can benefit from the down-to-earth advice in this book—advice like, "Never crack your knuckles," "Pee without getting any on your shoes," "Get someone else to clean your bathroom," "Take some time to eat the flowers," and so on. The book Binky inspired has sold more than 1 million copies, was on *The New York Times* best-seller list for twenty-two weeks, has been translated into over a dozen foreign languages, and has no doubt made the earth a better place to live. Binky also appears on greeting cards, posters, calendars, and T-shirts. Binky now has fame and fortune—and so does her mom. (And that is just one more endorsement for adopting a cat from a shelter.)

Birman ～ The Birman cat is known as the "Sacred Cat of Burma" and in ancient times they were kept in Buddhist temples. According to legend, before the time of Buddha, the Burmese people built temples to honor their gods. In one, the Temple of Lao-Tsun, a golden figure of the goddess Tsun-Kyan-Kse was kept, along with one hundred pure white cats. One night, a raider from Thailand attacked the temple, killing the old priest Mun-Ha as he worshiped before the goddess. His cat companion, Sinh, jumped on the body of his slain master and faced the goddess. The soul of the priest entered the cat, and the cat's white hair turned golden—like the goddess.

Sinh's eyes turned a deep blue and his feet remained pure white, to honor the purity of Mun-Ha's soul. The next morning the hair of all the other white cats had become golden. Sinh stayed at his post for seven days, at which time he died, carrying with him Mun-Ha's soul. Birmans were protected for years by the priests. It was believed that departed priests returned to the temple in the form of the cat.

There are various accounts of how the Birman came to Europe. According to one, two Birman were shipped to Major Gordon Russell in France in 1919 in appreciation of Russell's help in the escape of priests from Tibet. One cat did not survive the journey, but a pregnant female did and her kittens began the Birman line in France. In another account, the sacred cats were stolen by a greedy servant and sold for gold to a man in France. And yet another account claims that a woman in France imported the first Birman in 1925.

The Birman has a long thick body and coloring like a Siamese cat—bluepoint, chocolate point, lilac point, and seal point. The Birman was recognized for show in France in 1925, in England in 1966, and in the United States in 1967.

PERSONALITY: The Birman is an affectionate, friendly, and gentle cat. They are precocious, and adapt well to family life and other animals. *See also* BURMESE.

A Seal-point Birman, the "Sacred Cat of Burma." (PHOTOGRAPH BY ISABELLE FRANCAIS.)

Cats are mysterious beings . . . symbols of evil, gods of the Pharaohs. You never know if they love you or if they condescend to occupy your house. This mystery is what makes them the most attractive beast.

PAUL MOORE, Episcopal bishop of New York,
twentieth century

Black cat ∽ Black cats have been thought to be the source of either good luck or bad luck, depending on the time (century) and place. The origins of the black cat date back to the time of the ancient Phoenicians, when black cats were considered sacred. The Phoenicians smuggled some of the black cats out of Egypt and brought them to Europe, where they became quite common and popular.

During the Middle Ages, however, the black cat became associated with black magic and sorcery and was considered to be the personification of

Satan. They were massacred in various ways. On the Feast of St. John's day, the Christian Church organized annual ceremonies in which black cats (only those without a single white hair) were burned alive. Cats were even killed at Mass itself.

In the seventeenth century, black cats faced new threats. Myths developed that parts of black cats could cure a variety of illnesses. It was believed that if the tail of a black cat were buried under the doorstep of a house, the people living there would be protected from sickness. The English naturalist Edward Topsel believed that eye pains or blindness could be cured by burning the head of a black cat and blowing the ashes into the eyes three times a day.

It became customary in Europe to bury live black cats under fruit trees to stimulate the growth of the trees. In Transylvania and Bohemia black tomcats were killed and buried in the fields on Christmas Eve and at the sowing of the first seed in spring to prevent evil spirits from harming the crops.

In the East, Buddhists considered all cats lucky, but perhaps a black cat especially so. It was thought that if a black cat crossed your path and did you no harm you were incredibly lucky. A black cat entering your home could be turned into a stroke of good luck by treating the cat kindly. In that way the cat's master, the Devil, would be appeased and he would pose no threat to you.

Many other superstitions have persisted about black cats. There is an old British saying that goes, "Whenever the cat of the house is black, the lasses of lovers will have no lack." This had a definite sexual connotation. Because a female cat in heat would be surrounded by tomcat admirers, so would a lass or woman in the house attract a large circle of lovers or male admirers.

King Charles I of England was so convinced that his black cat brought him luck that he took

him wherever he went. Sure enough, the day after his black cat died, he was arrested and eventually beheaded.

Sailors' wives used to keep a black cat at home to ensure the safety of their husbands.

A French veterinarian, Fernand Mery, found a positive myth about the black cat in Brittany—that every black cat has one hair that is perfectly white. If one can find the hair, and pluck it out, it will serve as a unique good luck charm, which can render you great wealth or great love.

The superstition that letting a black cat cross your path brings bad luck is, in general, unique to America. In Asia and England, black cats are considered lucky.

Here are just a few of the other superstitions about black cats, and their origin where known.

· A strange black cat on your porch brings prosperity. (Scotland)

· If a black cat chooses to make its home with you, you will have good luck.

· If a black cat lies on the bed of a sick man, he will surely die.

· Dreaming of a black cat at Christmas foretells of a serious illness in the coming year. (Germany)

· If a black cat crosses your path, you will die in an epidemic. (Ireland)

· If a black cat is tied to where five crossroads meet, it will run to hidden treasure when it is released. (France)

In addition to their appearance in folklore, black cats have generated many stories and fables. In the French tale *Twelve Black Cats and the Red One*, a fisherman named Murdo MacTaggart went out to his boat to fish on Halloween night, despite warnings not to. Before he reached his boat, a terrible storm arose with fierce thunder and lightning and he ran to take shelter in a nearby small hut. There he started hearing queer sounds. When he looked out he saw twelve great black cats and another cat that was red and bigger than the rest. The cats entered the hut and sat in a circle around Murdo. After they sang a ritualistic death song, the red cat demanded payment—in the form of prey—for the song (which Murdo, of course, had not requested). Every time he found the animal required for payment, the cats devoured it, then sang another song and demanded more payment. When Murdo was about to be devoured by the cats, a priest heard Murdo's screams and ran to his rescue. Sprinkling holy water on the red cat, he shouted, "Begone, Satan and demons from hell. Begone! I bid you leave the soul and body of this man alone!" The red cat disappeared in a puff of foul-smelling smoke. Only the fur of the black cats remained.

One very well-known story is "THE BLACK CAT" by Edgar Allan Poe (which follows). A cat called Cataline is in Mark Twain's "A Cat's Tail"; the black cat Minnaloushe is in "The Cat and the Moon" by William Butler Yeats; in Walter de la Mare's short story "Broomsticks," the cat is Sam; and P. G. Wodehouse writes of a black cat named Webster in "Mulliner Nights."

Black cats have had quite a commercial career as well. In the twentieth century, they became one of the scary symbols of Halloween. The arched black cat is a familiar sight today on Halloween decorations, cards, costumes, and so on. They have been used in such games as Pin the Tail on the Cat and the Parker Brothers's The Black Cat Fortune Telling Game, which came out in 1897.

A number of businesses have used black cats in their logos. The most well known is probably the Cat's Paw Rubber Heel logo. Others include Charles of the Ritz–Lanvin's "My Sin," and Eveready Batteries.

Among the celebrity owners of black cats is tennis pro Jimmy Connors, whose black cat is named Kismet. Best-selling writer Sidney Sheldon's black cat, Birdy, likes to sit on the desk when Sheldon writes; Bandit lives with Donna Mills, who portrayed Abby Ewing on *Knots Landing*. The French novelist and philosopher THÉOPHILE GAUTIER, owned a black cat, Eponine, who was named for a character in Victor Hugo's *Les Miserables*. The poet W. B. Yeats also owned a black cat.

The black cat from the house next door
Waits with death in each bared claw
For the tender unwary bird
That all the summer I have heard
In the orchard singing.

CLIFFORD DYMENT, 1944

The Black Cat

For the most wild, yet most homely narrative which I am about to pen, I neither expect nor solicit belief. Mad indeed would I be to expect it in a case where my very senses reject their own evidence. Yet mad am I not—and very surely do I not dream. But tomorrow I die, and today I would unburden my soul. My immediate purpose is to place before the world, plainly, succinctly, and without comment, a series of mere household events. In their consequences, these events have terrified—have tortured—have destroyed me. Yet I will not attempt to expound them. To me, they have presented little but horror; to many they will seem less terrible than baroques. Hereafter, perhaps, some intellect may be found which will reduce my phantasm to the commonplace: some intellect more calm, more logical, and far less excitable than my own, which will perceive, in the circumstances I detail with awe, nothing more than an ordinary succession of very natural causes and effects.

From my infancy I was noted for the docility and humanity of my disposition. My tenderness of heart was even so conspicuous as to make me the jest of my companions. I was especially fond of animals, and was indulged by my parents with a great variety of pets. With these I spent most of my time, and never was so happy as when feeding and caressing them. This peculiarity of character grew with my growth, and in my manhood I derived from it one of my principal sources of pleasure. To those who have cherished an affection for a faithful and sagacious dog, I need hardly be at the trouble of explaining the nature or the intensity of the gratification thus derivable. There is something in the unselfish and self-sacrificing love of a brute which goes directly to the heart of him who has had frequent occasion to test the paltry friendship and gossamer fidelity of mere Man.

I married early, and was happy to find in my wife a disposition not uncongenial with my own. Observing my partiality for domestic pets, she lost no opportunity of procuring those of the most agreeable kind. We had birds, goldfish, a fine dog, rabbits, a small monkey, and *a cat*.

(continued)

This latter was a remarkably large and beautiful animal, entirely black, and sagacious to an astonishing degree. In speaking of his intelligence, my wife, who at heart was not a little tinctured with superstition, made frequent allusion to the ancient popular notion which regarded all black cats as witches in disguise. Not that she was ever *serious* upon this point—and I mention the matter at all for no better reason than that it happens, just now, to be remembered.

Pluto—this was the cat's name—was my favorite pet and playmate. I alone fed him, and he attended me wherever I went about the house. It was even with difficulty that I could prevent him from following me through the streets.

Our friendship lasted, in this manner, for several years, during which my general temperament and character, through the instrumentality of the Fiend Intemperance, had (I blush to confess it) experienced a radical alteration for the worse. I grew, day by day, more moody, more irritable, more regardless of the feelings of others. I suffered myself to use intemperate language to my wife. At length, I even offered her personal violence. My pets, of course, were made to feel the change in my disposition. I not only neglected but ill-used them. For Pluto, however, I still retained sufficient regard to restrain me from maltreating him, as I made no scruple of maltreating the rabbits, the monkey, or even the dog, when by accident, or through affection, they came in my way. But my disease grew upon me—for what disease is like Alcohol!—and at length even Pluto, who was now becoming old, and consequently somewhat peevish—even Pluto began to experience the effects of my ill temper.

One night, returning home, much intoxicated, from one of my haunts about town, I fancied that the cat avoided my presence. I seized him; when, in his fright at my violence, he inflicted a slight wound upon my hand with his teeth. The fury of a demon instantly possessed me. I knew myself no longer. My original soul seemed, at once, to take its flight from my body; and a more than fiendish malevolence, gin-nurtured, thrilled every fiber of my frame. I took from my waistcoat pocket a penknife, opened it, grasped the poor beast by the throat, and deliberately cut one of its eyes from the socket! I blush, I burn, I shudder, while I pen the damnable atrocity.

When reason returned with the morning—when I had slept off the fumes of the night's debauch—I experienced a sentiment half of horror, half of remorse, for the crime of which I had been guilty; but it was, at best, a feeble and equivocal feeling, and the soul remained untouched. I again plunged into excess, and soon drowned in wine all memory of the deed.

In the meantime the cat slowly recovered. The socket of the lost eye presented, it is true, a frightful appearance, but he no longer appeared to suffer any pain. He went about the house as usual, but, as might be expected, fled in extreme terror at my approach. I had so much of my old heart left, as to be at first grieved by this evident dislike on the part of a creature which had once so loved me. But this feeling soon gave place to irritation. And then came, as if to my final and irrevocable overthrow, the spirit of Perverseness. Of this spirit philosophy takes no account. Yet I am not more sure that my soul lives than I am that perverseness is one of the primitive impulses of the human heart—one of the indivisible primary faculties, or sentiments, which give direction to the character of Man. Who has not, a hundred times, found himself committing a vile or a silly action, for no other reason than because he knows he should *not?* Have we not a perpetual inclination, in the teeth of our best judgment, to violate that which is Law, merely because we understand it to be such? This spirit of perverseness, I say, came to my final overthrow. It was this unfathomable longing of the soul *to vex itself*—to offer violence to its own nature; to do wrong for the wrong's sake only—that urged me to continue and finally to consummate the injury I had inflicted upon the unoffending brute. One morning, in cold blood, I slipped a noose about its neck and hung it to the limb of a tree; hung it with the tears streaming from my eyes, and with the bitterest remorse at my heart; hung it *because* I knew that it had loved me, and *because* I felt it had given me no reason of offense; hung it *because* I knew that in so doing I was committing a sin—a deadly sin that would so jeopardize my immortal soul as to place it, if such a thing were possible, even beyond the reach of the infinite mercy of the Most Merciful and Most Terrible God.

On the night of the day on which this cruel deed was done, I was aroused from sleep by the cry of fire. The curtains of my bed were in flames. The whole house was blazing. It was with great difficulty that my wife, a servant, and myself made our escape from the conflagration. The destruction was complete. My entire worldly wealth was swallowed up, and I resigned myself thenceforward to despair.

I am above the weakness of seeking to establish a sequence of cause and effect between the disaster and the atrocity. But I am detailing a chain of facts, and wish not to leave even a possible link imperfect. On the day succeeding the fire, I visited the ruins. The walls, with one exception, had fallen in. This exception was found in a compartment wall, not very thick, which stood about the middle of the house, and against which had rested the head of my bed. The plastering had here, in great measure, resisted the action of the fire—a fact which I attributed to its having been recently spread. About this wall a dense crowd were collected, and many persons seemed to be examining a particular portion of it with very minute and eager attention. The words "Strange!" "Singular!" and other similar expressions excited my curiosity. I approached and saw, as if graven in bas-relief upon the white surface, the figure of a gigantic cat. The impression was given with an accuracy truly marvelous. There was a rope about the animal's neck.

When I first beheld this apparition—for I could scarcely regard it as less—my wonder and my terror were extreme. But at length reflection came to my aid. The cat, I remembered, had been hung in a garden adjacent to the house. Upon the alarm of

(continued)

fire, this garden had been immediately filled by the crowd—by some one of whom the animal must have been cut from the tree and thrown, through an open window, into my chamber. This had probably been done with the view of arousing me from sleep. The falling of other walls had compressed the victim of my cruelty into the substance of the freshly spread plaster; the lime of which, with the flames, and the ammonia from the carcass, had then accomplished the portraiture as I saw it.

Although I thus readily accounted to my reason, if not altogether to my conscience, for the startling fact just detailed, it did not the less fail to make a deep impression upon my fancy. For months I could not rid myself of the phantasm of the cat; and during this period there came back into my spirit a half sentiment that seemed, but was not, remorse. I went so far as to regret the loss of the animal, and to look about me, among the vile haunts which I now habitually frequented, for another pet of the same species, and of somewhat similar appearance, with which to supply its place.

One night as I sat, half stupefied, in a den of more than infamy, my attention was suddenly drawn to some black object, reposing upon the head of one of the immense hogsheads of gin, or of rum, which constituted the chief furniture of the apartment. I had been looking steadily at the top of this hogshead for some minutes, and what now caused me surprise was the fact that I had not sooner perceived the object thereupon. I approached it, and touched it with my hand. It was a black cat—a very large one—fully as large as Pluto, and closely resembling him in every respect but one: Pluto had not a white hair upon any portion of his body; but this cat had a large, although indefinite, splotch of white, covering nearly the whole region of the breast.

Upon my touching him, he immediately arose, purred loudly, rubbed against my hand, and appeared delighted with my notice. This, then, was the very creature of which I was in search. I at once offered to purchase it of the landlord; but this person made no claim to it—knew nothing of it—had never seen it before.

I continued my caresses, and when I prepared to go home, the animal evinced a disposition to accompany me. I permitted it to do so; occasionally stooping and patting it as I proceeded. When it reached the house, it domesticated itself at once and became immediately a great favorite with my wife.

For my own part, I soon found a dislike to it arising within me. This was just the reverse of what I had anticipated; but—I know not how or why it was—its evident fondness for myself rather disgusted and annoyed. By slow degrees these feelings of disgust and annoyance rose into the bitterness of hatred. I avoided the creature—a certain sense of shame, and the remembrance of my former deed of cruelty, preventing me from physically abusing it. I did not, for some weeks, strike, or otherwise violently ill use it; but gradually—very gradually—I came to look upon it with unutterable loathing, and to flee silently from its odious presence, as from the breath of a pestilence.

What added, no doubt, to my hatred of the beast, was the discovery, on the morning after I brought it home, that, like Pluto, it also had been deprived of one of its eyes. This circumstance, however, only endeared it to my wife, who, as I have already said, possessed, in a high degree, that humanity of feeling which had once been my distinguishing trait, and the source of many of my simplest and purest pleasures.

With my aversion to this cat, however, its partiality for myself seemed to increase. It followed my footsteps with a pertinacity which it would be difficult to make the reader comprehend. Wherever I sat, it would crouch beneath my chair, or spring upon my knees, covering me with its loathsome caresses. If I arose to walk it would get between my feet and thus nearly throw me down, or, fastening its long and sharp claws in my dress, clamber, in this manner, to my breast. At such times, although I longed to destroy it with a blow, I was yet withheld from so doing, partly by a memory of my former crime, but chiefly—let me confess it at once—by absolute *dread* of the beast.

This dread was not exactly a dread of physical evil—and yet I should be at a loss how otherwise to define it. I am almost ashamed to own—yes, even in this felon's cell, I am almost ashamed to own—that the terror and horror with which the animal inspired me had been heightened by one of the merest chimeras it would be possible to conceive. My wife had called my attention, more than once, to the character of the mark of white hair, of which I have spoken, and which constituted the sole visible difference between the strange beast and the one I had destroyed. The reader will remember that this mark, although large, had been originally very indefinite; but, by slow degrees—degrees nearly imperceptible, and which for a long time my reason struggled to reject as fanciful—it had, at length, assumed a rigorous distinctness of outline. It was now the representation of an object that I shudder to name—and for this, above all, I loathed, and dreaded, and would have rid myself of the monster *had I dared*—it was now, I say, the image of a hideous—of a ghastly thing—of the Gallows!—oh, mournful and terrible engine of Horror and of Crime, of Agony and of Death!

And now was I indeed wretched beyond the wretchedness of mere Humanity. And a brute beast—whose fellow I had contemptuously destroyed—*a brute beast* to work out for *me*—for me, a man fashioned in the image of the High God—so much of insufferable woe! Alas! neither by day nor by night knew I the blessing of rest anymore! During the former the creature left me no moment alone, and in the latter I started hourly from dreams of unutterable fear to find the hot breath of *the thing* upon my face, and its vast weight—an incarnate nightmare that I had no power to shake off—incumbent eternally upon my heart!

Beneath the pressure of torments such as these the feeble remnant of the good within me succumbed. Evil thoughts became my sole intimates—the darkest and most evil of thoughts. The moodiness of my usual temper increased to hatred of all things

(continued)

and of all mankind; while from the sudden, frequent, and ungovernable outbursts of a fury to which I now blindly abandoned myself, my uncomplaining wife, alas! was the most usual and the most patient of sufferers.

One day she accompanied me, upon some household errand, into the cellar of the old building which our poverty compelled us to inhabit. The cat followed me down the steep stairs, and, nearly throwing me headlong, exasperated me to madness. Uplifting an ax, and forgetting in my wrath the childish dread which had hitherto stayed my hand, I aimed a blow at the animal, which, of course, would have proved instantly fatal had it descended as I wished. But this blow was arrested by the hand of my wife. Goaded by the interference into a rage more than demoniacal, I withdrew my arm from her grasp and buried the ax in her brain. She fell dead upon the spot, without a groan.

This hideous murder accomplished, I set myself forthwith, and with entire deliberation, to the task of concealing the body. I knew that I could not remove it from the house, either by day or by night, without the risk of being observed by the neighbors. Many projects entered my mind. At one period I thought of cutting the corpse into minute fragments, and destroying them by fire. At another, I resolved to dig a grave for it in the floor of the cellar. Again, I deliberated about casting it in the well in the yard—about packing it in a box, as if merchandise, with the usual arrangements, and so getting a porter to take it from the house. Finally I hit upon what I considered a far better expedient than either of these. I determined to wall it up in the cellar, as the monks of the Middle Ages are recorded to have walled up their victims.

For a purpose such as this the cellar was well adapted. Its walls were loosely constructed, and had lately been plastered throughout with a rough plaster, which the dampness of the atmosphere had prevented from hardening. Moreover, in one of the walls was a projection, caused by a false chimney, or fireplace, that had been filled up and made to resemble the rest of the cellar. I made no doubt that I could readily displace the bricks at this point, insert the corpse, and wall the whole up as before, so that no eye could detect anything suspicious.

And in this calculation I was not deceived. By means of a crowbar I easily dislodged the bricks, and, having carefully deposited the body against the inner wall, I propped it in that position, while with little trouble I relaid the whole structure as it originally stood. Having procured mortar, sand, and hair, with every possible precaution, I prepared a plaster which could not be distinguished from the old, and with this I very carefully went over the new brickwork. When I had finished, I felt satisfied that all was right. The wall did not present the slightest appearance of having been disturbed. The rubbish on the floor was picked up with the minutest care. I looked around triumphantly, and said to myself: "Here at least, then, my labor has not been in vain."

My next step was to look for the beast which had been the cause of so much wretchedness; for I had, at length, firmly resolved to put it to death. Had I been able to meet with it at the moment, there could have been no doubt of its fate; but it appeared that the crafty animal had been alarmed at the violence of my previous anger, and forbore to present itself in my present mood. It is impossible to describe or to imagine the deep, the blissful sense of relief which the absence of the detested creature occasioned in my bosom. It did not make its appearance during the night; and thus for one night, at least, since its introduction into the house, I soundly and tranquilly slept; aye, *slept* even with the burden of murder upon my soul!

The second and the third day passed, and still my tormentor came not. Once again I breathed as a free man. The monster, in terror, had fled the premises forever! I should behold it no more! My happiness was supreme! The guilt of my dark deed disturbed me but little. Some few inquiries had been made, but these had been readily answered. Even a search had been instituted—but of course nothing was to be discovered. I looked upon my future felicity as secured.

Upon the fourth day of the assassination, a party of the police came, very unexpectedly, into the house, and proceeded again to make rigorous investigation of the premises. Secure, however, in the inscrutability of my place of concealment, I felt no embarrassment whatever. The officers bade me accompany them in their search. They left no nook or corner unexplored. At length, for the third or fourth time, they descended into the cellar. I quivered not in a muscle. My heart beat calmly as that of one who slumbers in innocence. I walked the cellar from end to end. I folded my arms upon my bosom, and roamed easily to and fro. The police were thoroughly satisfied and prepared to depart. The glee at my heart was too strong to be restrained. I burned to say if but one word, by way of triumph, and to render doubly sure their assurance of my guiltlessness.

"Gentlemen," I said at last, as the party ascended the steps, "I delight to have allayed your suspicions. I wish you all health and a little more courtesy. By the bye, gentlemen, this—this is a very well-constructed house" (in the rabid desire to say something easily, I scarcely knew what I uttered at all)—"I may say an *excellently* well-constructed house. These walls—are you going, gentlemen?—these walls are solidly put together"; and here, through the mere frenzy of bravado, I rapped heavily with a cane which I held in my hand, upon that very portion of the brickwork behind which stood the corpse of the wife of my bosom.

But may God shield and deliver me from the fangs of the Archfiend! No sooner had the reverberation of my blows sunk into silence than I was answered by a voice from within the tomb!—by a cry, at first muffled and broken, like the sobbing of a child, and then quickly swelling into one long, loud, and continuous scream, utterly anomalous and inhuman—a howl—a wailing shriek, half of horror and half of triumph, such as

(continued)

35

Bombay

~ The Bombay cat is named for the city of Bombay in India and for its resemblance to the Indian black leopard. It has a gleaming, jet-black coat that looks like patent leather and bright gold to vivid copper eyes. It was created by a prominent breeder in Kentucky, Nikki Horner, in the 1950s. The story goes that she decided to try to produce a "mini-panther" because she heard so many people say, "I'd love to own a panther." She bred a black American shorthair with a Burmese to create the panther-like Bombay. The Bombay is relatively rare outside of the United States.

PERSONALITY: The Bombay rarely stops purring, craves human companionship, dislikes being left alone, and is perfectly content to spend its entire life indoors. She is playful, curious, and intelligent.

Braun, Lilian Jackson

~ Any cat-lover who reads mysteries is familiar with the author of the very popular mystery series *The Cat Who...*, which features a crime-solving cat. Braun has always been a writer, though not always about cats. At the age of two she wrote—better make that dictated—her first poems.

When she was in high school and living in Detroit, the *Detroit Free Press* paid her twelve dollars a week to write a baseball poem during the Tigers' season. Although she won't reveal her age, she will tell you that she worked for eighteen years in advertising and public relations, starting in 1950 at the *Detroit Free Press* until retiring in 1979. Her first cat story was "The Sin of Madame Phloi," written when her two-year-old Siamese cat named Koko met a tragic death. (A much loved gift from her husband, Koko died after being pushed from a tenth-floor window of Braun's apartment by a senile woman.) She then went on to write the novels *The Cat Who Could Read Backwards*, *The Cat Who Turned On and Off*, and *The Cat Who Saw Red*, which was turned down in the late 1960s when the publisher decided cats were no longer "in." After an eighteen-year hiatus and encouragement from her husband, Braun submitted *The Cat Who Saw Red*, which was published and nominated for the Edgar Award.

In *The Cat Who...* series, Jim Qwilleran, a newspaper reporter on the *Daily Fluxion*, owns two cats—Yum Yum and Koko. The divorced Qwilleran adores his cats, though Koko is the favored and does the "detective" work. This paragraph from *The Cat Who Saw Red* (Qwill has just gotten home) captures his typical affection for them:

Qwilleran stroked each cat in turn, massaging Koko's silky back with a heavy hand and caressing Yum Yum's paler fur with tenderness. "How's the little Sweetheart?" He spoke to Yum Yum with an unabashed gentleness that his cronies at the Press Club would not have believed and that no woman in his life had ever had.

Here is the complete series of the *Cat Who . . .* mysteries:

- *The Cat Who Saw Red*
- *The Cat Who Could Read Backwards*
- *The Cat Who Ate Danish Modern*
- *The Cat Who Turned On and Off*
- *The Cat Who Played Brahms*
- *The Cat Who Played Post Office*
- *The Cat Who Had 14 Tales*
- *The Cat Who Knew Shakespeare*
- *The Cat Who Sniffed Glue*
- *The Cat Who Went Underground*
- *The Cat Who Talked to Ghosts*
- *The Cat Who Lived High*
- *The Cat Who Knew a Cardinal*
- *The Cat Who Moved a Mountain*
- *The Cat Who Wasn't There*
- *The Cat Who Came to Breakfast*

In case you have any doubts as to the popularity of Koko and Yum Yum, there is a Lilian Braun Fan Club which puts out two newsletters a year! (For a sample copy send stamped self-addressed envelope to Helen McCarthy, 4 Tamarack Road, Natick, MA 01760.) (Koko and Yum Yum get lots of fan letters themselves.)

Since the first Koko, Braun has always lived with cats. Here are some of her cat quotes that I particularly like:

"Cats . . . never strike a pose that isn't photogenic."

"To understand a cat, you must realize the he has his own gifts, his own viewpoint, even his own morality."

"Cats have a contempt of speech. Why should they talk when they can communicate without words?"

Indeed, why should they?!
See also Lydia ADAMSON.

Breakfast at Tiffany's ~ This 1961 Paramount movie, based on the novella by Truman Capote, stars Audrey Hepburn as Holly Golightly, a charming, wild and amoral free spirit. She has a tabby cat named Cat, who is unceremoniously kicked out into the rain when Holly falls on hard times. However, in a happy ending, Holly retrieves Cat and finds true love at the same time. The cat who played the role does in fact have a name: ORANGEY, a star in his own right, won a PATSY award from the American Humane Society for his work in this film.

Breeds ~ Over one hundred cat breeds are recognized throughout the world. Most breeds are the result of very careful planning and mating, pairing the best of the litters produced by plain, run-of-the-mill cats. Most breeds go back just one hundred years, when cats were first mated in order to produce animals with particular characteristics such as color and shape of the eyes; hair color, length, and pattern; personality; body type; and so on.

A cat that is characterized as an established breed is the result of the mating of two or more natural breeds (those which have developed on their own), which produces the same offspring when mated with the same hybrid breed. For example, the Himalayan is a new "breed" resulting from the original mating of the natural Siamese and Persian breeds. Once the breed is established, the Himalayan cats are mated with each other to continue the line.

The top cats in the United States according to the Cat Fanciers Association in 1993 were:

Breed	Registration
Persian	48,128
Maine Coon	3,557
Siamese	2,982
Abyssinian	2,361
Scottish Fold	1,284

Most purebred cats are registered, allowing them to compete in cat shows with others of the same breed. A cat must be registered with the particular association sponsoring the show.

These are among the most popular breeds commonly found today. (See individual entries for more detail.)

Abyssinian
American bobtail
American curl
American shorthair
American wirehair
Balinese
Bengal
Birman
British shorthair
Burmese
Burmilla
California spangled
Chartreux
Cornish rex
Cymric
Devon rex
Egyptian Mau
Exotic shorthair
Havana brown
Himalayan
Japanese bobtail

Javanese
Korat
Maine coon
Manx
Norwegian forest
Ocicat
Oriental shorthair
Persian
Ragdoll
Rex
Russian blue
Scottish fold
Siamese
Siberia
Singapura
Snowshoe
Somali
Sphynx
Turkish Angora
Turkish Van

The completed registration form, with your name, address, cattery name (not required), and the name of the kitten along with the fee should be sent to the appropriate association. (If the cat you buy was already registered, registration can be accomplished by completing the transfer of ownership on the owner's certificate.) If you want to register your cat in more than one association you can do that easily by making a photocopy of the cat's pedigree and both sides of the registration slip from the association in which the cat is already registered and send it to the new association with the appropriate fee. You should receive the registration within a few weeks. A cat's "papers" include the registration documents issued for the cat and the pedigree document listing the known names, titles, colors, and registration numbers of the first three to five preceding generations of the cat. (See index for cat and breed associations; *see also* SHOWS.)

Brindling ∽ The random mixture of different colored hairs in a cat's coat. *See* COAT.

British folktale ∽ The British have also developed numerous folktales about cats. Here's a particularly charming one. A year before a king and queen finally bore the daughter they so desired, they received a warning from a sorceress. If they were to have a daughter, she would die if she were to wed a prince. She told them to get three pure white kittens who would grow up with the princess. The kittens were to be given three balls of gold and three balls of linen thread. As long as the kittens played with the balls of thread, all would be fine. But if they should play with the gold balls, watch out! The little princess and three kittens grew up together and became best friends. When the princess learned to spin they were delighted, frolicking as they leaped for the spinning wheel. And they kept playing with the linen thread balls and ignoring the gold.

When the princess was sixteen and very beautiful, princes came from far and wide to woo her. But she declined every proposal. She seemed content to spend her days in the palace with her three companion white cats until one day a kind, wise, and handsome prince visited the palace. He kept bringing her gifts but never brought up the subject of marriage. Meanwhile, the princess fell madly in love with him and finally professed her feelings. The overjoyed prince expressed his love as well. No sooner had the prince and princess exchanged words of love than the cats, who had been playing with the linen balls in the tower room, started playing with the gold balls. The handsome prince whom the princess loved so dearly was suddenly afflicted with a strange malady that all the doctors summoned could not seem to cure—the prince was dying.

In desperation the princess sought out the original sorceress who had made the first dire prediction, who told her the only way she could save the prince would be by spinning ten thousand skeins of pure white linen by midnight Christmas, just twenty-seven days away. No hand but hers could spin the skein. The princess despaired of ever being able to complete such an enormous task, but started spinning immediately. After just one night she was discouraged and tired, as she gazed at how small a dent in the task she'd made. Crying, she told her cats she knew they'd help her if they could. The three cats told the princess they would help her, explaining that since they didn't have hands, they would be allowed to spin—with their paws. Each cat took to a wheel, spinning rapidly and beautifully. The only sound heard was the humming of the wheels. On Christmas day (lo and behold!) the ten thousand skeins were spun and the prince was on his way to a rapid recovery. In grateful appreciation, the princess gave the cats all her royal jewels, which they had always

admired. At the wedding feast, the cats, bedecked in their jewels, sat in a place of honor. They curled up in comfort and content and suddenly a pleasant hum was heard from all three. It was the wonderful, happy sound of purring, the gift the cats had received for helping the princess. And that is how the cat came to purr. (Of course, the prince and princess lived happily ever after.)

British Museum cat ～ An adored, admired, and very popular black cat named Mike reigned at the gate of the British Museum for some twenty years, from 1909 to 1929. When he died, a 165-page obituary was published and poems were written in his memory. Mike's popularity and fame surpassed that of his predecessor, Black Jack. Black Jack had had the habit of sitting upright on one of the desks in the Reading Room. When he wanted to go out, one of the library's patrons opened the door for him. One night, he was inadvertently locked in a room with bound volumes of newspapers. When he was finally released, it was discovered that during his time of "imprisonment" he had sharpened his claws on many of the book bindings, and he became persona non grata. It was decreed that he must go. He did. But after a time he returned and resumed his duties as the Reading Room Cat, to the great satisfaction of many. One day, Black Jack brought a small black cat to the museum. Mike became Black Jack's successor, and as already noted, gained even more fame.

> If it be true that nations have the cats they deserve, then the English people deserve well of cats, for there are none so prosperous or so friendly in the world.
>
> HILAIRE BELLOC, British novelist, poet,
> essayist, and historian (1870–1953)

British shorthair ～

The British shorthair may be the oldest natural English breed. Its ancestors came to northern Europe with Roman soldiers over two thousand years ago, and from northern Europe they immigrated to Great Britain. Though these hardy cats were called mongrel, or street, cats, during the last quarter of the nineteenth century British shorthairs appeared frequently in cat shows at London's Crystal Palace. The two world wars played havoc with the shorthairs.

Today, the British blue is an especially popular shorthair. But the British shorthair comes in many different colors as well, including solid colors—black, blue, cream, and white; bicolors—black and white, blue and white, red and white, and cream and white; and tabbies—classic, mackerel, and spotted.

The various types may have very different temperaments. Here are a few:

· British black shorthair—good-natured and very smart, an ideal household pet
· British white shorthair (includes the blue-eyed, orange-eyed, and odd-eyed)—intelligent, streetwise, and friendly, a good pet

This father and son were named Best Blue British shorthair in their association in 1993. (COURTESY LYNNE BOROFF, ADVENT HILL CATTERY, HARTLAND, VERMONT.)

• British cream shorthair—very good-natured, intelligent, and affectionate

• British blue shorthair—bright, very affectionate, and a bit on the quiet side

• British blue-cream shorthair—affectionate and lively

• British tabby shorthair (red classic, silver classic, and brown classic)—good-natured, affectionate, intelligent, and a good friend

• British tortoiseshell shorthair (tortoiseshell and white, blue tortoiseshell and white)—sharp, affectionate, charming, highly popular as a pet

• British spotted shorthair (most common types: brown, silver, and red)—good-natured, affable, and affectionate

• British bicolor shorthair (black and white "Magpie", cream and white, red and white)—intelligent, even-tempered, and friendly

• British smoke shorthair (black smoke, blue smoke)—good-natured, affectionate, intelligent

• British tipped shorthair—good-humored, affectionate, and intelligent

PERSONALITY: In general, British shorthairs tend to be reserved at first but soon overcome their shyness. They are very loyal, intelligent, untemperamental, and loving. They have a quiet voice and are quite hardy and resistant to cold.

Burmese ~ The Burmese is thought to have originated in Southern Asia, in Burma, where brown cats called Rajas dwelled in Buddhist temples in the fifteenth century. It was believed that the soul of someone who died lived on for a period of time in the body of a sacred cat, before going on to total perfection in the next life; and that when a cat dies, he will speak to the Buddha on behalf of the owner. Besides their role in the transmigration of souls, these cats were also thought to guard the temple.

The Burmese was the first pedigree breed to be developed completely in the United States—and one of the first in which a thorough genetic study played a role. The "first" Burmese cat, called Wong Mau, was brought into this country in 1930 from Rangoon and purchased by Navy psychiatrist Dr. Joseph Thompson, who mated her with a Siamese tom. The Burmese was first registered in 1936.

Her short, glossy coat, lying very close to the skin, comes in a number of different colors: sable—a rich, warm brown; champagne—a warm honey beige; medium blue; and a pale silvery gray. Among the varieties of Burmese are the sable Burmese, red Burmese, American sable Burmese, blue tortoiseshell Burmese, and the platinum Burmese.

PERSONALITY: The Burmese is agile, energetic, playful, devoted, and smart. Burmese cats love people. *See also* BIRMAN.

Burmilla ~ What do you get when you combine a Burmese and Chinchilla? You get a burmilla. That's what happened in 1981 in Great Britain when two of Baroness Miranda von Kirchberg's cats—a lilac Burmese and a chinchilla—were accidentally mated. Three years later a breed club was started for the Burmilla and it is now one of the most popular new breeds.

The burmilla comes in silver or gold with tips in a variety of colors. Its tail has distinct rings.

PERSONALITY: The burmilla is noted for its wonderful, even-tempered, and playful disposition.

California Spangled Cat ~ This shorthair cat, with spots like a wild cat, was first bred by Paul Casey, a TV writer in Burbank. In 1971, he bred a Siamese and a spotted silver angora. Eventually he produced the spangled cat which now comes in nine colors—silver, bronze, black, white, charcoal, gold, red, blue, and brown. As of 1992, kittens were selling for $3600, and there is a waiting list.

Cartoon Cats ~ Cats have had many roles in comic strips, comic books, paperback books, animated cartoons, full-length animated films, television series, and commercials. Though most of the cartoon cats are intended for a young audience, adults enjoy many of them as well (often on a different level), and some are even X-rated, for adults only. Cartoon strips originated in the late 1800s, as did motion pictures. Virtually every animal imaginable can be found in cartoon form somewhere.

Cats have both starred in their own cartoons and have appeared in the cartoons of other animals or humans, as aids or enemies. Some cats are heros while others are oafs, always being outwitted by a mouse, bird, or the like. Some of the cartoon cats made brief appearances in animated films or comic strips; others, like HEATHCLIFF, GARFIELD, KRAZY KAT, and SYLVESTER, have enjoyed long popularity.

FELIX THE CAT, who made his first appearance in 1919, was the first true animated film star. Felix was so popular that Walt Disney, who was thinking of developing a cat cartoon character, feared the competition with Felix would be too great and switched to a mouse (good move, Walt!). In the late 1940s and 1950s, the Sylvester the Cat cartoons were so popular that many people went around saying "I tawt I taw a putty tat," Tweety Bird's signature line.

Here are some of the more noteworthy cartoon cats:

Azrael ~ Featured in the cartoon world of the Smurfs, created in 1957 by Belgian cartoonist Pierre "Peyo" Culliford, Azrael belongs to the sorcerer Gargamel, who frequently tries to capture the Smurfs, but Azrael often gives the trap away by meowing excitedly.

Baggy Pants ~ Dressed like Charlie Chaplin's Tramp, Baggy Pants appeared in 13 episodes of "Baggy Pants and Nitwits" on NBC in 1977.

Beans ~ This chubby cartoon cat made his debut in 1935 with Porky Pig. Over the next nine years, Beans starred in seven Warner Brothers cartoons.

Boo ~ This ghostly cat appeared in the 1971 ABC series, "Funky Phantom."

Cap'n Catnip ~ Cap'n Catnip is the crime-fighting alter-ego of Cheshire A. Catt in Charlton Comic's animated 1981 film, *Charlton Bullseye*.

Captain Jack ~ Created by Mike Kazaleh, this cat appears in the future world (2200) in *The Adventures of Captain Jack*, published by Fantagraphic Books.

Claude Cat ~ This gray-brown cat made his debut in the Oscar-nominated short *Mouse-Wreckers* in 1949 and had major roles in *The Hypo-condri-cat* and *Two's a Crowd* the following year.

Creepy Cat ~ This inept orange cartoon cat appeared in two issues of the Marvel Comic's *Film Funnies* in 1949 and 1950. Creepy has just one job at the house where he lives—to find and destroy the mouse who cohabits the quarters—he is always outwitted.

Esmeralda ~ Esmeralda was the cat star in the comic strip *Cicero's Cat*, a spinoff of the cartoon "Mutt and Jeff" begun in 1933. Cicero is Mutt's son. Esmeralda was able to talk and would generally use that skill to get what she wanted with no regard for anyone else (an inspiration for clever and independent cats like Garfield and others who emerged later). *Cicero's Cat* was drawn by Al Smith who was the assistant of the Mutt and Jeff creator, Bud Fisher, and was produced by the Bell Syndicate until it met its demise about 30 years later.

Jane Feline ~ Created by Nona Bailey, Jane Feline debuted in a cartoon strip syndicated in health club newsletters in 1982 and ran for seven years. Jane lives with an aerobics teacher but hates exercise.

Julius the Cat ~ Julius appeared in about fifty shorts for Walt Disney between 1924 and 1927.

Kamikaze Cat ~ Created by Mark Hamlin and Roger McKenzie, Kamikaze appeared in a 1983 comic book. Known as KC, the sleuth appeared in trenchcoat and fedora, with a cigarette dangling from his lips.

Kat Karson ~ This cartoon cowboy cat appeared in the comic book *Cowboys 'n Injuns*, published off and on by Comix between 1946 and 1952.

Kitty ~ Created by cartoonist Cliff Sterrett, this light-gray alley cat debuted in the comic strip *Polly and her Pals* in 1912.

Klondike Kat ~ Klondike Kat appeared in twenty-six television episodes of CBS's "Tennessee Tuxedo" and "Go Go Gophers" in the 1960s. He was a mountie stationed in the Northwest, at Frot Frazzle and reporting to Major Minor.

Motley the Cat ~ This fluffy white cartoon cat was created in 1980 by Larry Wright for his strip *Wright Angles*. Motley is notable for his cleverness and sense of humor, as in this quip, "One more mouse this year would put me in a higher tax bracket."

Poosy Gato ～ Poosy first appeared in the strip *Gordo*, created by Gus Arriola, in 1941. Gordo is a former Mexican farmer turned tour-bus driver, and Poosy accompanies him on his adventures.

Sebastian ～ Sebastian appeared in the comic book *Josie* from 1963 to 1982 as the mascot of the teenager Josie and her rock group, the Pussycats. She also appeared in "Josie and the Pussycats," on CBS from 1970 to 1972, and "Josie and the Pussycats in Outer Space," 1972–1974.

Spooky ～ This resourceful scrawny black cat, created by Bill Holeman in *Smokey Stover*, first appeared in 1935 and then in his own comic strip for ten years, as well as in the daily adventures of *Nuts and Jolts*.

Streaky the Super-Cat ～ Streaky first appeared in DC Comics' *Action Comics* in 1960. Because of his encounter with X-kryptonite, he is able to do incredible feats and he accompanies Supergirl on many of her adventures.

Superkatt ～ Created by Dan Gordon in American Comic's *Giggle Comics* in 1944, Superkatt often pronounces "Make way for the cat what is super!" What he doesn't realize is that as he shouts out his warning, some other disaster is ensuing that causes people to indeed heed his advice.

Waldo Kitty ～ Waldo appeared in thirteen episodes of "The Secret Lives of Waldo Kitty" on NBC in 1975. Based of course on James Thurber's "The Secret Lives of Walter Mitty," Waldo regularly

fantasizes himself as the hero fighting desperate villains, such as supercat Catman, jungle hero Catzan, the legendary archer Robin Cat, or Captain Herc in "Cat Trek."

See separate entries for these other famous cartoon cats: BILL THE CAT, COSMO, COURAGEOUS CAT, FIGARO, FRITZ THE CAT, HODORI, *OLIVER & COMPANY*, TOM (AND JERRY), TOP CAT.
See also BINKY, B. KLIBAN.

Illustration from Lippincott's First Reader, *1882.*

Cat ～ There are various theories on the derivation of the word *cat*. One theory is that the word's origin is Arabic, and the oldest use of it may be in northern Africa, where the word is *gattus*. In Rome the cat was originally called *felis*, from felix, which means a good and auspicious omen. Later, the Romans started using the name catta, which may have come from the word *catta*, which means weasel, since both cat and weasel catch vermin; or it may have been derived from the Egyptian word *kadis*. *Puss* or *pussy* appears to be from the Egyptian word *Pasht* or *Posjt*, which were names for the goddess Bastet, Egypt's cat-headed god. However, others contend that *puss* or *pussy* are from the latin words *pusus* and *pusa*, which mean little boy and little girl. The general name for a cat in Turkey is *kedi*—which very well may have turned into the word *kitty*. Following are some of the variations of the word *cat* in different languages:

Arabic—kitte
Armenian—gatz
Basque—catua
Chinese—miu or mio
Dutch—kat
Egyptian—mait or mau
French—chat
German—katze, katti or ket
Greek—kata or catta
Icelandic—kottur
Italian—gatto
Japanese—neko

Latin—felis or cattus
Norwegian—katt
Polish—kot or gatto
Portuguese—gato
Rumanian—pisica
Russian—kots or koshka
Spanish—gato
Swahili—paka
Swedish—katt
Welsh—kath
Yiddish—gattus and chatul

This detail from a hanging scroll, Seated Cat *by the Chinese artist Chu Ling, dates from the Ch'ing Dynasty, c. 1800.*
(COURTESY THE METROPOLITAN MUSEUM OF ART, ROGERS FUND, 1956.)

In 1911, Ambrose Bierce defined cat in this way: "a soft, indestructible automaton provided by nature to be kicked when things go wrong in the domestic circle." He based his definition on Descartes's theory that only humans have intelligence and that all animals are automatons, unfeeling objects whose sole existence was for their use and pleasure to people. Descartes had some good ideas, but this was not one of them. Today numerous studies show that many animals, certainly cats, do have intelligence. (And I can personally vouch this is true for my cats Miel and Molly.)

In *Webster's New World Dictionary*, Third College Edition, revised in 1988, one definition for *cat* is "a small, lithe, soft-furred animal (*Felis cattus*) of this family domesticated since ancient times and often kept as a pet or for killing mice." And in the *Random House Dictionary*, published in 1978, a cat is defined as "a domesticated carnivore, popular as a pet, bred in a number of varieties."

The word *cat* has some other definitions as well. It is slang for a jazz musician and it is sometimes used as a term for a person, generally a woman, who makes spiteful remarks.

Cat-a-Muse ～ This cat trivia board game, for two to six players, adults and families, was invented in 1993. The object of the game is to be the last cat surviving on the Catwalk. Each cat, of course, has nine lives. Anytime you give the wrong answer to a Cat-egory (trivia) or Cat-Fact you lose a life. There are also Cat-astrophes in which a life can be lost such as "tail accidentally grabbed by Olympic disc thrower," "attempted to be the first cat to go over Niagara Falls in a catamaran," and "booked a stateroom on the Titanic." A life can also be lost in a "cat fight," which can result if your cat lands on a space already occu-

pied. (*See* CAT IN THE BOX game.) You can advance or retreat by way of Cat-alyst cards which have commands like "Spring Forward 2" or "Leap Back 5." If you are a trivia fan, or just crazy about cats, this is a game for you, full of cat information, lore, and fact. Besides skill, however, this game requires a fair amount of "throw of the dice" luck.

According to GAMES 2000, the distributor, a portion of the profits from the game is being donated to aid domestic cats. For information on where to get Cat-a-Muse call 510/455-8233.

Cat City ～ This animated feature film was made in Hungary in 1987 at Budapest's top animation studio (with English subtitles). When the entire mice population is threatened with extinction by a group of nasty cats, Intermaus, an international mouse intelligence agency, uses its top agent to find the blueprints for the secret weapon the cats have developed. The mice are saved and the cats lose their prey.

Cat Collectors ～ This international organization was founded in 1982 by Marilyn Dipboye in Michigan, after she saw an ad in the paper about an owl collectors club. Being a cat owner and a collector of cat items, she hunted for a similar club for cat collectors. When she couldn't find one, she started one! As of 1993 there are over a thousand members in the United States as well as Australia, France, Canada, New Zealand, Germany, Holland, Switzerland, and Sweden.

Besides interesting bits of news and articles in the bimonthly newsletter for members, *Cat Talk*, a cat collectors catalog is also included in membership—for serious collectors as well as the cat lover who is not a serious collector but likes an occasional cat mug, T-shirt, cat figurine, stamps, jewelry, and so on. The catalog has pictures with descriptions and prices of numerous cat items for sale, many one-of-a-kind antiques. Among the least expensive items in the 1993 spring edition were decks and mini-decks of cards, some new and some used, for between $4.00 and $6.50. On the more pricey side, for $195 you could get a figurine of "Nadal handcrafted Spanish porcelain"—a dark-skinned peasant girl in an aqua dress, blue apron, and pink bonnet carrying a basket containing a creamy colored kitten. And for $260 you could pick up forty-seven books on cats in soft and hard cover, mostly new and in dust jackets, some older and some for children (I was tempted!).

Books (on or about cats, of course) are also reviewed and members are welcome to become pen pals with other members. Cat Collectors is at 33161 Wendy Drive, Sterling Heights, MI 48310.

Cat Dancer

～ The Cat Dancer is a simple toy for cats and their owners invented by Jim Boelke of Neenah, Wisconsin. It is a three-foot piece of 20-gauge oil-tempered spring steel, with twisted strips of cardboard on each end. In 1992 about three hundred thousand were sold. But the toy hadn't always been so popular.

In 1978, Mr. Boelke was sweeping the floor in a factory in Oshkosh, Wisconsin, when he noticed a strip of scrap metal. He took it home and waved it at his cats, Jake and Elwood, who sprang into action. He then started entertaining friends at parties with his little contraption and his dancing cats. Over the next four or five years he gave away thousands of his "little" invention.

In 1983, he decided he'd go for it. With $1500 he'd saved he went into business. It didn't hurt having Calvin Klein's cat, Max, appear on a celebrity-cat calendar proclaiming that the Cat Dancer was his favorite toy. Today, thousands of cats throughout the United States are running, jumping, and dancing with this simple and inexpensive toy—and Jim Boelke says he is not rich, but comfortable.

Cat fancy

～ This term refers to virtually anything connected with an interest, or more accurately love, of cats. It probably originated in Great Britain in the late nineteenth century, when cats were achieving new status and desirability. The word *fancy* could refer to breeds as well as to its other meaning, which is "to have a yearning for." In London you might hear something like, "I fancy a cup of tea right now." The magazine *Cat Fancy* is for cat owners, breeders, and lovers. It contains all kinds of information about felines.

Cat Festival

～ An annual Cat Festival, with medieval roots, takes place in Ieper, Belgium, on the second Sunday in May. It features a Parade Cat (kattestoet) with as many as 2500 marchers dressed as cats—on floats, skateboards, horses, on foot, and in carriages. You're likely to spot a witch or two as well, and images from the entire history and mythology of catdom are on display. For example, the divine cat Bastet, worshiped by the people of Egypt, will be represented, as will two giant cats pulling the chariot of Reya, the Germanic goddess, and cats portraying different proverbs and fables, such as Puss in Boots.

According to legend, the festival was started by Baudouin III, the count of Flanders in 962, when he ordered that two or three cats be thrown from the tower of his castle. At that time cats were sacrificed because of the pagan belief that had made the cat into a divine creature—usually of fertility. By ordering the cats thrown from his castle, Baudouin showed that the people of Ieper had totally renounced these pagan superstitions. Although there have been fairly frequent and sometimes long interruptions, the custom persisted over the centuries, and was not stopped until 1817. In 1938 the tradition resumed, with live cats being replaced by manmade plush ones!

In 1955 the parade was added to the festival. The parade starts at three o'clock P.M., and is followed by a jester tossing the cats from the belfry while spectators try to catch them. (It is said that if you return from the festival with one of the fool's cats, you will have a year of happiness.) The festival concludes with fireworks.

Cat from Outer Space, The ～

This 1987 Walt Disney film features a spaceship commanded by an alien cat named Jake who possesses extraterrestrial powers. When Jake's craft runs into some engine trouble and he is forced to land on earth to make repairs, he finds a friendly physicist who helps him get the money needed for the repairs, and he is able to rejoin his space fleet.

Cat House in Henfield ～ This

sixteenth-century cottage in Henfield, England, gets its name from the thirteen black cats that are painted on the paneled walls close below the thatched roof. Each cat is holding a bird in its paw. The story goes that during the last century, the owner of the house, Bob Ward, owned a canary that was his treasured companion. Canon Nathaniel Woodward, who lived nearby, also had a treasured companion—his cat. One day the canary got out of its cage and flew out the window just as the canon and his cat were passing.

The canary met a quick and violent death. As a constant reminder of the horrible deed his cat had done, Bob painted black cats on his house and rigged up a set of scallop shells on wires that he jangled to get the canon's attention every time he passed by. And though Bob and the canon are long gone, the cats on the house are still there. The tale continues to attract tourists who are visiting Sussex County. *See also* THE FELIX GALLERY, also in Sussex.

Cat House in Key West ～ This

store is filled with all kinds of cat items for sale for cats and their owners. It is located in the historic district in Old Town in the very building that at one time was the most popular CATHOUSE in the city. At that time it wasn't fancy cat T-shirts, posters, or pictures that drew the people in. That cathouse was known for having some of the most beautiful prostitutes in the town. Today, Purrle the cat, wearing a rhinestone collar, reigns. Address: 411 Green St. Key West, FL 33040. *See also* HEMINGWAY.

Cathouse Restaurant ～ This restaurant

contains over four thousand cat figurines, photos, and paintings. It was opened in Sebring, Florida, in 1972 by cat fanciers Norman Peck and Charles Cox. It was billed as "The World Famous Cathouse—Florida's Only Legal Cathouse." The sign for the restrooms points to the "Sandbox," and the private dining room is the "Persian Room." The current owners, Betty and Joe Reaves, bought the Cathouse in the mid-1980s. They do not buy any of the mementos found in the restaurant. Visitors bring in the cat-ifacts from all over the world on a daily basis. Ironically, the Reaves do not own a cat—but they do have dogs.

Cat-in-the-box ～ This is a very inexpensive game (usually free) which can keep your cats occupied for hours. In addition, they rarely outgrow it and never cease to enjoy it. Your role is minimal and entails supplying an empty box, preferably cardboard. The box can range in size from one your cat can just manage to squeeze into, to one in which the cat can perform various acrobatics, including chasing his tale, repeatedly. After supplying the box, your presence is not needed. The cat plays this on his own, the exception being when there is another cat around who is also interested in the box. In that case a game of musical box may ensue with one cat (not very playfully) chasing the other cat out of the box. "Cat-in-the-bag" is similar to "Cat-in-the-box" but requires a paper shopping bag. Should the box or bag become worn out or tattered, it is easily replaced. I have not been able to find any historical reference for this very common game nor an explanation for its continued fascination to cats. However, it is cheaper than catnip and store-bought toys that end up under the refrigerator and other inaccessible places, and most cats love it.

Cat-Lovers Cookbook, The ～ Though I admit I haven't tried any of the recipes yet, Tony Lawson's book includes such recipes for your fine feline friends as Sardines and Rice (Kitty Heaven), Meow Sushi, Chicken Soup, Chicken and Asparagus Casserole, Kitty Pizza, and Kitty Tacos. Some of these dishes your cats may be willing to share with you. They do take a smite more work than just opening a can, but doesn't your kitty deserve it? (Surely she'd do the same for you if you gave her this book and the necessary ingredients.) In a section called "Tandem Cooking," you'll find recipes designed for both you and your cat. There are also special diets and a few other little odds and ends, such as

how to make a kitty gift bag. The amusing illustrations are done by Tony's wife, Paté. The Lawsons live on the west coast in California. This book is a must for anyone who *really* cares about their cat!

Catnap ～ *See* SLEEPING.

Catnip ～ A perennial herb (*Nepeta cataria*) that is a member of the mint family, it is also known as catmint. The word *catnip* was first used in America in the early eighteenth century. Catnip has a strong scent that is very attractive to some cats, causing euphoric, uninhibited behavior as well as relaxation. The chemical in the catnip which is so exciting to your cat is nepetalactone, which is activated by smell and works on a cat's nervous system. It is nonaddictive and safe, although a cat who is exposed frequently can become immune to its effects.

The common response to catnip is sniffing; licking and chewing with head shaking; chin and neck rubbing; rolling over and body rubbing—in that order. Typically, the effect lasts five to fifteen minutes. About 70 percent of cats show some response to catnip, whether partial or total. Females and males appear to be equally affected. Other animals, like people, do not respond.

Catnip grows wild or can be grown in pots at home. It does best in direct sunlight. There are some hybrid varieties of catnip. The most common, *Nepeta cataria*, can be grown from seeds. If you are growing your own, the leaves should be picked in the early spring, on a warm sunny day. Flowers should be picked in mid- to late summer, when they are at their fullest. To dry the leaves or flowers, they should be placed in a single layer in a dark, warm, well-ventilated place for two to three weeks. Dried catnip is, of course, available in pet stores, where you will also find a variety of small toys stuffed with catnip.

Cats ～ This award-winning Broadway musical is based on T. S. Eliot's collection *Old Possum's Book of Practical Cats*, with music composed by Andrew Lloyd Webber. The show, Webber's inspiration, originally opened at the New London Theatre in 1981, where it became the longest-running musical in the history of British theater. *Cats* opened in New York City in October 1982, and as of early 1994 was still going strong. It is the longest-running musical on Broadway today, and the third longest-running production in Broadway history.

Cats has also played in Japan, Germany, Hungary, Austria, Canada, Australia, Norway, Finland, the Netherlands, Sweden, France, and Mexico.

The most well-known song from *Cats*, "Memory," has been recorded by over 150 singers, including Barbra Streisand, Barry Manilow, Johnny Mathis, Judy Collins, Eddie Fisher, and Liberace.

Cats has a cast of thirty-five actors and actresses all spectacularly costumed. Among the T. S. Eliot cats they play are Mister Mistoffelees the Magical Cat, Skimbleshanks the Railway Cat, Jellicles, Macavity, Gumbie Cat, and Old Deuteronomy, the patriarchal leader.

In the eleven years the *Cats* production has been staged in New York, it has consumed 33,280 condoms (used to protect body microphones); 1,870 pounds of Yak hair; 16,180 wig caps; 1,471 pounds of hairpins; and 8,415 pairs of socks.

Cat's cradle ～ This is a game played by two people who make different patterns with a string looped around their fingers by passing it back and forth. The pattern that begins the game is called the cradle. The cat's cradle has been around for many years and there are various explanations for its origins. Some say that the game has nothing at all to do with a cat—that *cat* is derived from *catch*, which is from the French word *crèche*, or manger. Another explanation is that the game relates to an old Eastern European custom. At the time, it was believed that a cat could increase a newlywed couple's chances of conceiving. (This was very likely, based on the fact that cats have no trouble reproducing.) One month after the wedding, a cat in a cradle was brought to the home of the newlyweds, where it was rocked back and forth in front of them. This was supposed to guarantee an early pregnancy for the bride. Yet another explanation focuses on the mysterious and magical powers of the cat around the world. In the Congo, the string patterns were changed in order to influence the path of the sun, to persuade the sun to rest. The string patterns were used by the Eskimos for the opposite reason, to trap the sun in the strings and increase its presence in the winter. The sun was seen as a "solar cat," to be symbolically caught in the cradle of string. The association with the sun may date back to ancient Egypt, when the great sun god Re or Ra was thought to take the form of a cat. According to James Frazer in *The Golden Bough*, Eskimo boys were not allowed to play the string game because it was thought that it might magically result in their fingers getting entangled in harpoon lines when they became adults.

Cat's Eye ～ In this 1985 movie based on a Stephen King story, a pet tabby named General protects a young girl from a troll that lives in her bedroom wall. Six identical cats were cast to play the coveted role. That way, if one cat wasn't working out, another could be substituted with no one the wiser. Burbank and Floyd, identical brown tabbies, most frequently played General. Named for the shelter where he was found, Burbank went on to play a starring role in the TV series *Frank's Place* with Tim Reid.

Cat Words

Because of the cat's long presence in our history and its unique and enigmatic personality, many words we use to describe other people or characteristics make reference to the cat. Here are some of cat-related words that have entered our lexicon.

cat around—a slang expression used to describe someone who is seeking a sexual partner.

catbird—a slate-colored songbird of north America known for its mewing call. In Australia, the term is used to describe someone who is seeking a sexual partner.

catburglar—lithe, agile, and quiet thieves adept at coming and going without attracting attention, like a cat. Cary Grant plays a former cat burglar in the Hitchcock film *To Catch a Thief.*

cater-cornered/kitty-cornered—used to describe something positioned diagonally across from another site, derived from the French *quartre*, or four-cornered. In the South, the term is cattywampus or catawampus.

catgut—This strong string used for tennis rackets, stringed instruments, bowstring, and sutures is in fact made from sheep's intestines. It appears to have been given its name because when it was used on instruments like the violin the sound created, by less talented musicians, was like that of a cat crying.

cathouse—slang term for brothel. Prostitutes have been called "cats" since the fifteenth century, when it was observed that a female cat in heat attracts many male cats. As early as 1400, men were warned to stay away from the "cattis tailis," or cat's tail.

cat-o'-nine-tails—a whip, usually having nine knotted lines or cords fastened to a handle and used for flogging, so named because of the catlike scratches it makes.

cat's paw—someone who is duped by another to serve his own purposes, derived from fables told by Aesop and LaFontaine in which a monkey persuades a cat to retrieve hot chestnuts from a fire for him. In his play, *L'Etourci*, Moliere includes the line "To pull the chestnuts from the fire with a cat's paw."

catty—used pejoratively to describe someone who is quietly or slyly malicious, frequently a gossip.

copycat—someone who imitates or mimics someone else. Sometimes a crime is called a copycat crime when it imitates another recent crime.

fat cat—an important, influential, famous and/or wealthy person, often in politics, no doubt because the cat symbolizes the good, plush or luxurious life.

hep cat—originating in the 1920s to describe jazz musicians and others who were "cool," "with-it", and "in the know."

kittenish—playful, frisky, playfully coy—like a kitten.

pussyfoot—to move in a stealthy or cautious manner in a catlike way, or to shy away from making a commitment or taking a stand.

Cat's-eye ～ Resembling the eye of a cat, this gemstone has a changeable luster. In medieval times, it was considered a very effective amulet that would protect one from the evils of witchcraft. According to E. A. Wallis Budge, an Egyptologist, Arabs believed the cat's-eye could make its owner invisible, and in some regions it was used for birth control. When a man was about to go to war he would wash the stone in some milk, which he would then give his wife to drink. Though this potion would not prevent the wife from having affairs while he was gone, it would prevent her from becoming pregnant.

Cat's Little Instruction Book, A ～ This book, and it is little, contains 201 pieces of advice for cats (just the right number). Author Leigh W. Rutledge is certainly in a position to give advice—he shares his Colorado home with twenty-eight cats. There is not sufficient space to list all his recommendations, but here are a few representative examples:

- Worry about courage, cleanliness, and hairballs.
- Stay out of automobile engines.
- The three Great Lies of Life are:
  1. "The check is in the mail."
  2. "All I want is one kiss."
  3. "It'll be all right, just get in the carrying case."
- No matter what you've done wrong, always try to make it look like the dog did it.

I have offered these suggestions to my cats and they have both been very appreciative, and there are another 197 pieces of appropriate and helpful advice. The book makes a good stocking stuffer for your cat, and if your cat cannot read it on his own, it affords you the opportunity to enjoy quality time together.

Cat Socializer program ～ By 1993 this three-year-old program at the San Francisco Society for the Prevention of Cruelty to Animals had eighty volunteers. The volunteers come on a regular basis and visit with kittens and cats at the shelter, where as many as one hundred cats may be waiting to be adopted. 2500 16th St. CA 94103; 415/554-3087

Cattery ～ a place where cats are bred and/or boarded.

Celebrity cats ～ Celebrity cats and other "cat people" of note include:

Denise Alexander—the actress who stars on the popular soap opera *General Hospital* is an animal lover. Her favorite may be Charlie, her orange tabby.

Confucius (551–479 B.C.)—The great Chinese sage who devoted his life to relieving suffering among the poor is said to have had a pet cat.

Ann-Margret—The Swedish-born star of the stage and screen is a lover of cats and the owner of many, including Big Red and a tabby named Tuffy.

Warren Beatty—This handsome actor was introduced to the world of cats by his former companion, Diane Keaton. She convinced him to adopt one, which he named Cake.

Polly Bergen—The singer, actress, and cosmetics businesswoman owns an Abyssinian whom she calls—what else?—Abby.

Raymond Chandler—The mystery writer's cat was a black Persian named Taki. He often referred to Taki as his "secretary" because she would sit on a manuscript as he worked on revisions. He talked to Taki as if she were a person.

Robert De Niro—The actor brought seven cats with him when he went to California to shoot *The Last Tycoon*. He and his cats stayed at the Beverly Hills Hotel. (Well, wouldn't you?)

Linda Evans—The star of *Dynasty* has a cat named She, as well as a collection of ceramic cats.

Faith Ford—The actress who plays Corky on the prime time TV series *Murphy Brown* owns a Russian Blue named Newman. (Perhaps after actor Paul.)

Michael J. Fox—The star of the hit movie *Back to the Future* and TV show *Family Ties* has ties to a black and white cat who shares his life.

Janet Leigh—The actress who starred in Hitchcock's *Psycho*—she was the one in the shower—has a cat whose name is Turkey.

Martin Mull—Mull's cat Alice is the butt of many of the comedian's jokes. Mull is also an actor who enjoys painting. I would certainly be surprised if Alice, who loves to watch him paint, has not found herself the subject of at least one masterpiece.

Aaron Neville—The jazz musician and Grammy winner lets his cat Tiger sit right beside his Grammy award.

Bernadette Peters—This versatile star of the stage, screen, TV, and cabaret is the owner of Murphy, a handsome Himalayan cat with blue eyes.

Pope Pius (1846–1878)—He had a very polite cat who patiently waited for the pope to finish dinner. That was when the pope himself would serve his cat food, at his table.

Sally Jessy Raphael—The TV talk show host has a blue-eyed cat named Sheba. Sally keeps a portrait of herself nearby so that Sheba won't be lonely while Sally is away talking with her guests and thousands of viewers.

O. J. Simpson—The Heisman Trophy winner, actor, and sports commentator calls his cat Sheena.

Gloria Steinem—The well-known feminist and author is the owner of Magritte, a big fluffy cat with big golden eyes.

Joan Van Ark—The longtime star of *Knots Landing*, who won acclaim for her role of Valene on the long-running prime time soap opera, named her cat Snug Harbor.

Queen Victoria (1819–1901)—The queen doted on cats. During her reign they came into great favor in England and were highly romanticized. After she died, her cat, White Heather, was cared for by the royal family. White Heather enjoyed a long and loving life in Buckingham Palace, dying during the reign of Edward VII.

H. G. Wells (1866–1946)—The English social critic, journalist, and author of such books as *The Time Machine* and *The War of the Worlds* had a cat named Mr. Peter Wells, who was known to friends as Mr. Peter. Legend has it that when Mr. Peter thought a guest was talking too long or too loudly, he would jump down and march noisily toward the door. No mention is made of the effectiveness of Mr. Peter's intervention.

Taboo—This cat owes its celebrity to his neighbor, superstar Michael Jackson, in Encino, California. Taboo has been catnaped more than once by enthusiastic fans who thought he was Michael's cat. The first time Taboo disappeared, his owners, Helen and Dave Arthur, were upset and worried until several days after Taboo's disappearance they got a phone call asking for Michael Jackson. Taboo's collar had the name Arthur on it and the Arthurs' phone number. The disappointed fans, who had taken Taboo to San Diego, drove the two hours back to Encino to return him.

See also CHAUCER, GEOFFREY; CHURCHILL, SIR WINSTON; and HEMINGWAY, ERNEST

Charlotte's cats ～ Charlotte Wright, in

Robertsdale, Alabama (population 2,400) takes in cats with feline leukemia, well aware that they have the fatal disease. Charlotte grew up with cats. In the early 1980s she adopted three kittens who were abandoned near the school where she taught. One of the kittens died of feline leukemia when he was six months old and the other two tested positive for the leukemia. Her veterinarian advised her not to get other cats because the virus is contagious. Seeing her disappointment, he asked if she'd consider adopting other cats with feline leukemia so that they would not have to be euthanized. She has had as many as forty-five cats at a time. The cats are housed in a special structure. Family and friends are supportive and help Charlotte feed and care for her pets. Charlotte also has a service called Critter Sitters, taking care of pets and sitting with them when their owners are away. As great a comfort as she is to the cats she cares for, they are in turn a great comfort to her. "There's nothing like a cat," she says. "I love those cats."

Chartreux ～ The Chartreux cat origi-

nated in France and there are numerous references to her in French lore and literature. Legend has it that Carthusian monks in France developed the Chartreux cat at their monastery, Le Grand Chartreux, during the seventeenth century. However, there is no mention of the Chartreux in Carthusian archives and no evidence that they were cat breeders.

The earliest recorded use of the name was in 1723 when the *Universal Dictionary of Commerce* used Chartreux to describe cats with blue hair.

The Leger sisters, who lived on a small Brittany island, are the first known breeders of the Chartreux. When they moved to the island Belle-Ile-sur-Mer in the 1920s, they found a large population of blue-gray cats in the capital city of the island. The first Chartreux was shown by the Legers in 1931 in Paris. The first Chartreux came to the United States in 1970.

The Chartreux is one of the rarest breeds in the world. Its population was diminished during the first and second world wars. Many were left homeless, to fend for themselves. Others were killed for badly needed food or for their plush, woolly, blue-gray coats.

PERSONALITY: Chartreux speak in a tiny voice and come when called. They are quiet, gentle, and very devoted. It is not unusual for a Chartreux to prefer the company of people and dogs to other cats.

Chaucer, Geoffrey ～ (1340–1400) The

British author of *Canterbury Tales* included cats in his famous stories. Some of the pilgrims bring cats with them on the journey from England to Canterbury, and in "The Manciple's Tale," Chaucer speaks of the merits of the cat:

> Lat take a cat and fostre hym wel with milk
> And tendre flessch and make his couche of silk,
> And lat hym seen a mouse go by the wal,

Anon he weyvith* milk and flessch and al,
And every deyntee that is in the hous,
Swich appetite hath he to ete a mous.
Lo, heere hath lust his dominacioun,
And appetit fleemeth** disrecioun.

 * weyveth = abandons
** fleemeth = banishes

Cherry Pop ~ This red Persian cat may very well be the most pampered cat in the land. She is owned by—or perhaps a better way of putting it is that she owns—Vi and Huey Vanek of Fort Lauderdale, Florida. The millionaires spent $150,000 and racked up some 260,000 frequent flyer miles in 1987 and 1988 taking Cherry Pop to cat shows around the country, where she took many top prizes. When Cherry Pop visited San Francisco, she was given the keys to the city. When she went to Los Angeles she met Doris Day, Angie Dickinson, and Betty White. When she traveled to Boston she was crowned Queen of the City by the mayor.

Back in Fort Lauderdale, Cherry Pop resides with the Vaneks in a $400,000 home which was designed with her in mind. She can lounge on a concrete perch in front of a giant picture window and watch the aviary and squirrel area that was built just for her viewing pleasure. She dines on choice lean steak twice a day and drinks Evian water and skim milk. Should Cherry Pop outlive her owners, she will never want. The Vaneks have willed their estate to her (and the other two cats they own) and enough money to a cat lover so that their heirs can live in the luxury to which they have become accustomed for the rest of their lives.

Resembling the British Blue shorthair, the Chartreux is said to have originated at the monastery of La Grande Chartreuse in France in the Middle Ages. (PHOTOGRAPH BY ISABELLE FRANCAIS.)

The Cheshire cat, by John Tenniel from Alice's Adventures in Wonderland, *1865.*

Cheshire cat

One of the most well-known cat figures in all of literature, the enigmatic Cheshire cat makes its appearance—and disappearance—in Lewis Carroll's *Alice's Adventures in Wonderland*, published in 1865. Alice first encounters the cat grinning ear to ear in the Queen's kitchen:

"Please would you tell me," said Alice a little timidly, for she was not quite sure whether it was good manners for her to speak first, "why your cat grins like that!"

"It's a Cheshire cat," said the Duchess, "and that's why. Pig!" She said the last word with such sudden violence that Alice quite jumped; but she saw in another moment that it was addressed to the baby, and not to her, so she took courage, and went on again:—

"I didn't know that Cheshire cats always grinned; in fact, I didn't know that cats *could* grin."

"They all can," said the Duchess; "and most of 'em do."

"I don't know of any that do," Alice said very politely, feeling quite pleased to have got into the conversation.

"You don't know much," said the Duchess; "and that's a fact."

Later, Alice converses with the cat:

The Cat only grinned when it saw Alice. It looked good-natured, she thought: still it had *very* long claws and a great many teeth, so she felt it ought to be treated with respect.

"Cheshire Puss," she began, rather timidly, as she did not at all know whether it would like the name: however, it only grinned a little wider. "Come, it's pleased so far," thought Alice, and she went on, "Would you tell me, please, which way I ought to walk from here?"

"That depends a good deal on where you want to get to," said the Cat.

"I don't much care where——" said Alice.

"Then it doesn't matter which way you walk," said the Cat.

"——so long as I get *somewhere*," Alice added as an explanation.

"Oh, you're sure to do that," said the Cat, "if you only walk long enough."

Alice felt that this could not be denied, so she tried another question. "What sort of people live about here?"

"In *that* direction," the Cat said, waving its right paw round, "lives a Hatter: and in *that* direction," waving the other paw, "lives a March Hare. Visit either you like: they're both mad."

"But I don't want to go among mad people," Alice remarked.

"Oh, you can't help that," said the Cat: "we're all mad here. I'm mad. You're mad."

"How do you know I'm mad?" said Alice.

"You must be," said the Cat, "or you wouldn't have come here."

Alice didn't think that proved it at all; however, she went on: "and how do you know that you're mad?"

"To begin with," said the Cat, "a dog's not mad. You grant that?"

"I suppose so," said Alice.

"Well then," the Cat went on, "you see a dog growls when it's angry, and wags its tail when it's pleased. Now *I* growl when I'm pleased, and wag my tail when I'm angry. Therefore I'm mad."

"*I* call it purring, not growling," said Alice.

"Call it what you like," said the Cat. "Do you play croquet with the Queen to-day?"

"I should like it very much," said Alice, "but I haven't been invited yet."

"You'll see me there," said the Cat, and vanished.

Alice was not much surprised at this, she was getting so well used to queer things happening. While she was still looking at the place where it had been, it suddenly appeared again.

"By-the-bye, what became of the baby?" said the Cat. "I'd nearly forgotten to ask."

(*continued*)

"It turned into a pig," Alice answered very quietly, just as if the Cat had come back in a natural way.

"I thought it would," said the Cat, and vanished again.

Alice waited a little, half expecting to see it again, but it did not appear and after a minute or two she walked on in the direction in which the March Hare was said to live. "I've seen hatters before," she said to herself: "the March Hare will be much the most interesting, and perhaps as this is May it won't be raving mad—at least not so mad as it was in March." As she said this, she looked up, and there was the Cat again, sitting on a branch of a tree.

"Did you say pig, or fig?" said the Cat.

"I said pig," replied Alice; "and I wish you wouldn't keep appearing and vanishing so suddenly: you make one quite giddy."

"All right," said the Cat; and this time it vanished quite slowly, beginning with the end of the tail, and ending with the grin, which remained some time after the rest of it had gone.

"Well! I've often seen a cat without a grin," thought Alice; "but a grin without a cat! It's the most curious thing I ever saw in all my life!"

The name Cheshire cat may have originated in Cheshire, England, where local coats of arms were emblazoned with a lion's face which over time began to appear as a grinning cat.

Chessie ∼ This charming picture of a sleeping kitten, drawn by Austrian artist Guido Gruenwald, became the symbol for the Chesapeake and Ohio Railroad in 1934. The original illustration was bought in 1933 by Lionel C. Probert, a C&O executive, at a New York art gallery. He thought the picture of the adorable sleeping kitten could be the perfect symbol for the smooth ride the C&O offered passengers.

The kitten, given the name Chessie, made her debut in 1934 in an ad in *Fortune* magazine, accompanied by the slogan, "Sleep like a kitten." Within two days of publication the magazine received over three hundred requests for copies of the print. When the company issued a free Chessie calendar that same year, forty thousand copies disappeared virtually overnight. Since then, Chessie has appeared in many ads and on millions of calendars, as well as on jewelry, hats, vests, pocket knives, tape measures, pens, scarves, playing cards, T-shirts, tote bags and so on. At one point, the slogan changed to "Purr-fect transportation."

When the C&O, B&O, and Western Railroads became affiliated, it became the Chessie System.

Gruenwald, the artist, never knew what a popular figure Chessie had become. Though he knew that an American railroad company had purchased full reproduction rights to his print *Good*

Night, neither he nor his agent ever learned of Chessie's great success. They died in 1935 and 1937.

Children's cat books ～ Cats have

been very popular in children's literature from early on. One of the most well-known tales, "PUSS IN BOOTS," first appeared in Giovanni Francesco Straparola's book of fairy tales and fables. Though Charles Perrault's version, published in France in 1696, has became a classic. Since then *Puss in Boots* books have come out in many different versions, perhaps the latest "Puss in Boots," but

Chessie, who at peaceful sleep became the symbol for the Chesapeake and Ohio Railroad.

certainly not the last, is the version by Lincoln Kirstein a founder of the School of American Ballet and the New York City Ballet, published in 1992. Artist Alain Vaës, internationally known for his costume and set designs for the New York City Ballet, painted the water-color illustrations.

Similarly, there are numerous versions of the English fable, DICK WHITTINGTON AND HIS CAT, published by G. P. Putnam's Sons in 1892, although no doubt it was around for many years before that. In both stories the cats are the heros, making their owners successful, wealthy, and famous.

Many of the fables and folklore which have been passed down parents to child, from generation to generation, on every continent, all over the world, feature cats. AESOP'S FABLES, written around 500 B.C. by the Greek writer Aesop, include many cats, such as "The Cat and the Fox," "The Eagle and the Cat," "Venus and the Cat," "Cat and the Cock," "The Cat, the Cock, and the Young Mouse." Two German brothers, Jakob and Wilhelm GRIMM, researched and recorded hundreds of stories between 1812 and 1815 and published their collection in *Fairy Tales*. Some of the fairy tales featuring cats are "The Companionship of the Cat and the Mouse," "The Fox and the Cat," and "The Miller's Drudge and the Cat." In the first one the cat outwits the mouse. In the second tale, the cat "outfoxes" the fox. And in the third tale, a cat is the hero as well. In this volume you'll find examples of cat folklore from nationalities around the world: African, American Indian, Arabic, Chinese, English, French, Irish, Italian, Japanese, Rumanian, and Russian.

Children's books about cats have prospered and proliferated in the modern era as well, especially as cats have joined more and more households. Wanda Gag's *Millions of Cats*, first published in 1928, has sold hundreds of thousands of copies and if it hasn't sold a million copies yet, no doubt it soon will. It is still found on bookstore shelves and on bookshelves (or on the floor) in many children's rooms. *Millions of Cats* won the Newbery Honor Book award in 1929. Does the number of cats in the book have anything to do with its popularity? Probably not, but the authors of *A Castle of a Thousand Cats*, *House of Thirty Cats*, and *Twenty-seven Cats Next Door* weren't taking any chances.

Another popular, well-known book is *The Cat in the Hat* by Dr. Seuss (THEODORE SEUSS GEISEL). This volume, published in 1957, and its sequel, *The Cat in the Hat Comes Back* (1958) are just two of the author's hilarious, illustrated, rhyming books which children, and adults, have come to love.

Some of the other older titles you'll probably recognize are *Anatole and the Cat* by Eve Titus (1957); *A Cricket in Times Square* by George Selden (1960); *Cat Who Went to Heaven* by Elizabeth Coatsworth (1930); and *Blue Cat of Castletown* by Catherine Kate Coblentz (1949).

And one of the most well-known fictional cats, the CHESHIRE CAT, plays a very prominent role in Lewis Carroll's *Alice in Wonderland*.

Cats have also played a prominent role in comic books. Some have even had their own such as Heathcliff, Creepy Cat, and Felix.

Perhaps there are so many books about cats because many writers for children have cats themselves, or because cat books seem to have a long, long life (*Puss in Boots* is still going strong) or because books about cats sell well. Editors have noted that typically when two children's books by the same author are released, if one stars cats and the other doesn't, the cat book far outsells the other book. (Could another reason that cat books sell so well be that mothers, who most frequently buy books for their children, have long been known to be partial to cats while men are partial to dogs?)

Cats make good subjects for children's books for a number of reasons. Being independent, they can serve as a role model for their young readers. Because cats' personalities are so varied, the stories about them can be as well. Cats are seen as mysterious, sweet, gentle, magical, adventurous. Writers can, therefore, depict cats doing virtually anything—and it is not out of character, outrageous, or absurd.

There are children's cat books which tell real-life stories—the experiences we face with our own cats, how they entertain themselves, how their mommy feeds and takes care of them; fantasy stories about hero cats who save lives, cats who fly to the moon, talk, procure a title and great fortune for their owner; and how-to stories that describe the different kinds of cats, how to take care of them, their habits and so on.

As with just about anything else, there are people who collect cat books written for children. You may want to check your attic for Beatrix Potter first editions; in the late 1980s *The Pie and the Kitty Pan*, published in 1905 went for $125, *The Tale of Tom Kitten* published in 1907 for $150 and, *The Story of Miss Moppet*, published in 1906, for $295.

Many authors of "adult" books have also written books about cats for kids including Pearl Buck, T. S. Eliot, Peter De Vries, and Rudyard Kipling.

Chinese folktale ∼ A cautionary cat tale survives from China. In "The Helpful Animals," while fishing, a poor boy catches a broken piece of an iron pot on his line instead of a fish. Realizing that it is a treasure, he brings it home and hides it in a box, which he hangs from the ceiling. From that day on he becomes richer and richer, and hires a servant. Thinking that there must be some reason his master has become so rich, the servant finally finds the piece of iron and flees with it. Thereupon the young man's fortunes change.

Noticing their reduced circumstances, one

Cats were widely admired in China, as they were in much of Asia. This detail from Spring Play in a T'ang Garden, *a silk handscroll by an unknown artist, is a copy of a painting attributed to Hsuan Tsung of the Ming Dynasty (1368–1644).* (COURTESY THE METROPOLITAN MUSEUM OF ART, FLETCHER FUND, 1947.)

day his cat says to his dog, "Master always used to give us meat and rice and some of what he ate. Why do we only get some soaked rice now?" The dog explains about the stolen lucky treasure and both agree they must retrieve it for their master. They quickly leave and after crossing a sea and a river they find the runaway servant's house. Around midnight the cat creeps in and approaches a mouse hole. "Will you help us steal the treasure?" he asks the mice. "Certainly," they reply, climbing to the beam from which the hidden treasure is hung in the box. Gnawing through the rope from which it hangs and then through the box, the mice retrieve the charm and give it to the cat and dog.

On the way home the dog drops the lucky piece of iron pot into the sea. When the dragon king hears what has happened, he orders a servant to return the fragment to them—obviously not recognizing it for the treasure that it is. The grateful cat and dog finally arrive home with the charm and put it on the table. When the wife sees the now bedraggled cat she flies into a rage and shouts, "Monster: now that we are poor you animals have become foul as corpses!" whereupon she gives the poor cat such a hard blow that she kills her. Then she does the same to the dog.

When they are both dead, the treasure returns to the place it had come from—that is to say, the sea.

Churchill, Sir Winston ～ (1874–1965)

An exemplary cat lover, the British statesman and writer brought his cat Nelson with him to Ten Downing Street in 1940, when he began his term as prime minister. Nelson would crawl under the bed and retreat to the farthest corner when London was being bombed. Churchill's cat Jock slept with him and ate with him. When it was time for dinner, Churchill would often send servants to find Jock and would not eat until Jock

was present. Jock was also a frequent visitor to numerous wartime cabinet meetings held at the prime minister's residence. Churchill would personally take Jock to a safe place during a blitz in London. Churchill's cat refused to leave his owner's bedside during Churchill's final illness. But just hours before Churchill died, the cat suddenly left the house, as though he knew his owner would soon depart.

Cinderella ～

This animated Disney feature film, released in 1950, included in the cast a mean, nasty cat named Lucifer. Belonging to Cinderella's wicked stepmother and stepsisters, Lucifer walks with his nose in the air when near Cinderella. In the end, though, Cinderella wins her prince and Lucifer plunges to his death after being tossed through a window by Cinderella's dog, Bruno.

> The cat lives alone, has no need of society, obeys only when she pleases, pretends to sleep that she may see the more clearly and scratches everything on which she can lay her paw.
>
> FRANÇOIS-AUGUSTE-RENÉ DE CHATEAUBRIAND, French writer (1768–1848)

> A whisker first, and then a claw,
> With many an ardent wish,
> She stretched in vain to reach the prize—
> What female heart can gold despise?
>
> THOMAS GRAY (1716–1761), "Ode on the Death of a Favourite Cat"

> Those who'll play with cats must expect to be scratched.
>
> MIGUEL DE CERVANTES, Spanish writer
> (1547–1616)

Claws ∽ It is thought by many cat owners that cats scratch the fabric of the couch or chair in order to sharpen their nails, but it is actually another way of grooming. The old claw is removed leaving a new, healthy claw. It's like a snake shedding its skin. Cats only claw with their front paws. They use their mouths to bite and groom the nails on their hind legs.

The scratching also serves as exercise, making the retraction and protrusion reflexes of the claws stronger. The cat's claws are a vital instrument for catching prey, defending itself, and climbing.

Another function that scratching plays is that of scent marking. Underneath the cat's front paws are scent glands. The rubbing produces a scent which is rubbed onto the fabric, putting the cats personal "signature" on the item of furniture. Cats who have been declawed will continue to scratch at the furniture, but with much less dire results.

Cleopatra ∽ (68–30 B.C.) The queen of Egypt (51–49 and 48–30 B.C.) and the mistress of Julius Caesar and Mark Antony, Cleopatra was also a cat fancier. Her cat was named Charmian and it was said that she copied the shape and style of her cat's eyes in her own makeup and facial decorations; she also adapted the same aloof attitude as her cat. See EGYPT.

Coat ∽ The coat of the cat is one of the major components in judging cats in competition—and in choosing a pet for a home—and is often what is noticed first about any cat. Generally, cats have long hair or short hair, with shorthair cats being more popular. (Even the "hairless" sphynx cat has some hair. As an adult, she has a soft fuzz of down hair on her paws.)

> The tortoise-shell cat
> She sits on the mat,
>   As gay as a sunflower she.
>
> PATRICK CHALMERS, American writer,
> twentieth century

Ode to a Cat

> All your wondrous wealth of hair,
>   Dark and fair,
> Silken-shaggy, soft and bright
> As the clouds and beams of night,
> Pays my reverent hand's caress
> Back with friendlier gentleness.
>
> A. C. SWINBURNE, British poet and critic
> (1837–1909)

Cats usually have four types of hair: down hair, awn hair, guard hair, and vibrissae. Down hair is soft, thin and short. It is closest to the body of the cat and serves as insulation, keeping the cat warm—kind of like a down coat keeps you warm. Awn hairs are the middle hairs—between the down and guard hairs. They are bristly with a slight swelling toward the tip before tapering off. Guard hairs are the longest and thickest of the ordinary body hairs, forming the protective topcoat. They keep the underlying hair dry and snug. Guard hairs are straight and evenly tapered. Vibrissae are the whiskers, greatly enlarged and toughened hair. (*See* WHISKERS.) (Through breeding, some cats have an "abnormal" number of one or more types of the hair, and some cats don't have the four types.)

Your cat's beautiful coat is also very functional. It protects the cat from heat and cold, physical injuries, too much sun, and harmful chemicals. A cat can have as many as 130,000 hairs per square inch on her belly and about half that amount on her back. In the summer a cat's coat thins; in the winter, when it is cold, the coat fluffs out. A thick layer of heated hair which is trapped near the skin keeps the cat warm.

The cat's hair is more than "dark and fair." Cats' coats come in a virtually unlimited number of different colors, shadings, and patterns. Pedigreed cats who are shown are judged by very specific breed standards, but domestic, unpedigreed cats also display just as great a variety of markings.

There are about half a dozen basic colors of cat hair: black or ebony; blue; chestnut or chocolate brown; cinnamon; cream, lavender or lilac; red; and white. When a cat has all the same colored hairs, from the roots to the tips, the coat is called solid- or "self"-colored. When the individual hairs have bands of several different colors, the pattern is known as ticking. (The best known ticked cat is the Abyssinian.) Brindling is the random mixture of different colored hairs in a cat's coat.

The most common solid color cat is the black cat. Most cats are not solid-colored, however, and have shadings and patterns. Cats with "shading" display a gradual variation in the color of the coat, usually cream or white, from belly to back. If the hair is fairly long, the cat may appear to have a solid coat, but when she moves it is evident the color of the hairs actually varies.

The patterns of a cat's coat also come in a great variety. The most common is the classic tabby, with symmetrical stripes and spirals circling up her legs, ringing her tail, and falling horizontally over her back. A characteristic "M" marks the forehead, dark unbroken lines extend from the outer corner of each eye. A mackerel tabby has more narrow, clearly defined stripes than the classic tabby. A patched tabby, which is also called a torbie, displays patches of red and/or cream in her coat. A spotted tabby has spots in the coat that may vary in size and shape. A ticked tabby has a coat with hairs having two or three bands of color.

Cats may also be marked with points, in which particular parts of the cats body are a darker color. The points on a cat are the mask (the hair around the eyes and nose), ears, paws, tail, and sexual organs (in the male cat). The cats most noted for points are the Siamese, which are identified by the color of the accents: blue point, chocolate point, lilac point, and sealpoint.

Other patterns include white with patches of white, black, blue, red, or cream; calico, a white coat with patches of red and black; the tortoise shell, black with red and cream patches; and the cameo, with darker color on the tips of the hair than underneath.

Contraceptives ～ Contraceptives for cats? The most common way in the United States of rendering a cat infertile is the surgical removal of the cat's sex organs. Females are "spayed" and males are "castrated." However, this is not the only way to prevent reproduction, and an effort was made to develop contraceptive pills for cats—similar to the ones used by humans. The pill was tried with stray cats, but there were unwelcome side effects. And the method was far from foolproof, since many cats avoided the food containing the pill. Israel claims to prevent the birth of some twenty thousand kittens a year using the pill. Stay tuned . . .

Colette

The French author (1873–1954) wrote about her cats in her books and was very devoted to them. Her cats had names like Fanchette, Zwerg, and La Chatte, which is the feminine of the French word for *cat*. Chartreux was the last cat she owned. When her cat Zwerg died, she wrote to a friend, "We ought only to allow ourselves to become attached to parrots and tortoises."

Colette obviously felt strongly about the positive qualities of cats. She has written, "The only risk you ever run in befriending a cat is enriching yourself," and, "There are no ordinary cats." In one of her novels, *The Cat*, the protagonist must choose between Saha, an exquisite Russian blue, and his bride. He chooses Saha. Here is one charming example of her stories about cats.

The Long-cat

A short-haired black cat always looks longer than any other cat. But this particular one, Babou, nicknamed the Long-cat, really did measure, stretched right out flat, well over a yard and a quarter. If you did not arrange him properly, he was not much more than a yard. I used to measure him sometimes.

"He's stopped growing longer," I said one day to my mother. "Isn't it a pity?"

"Why a pity? He's too long as it is. I can't understand why you want everything to grow bigger. It's bad to grow too much, very bad indeed!"

It's true that it always worried her when she thought that children were growing too fast, and she had good cause to be anxious about my elder half-brother, who went on growing until he was twenty-four.

"But I'd love to grow a bit taller."

"D'you mean you'd like to be like that Brisedoux girl, five-foot-seven tall at twelve years old? A midget can always make herself liked. But what can you do with a gigantic beauty? Who would want to marry her?"

"Couldn't Babou get married, then?"

"Oh, a cat's a cat. Babou's only too long when he really wants to be. Are we even sure he's black? He's probably white in snowy weather, dark blue at night, and red when he goes to steal strawberries. He's very light when he lies on your knees, and very heavy when I carry him into the kitchen in the evenings to prevent him from sleeping on my bed. I think he's too much of a vegetarian to be a real cat."

For the Long-cat really did steal strawberries, picking out the ripest of the variety called Docteur-Morère which are so sweet, and of the white Hautboys which taste faintly of ants. According to the season he would also go for the tender tips of the

(continued)

asparagus, and when it came to melons his choice was not so much for cantaloupes as for the kind called Noir-des-Carmes whose rind, marbled light and dark like the skin of a salamander, he knew how to rip open. In all this he was not at all exceptional. I once had a she-cat who used to crunch rings of raw onions, provided they were the sweet onions of the South. There are cats who set great store by oysters, snails, and clams.

When the Long-cat went off to poach strawberries from our next-door neighbor, Monsieur Pomié, he went by way of the wall, which was covered with such dense ivy that the cats could walk along under cover, their presence revealed only by the quivering of the leaves, the mist of yellow pollen and the golden cloud of bees.

He loved his leafy tunnel but, do what he would, he had to come out of it at the end since Madame Pomié kept the top of the wall bare where it overlooked her garden. Once out in the open, he adopted a very off-hand manner, especially if he met Madame de Saint-Aubin's beautiful cat, who was black, with a white face and belly. I found this wall a good place to study tomcats, not so much their habits as their ceremonial procedure, governed by a kind of choreography. Unlike the females, they are more noisy than warlike and they try to gain time by palavers. Hence all the snarling preambles. Not that they do not know how to fight cruelly once they come to grips; but as a rule they are far removed from the silent and furious grapplings of the females. The she-cat we had at the same time as the Long-cat literally flew into battle if a female ventured into her haunts. Barely touching the ground, she would pounce on the enemy, even if it were her own offspring. She fought as a bird does, going for her adversary's head. I never saw her chastise a male, except for a few cuffs, for as soon as the males saw her they fled, while she followed them with a look of inexpressible contempt. When July and January came, she settled her amorous encounters in forty-eight hours. On the morning of the third day, when the chosen partner, in fine fettle and with renewed appetite, approached her with a self-confident, prancing gait and a deep-throated song, she would root him to the spot with a mere look.

"I've come," he would begin. "I . . . I came to resume our agreeable conversation of yesterday . . ."

"Excuse me," the she-cat interrupted, "you were saying? I didn't quite catch. What agreeable conversation?"

"Why . . . the one we had at ten o'clock in the morning . . . and the one at five in the afternoon . . . and especially our conversation at ten in the evening, near the well."

The she-cat, perched on top of the pergola, raised herself a little on her delicately-boned paws.

"Near the well, a conversation, you, with *me*? Who do you suppose is going to believe that? You don't expect *me* to! Take yourself off! It'll be the worse for you if you don't, I can tell you. Take yourself off!"

"But . . . but I love you. And I'm ready to prove it to you again."

Standing upright there the she-cat towered over the tom as Satan, jutting out from Notre Dame, broods over Paris. The look she cast on him from her tawny-gold eyes was such as he could not long endure; and the outcast would make off with the shambling gait of someone who has been driven away.

As I was saying then, the Long-cat, impelled by a vegetarian craving which those who have not experienced it can never understand, would go after the strawberries, the melons and the asparagus. On his return, a little green or rosy pulp remained, as evidence of his pillagings, in the grooves between his curved claws, and this he licked casually during his siesta.

"Show your hands!" my mother used to say to him, and thereupon he surrendered to her a long front paw, adept at every kind of mischief, with pads as hard as a road parched with drought.

"Have you been opening a melon?"

I dare say he understood. His gentle yellow eyes met Sido's penetrating look, but since his innocence was only assumed, he could not help squinting a little.

"Yes, you *have* opened a melon. And I expect it was the pretty little one I had my eye on, the one that looked like a globe with yellow continents and green seas." She released the long paw which fell back limp and expressionless.

"That deserves a good slap," said I.

"I know. But just think that instead of a melon he might have slit open a bird, or a little rabbit, or have eaten a chick."

She scratched the flat skull which he stretched up against her hand, and the half-bald temples which showed bluish between the sparse black hairs. A tremendous purring rose from his thick neck with its white patch under the chin. The Long-cat loved no one but my mother, followed no one but her and looked to her for everything. If I took him in my arms he would imperceptibly glide out of them as though he were melting away. Except for the ritual battles and during the brief seasons of love-making, the Long-cat was nothing but silence, sleep and nonchalant night-prowlings.

I naturally preferred our she-cats to him. The females of the feline tribe are so unlike the males that they seem to regard the tom as a stranger and often as an enemy. The only exceptions are the cats of Siam who live in couples like the wild beasts. Perhaps it is because the cats in our countries are such a hybrid collection of every coat and color that they develop a taste for change and fickleness. In my home we were never without two or three she-cats who graced the lawns, crowned the pump and slept in the wisteria, which they had hollowed into a hammock. They confined their charming sociability to my mother and myself. As soon as January and July, the compulsory seasons of love, were over, they regarded the male once again as a suspect, a lout, and a wicked devourer of newly-born kittens, and their conversations with the Long-cat

(*continued*)

consisted chiefly of crisp insults, whenever he assumed the bland, gentle manner and the innocent smile of the cat who has never harbored any evil intentions, or even thoughts. Sometimes they seemed about to play, but this never came to anything. The females took fright at the strength of the male, and at that furious excitement which, in an uncastrated cat, turns playfulness into a murderous combat.

By virtue of his serpent-like build, the Long-cat excelled at strange leaps in which he nearly twisted himself into a figure of eight. In full sunlight his winter coat, which was longer and more satiny than in summer, revealed the waterings and markings of his far-off tabby ancestor. A tom will remain playful until he is quite old; but even in play his face never loses the gravity that is stamped on it. The Long-cat's expression softened only when he looked at my mother. Then his white whiskers would bristle powerfully, while into his eyes crept the smile of an innocent little boy. He used to follow her when she went to pick violets along the wall that separated M. de Fourolles' garden from ours. The close-set border provided every day a big bunch which my mother let fade, either pinned to her bodice or in an empty glass, because violets in water lose all their scent. Step by step the Long-cat followed his stooping mistress, sometimes imitating with his paw the gesture of her hand groping among the leaves, and imitating her discoveries also. "Ha, ha!" he would cry, "me too!" and thereupon show his prize: a bombardier beetle, a pink worm or a shriveled cockchafer.

"My goodness, how silly you are," Sido would say to him, affectionately. "Never mind, what you've found is very pretty."

When we rejoined my elder brother in the Loiret, we took with us our favorite she-cat and the Long-cat. Both of them seemed to mind much less than I did exchanging a lovely house for a small cottage, and the vast grounds of our family property for a narrow garden. I have referred elsewhere to the stream which danced at the end of this garden. Left to itself, it was sufficiently clear and sparkling, and had enough soap-wort and wild radishes clinging to the walls which hemmed it in, to beautify any village, if the village had respected it. But those who lived on its banks polluted it.

At the end of our new garden there was a little wash-house which protected the straw palliasse on which the washerwomen knelt, the sloping board, white as a scraped bone, where they pressed the frothing linen, the washerwomen's battledores, the brushes made of couch-grass and the sprinklers. Soon after our arrival the she-cat laid claim to the palliasse, gave birth to her litter on it, and brought up there the one little tabby which we left her. Whenever the sun shone I joined her there and sat on the soaping-board. The tabby kitten, soft and heavy with milk, watched the reflections of the little river forming broken rings, gold serpents and wavelets on the tiled roof of the penthouse. At six weeks he was already trotting, and following the flight of the flies with eyes that were still blue, while his mother, with a coat as finely marked as his, saw herself mirrored in the beauty of her son.

Excluded though he was from this family happiness, the Long-cat for all that adopted an air of serenity that was vaguely patriarchal, the detached bearing of those fathers who are content to leave the care of their offspring to their worthy spouse. He confined himself to the parsley bed which the she-cat let him have, and there he would sprawl, warming his long belly, with its withered teats, in the sun. Or else he would drape himself over the heap of firewood, as if the spiky faggots were wool and down. For a cat's idea of what is comfortable and what is not is incomprehensible to a human.

Spring drenched our retreat with precocious warmth, and in the light air of May the scents of lilac, young tarragon and red-brown wallflower intermingled. I was at that time a prey to homesickness for my native village, and this I nursed in silence in the new village, amidst the bitterness of spring and its first flowers. There I sat, an anemic young girl, leaning my cheeks and my little waxen ears against a wall already warm, the end of one of my over-long plaits always trailing far from me over the fine, sieved leaf-mold of a seed-bed.

One day when we were all dozing, the she-cat on her palliasse, the tom on his couch of spiky firewood-bundles, and I at the foot of the wall where the sun lingered longest, the little cat, who was wide awake and busy chasing flies on the edge of the river, fell into the water. True to the code of his tribe, he uttered no cry and began to swim by instinct as soon as he came to the surface. I happened to see him tumble in, and just as I was setting off for the house to seize the butterfly net, run down the road, and rejoin the river at the first little bridge, where I could have fished out the swimming kitten, the Long-cat threw himself into the water. He swam like an otter, ears flat and only his nostrils out of the water.

It is not every day that one sees a cat swim, swim of his own free will, I mean. He can glide unerringly through the water like a serpent, but he never makes use of this gift except to save his life if he is in danger of drowning. Helped by the current, the Long-cat forged ahead strongly in pursuit of the kitten, the swift, transparent water of the pent-up river on its bed of pebbles and broken shards making his long body look like a leech. I lost half a minute through stopping to watch him.

He seized the little cat by the scruff of its neck, turned right round and set off upstream, not without effort, for the current was strong and the kitten, inert like all little cats when you hold them by the scruff of their necks, weighed his full weight. The sight of the Long-cat struggling nearly made me jump into the water too. But the rescuer clambered on to the washing-board and laid his dripping burden on the bank, after which he shook himself and looked in stupefaction at the drenching kitten. That was the moment when the rescued one, silent hitherto, elected to cough and sneeze and set up a terrific shrill lamentation which awoke the mother cat.

"Horrors!" she cried. "What do I see? You baby-snatcher! You wrecker, you devourer of infants, you stinking beast, what have you done to my son?"

(continued)

Even as she jerked out these insults at the top of her voice, she was already encircling the little cat with her own body and sniffing him, finding time to turn him all over and lick the river water off his coat.

"But," ventured the Long-cat, "but . . . but on the contrary, I jumped into the water to get him. Now I come to think of it, I don't know what made me do it!"

"Out of my sight! Or in another moment I'll bite your nose off and crush the breath out of you! I'll blind you, I'll slit your throat, I'll . . ."

She made ready to suit the action to the word, and I admired the furious beauty which animates a female when she pits herself against danger or an adversary bigger than herself.

The Long-cat took to his heels and, still dripping, gained the ladder leading to the cozy hay-loft warm under its tiled roof. The she-cat, changing her tone, led her son to the palliasse where he found once again the warm maternal belly with its milk, healing care and restoring sleep.

But the she-cat never forgave the Long-cat. Whenever she met him she never forgot to call him "baby-snatcher, drowner of little cats, assassin," accompanying this with snarls and yells, while the Long-cat strove each time to clear himself: "Now look here! I tell you that, on the contrary, it was I who, obeying only my own heart, overcame my loathing for cold water . . ."

I genuinely pitied him and used to call him "poor, misunderstood Long-cat."

"Misunderstood," said my mother, "that remains to be seen."

She could see deep into souls; and she was not one to be taken in by the equivocal meekness, the flickering yellow gleam in the eye of a tomcat, whenever it lights on tender, defenseless flesh.

Coolidge, Calvin ～ (1872–1933) The thirtieth president of the United States, Coolidge served from 1923 to 1929 along with his three cats, Blackie, Tiger, and Timmie. Timmie would allow a canary named Caruso to walk over his back and sleep between his claws. When one of his cats disappeared, Coolidge went on a Washington radio station to appeal for his return. Coolidge also owned a terrier, an Airedale, a collie, a sheepdog, two chow dogs, a bulldog, a police dog, three canaries, a pair of raccoons, a thrush, a goose, a donkey, a wallaby, a pigmy hippo, some lion cubs, and a bear.

Cornish rex ～ The first rex cat was one of a litter of five kittens born to a barn cat in Cornwall, England, in 1950. It was a cream-colored kitten with short, curly fur. Since Nina Ennismore, its owner, had bred rex rabbits, which also have curly coats, the cat was called rex and became known as a Cornish rex. Ennismore named the cat Kallibunker. Ennismore assumed that the kitten's strange coat was the result of a spontaneous mutation. The Cornish rex now comes in variety of coats, including the chocolate tortoiseshell and the blue Cornish.

The Cornish rex differs from the DEVON REX in

several ways: he has a longer, plusher, and wavier coat and a roman-style nose whereas the Devon rex has a decided top to its nose.

PERSONALITY: The Cornish rex is usually playful and affectionate. *See also* REX.

Cosmo ～ Cosmo was created by Pat Adams and made his first appearance in Fox Publication's *All Top* in 1945. The cartoon supercat Cosmo lives in a secret lab on the moon and gets his power from cosmic catnip capsules. He uses the "telefinder" to locate those on earth needing his help, to whom he will fly in his powerful rocket. When he reaches earth he has superspeed (he can fly), superstrength (he can throw a bull), and superskin (buzzsaws only tickle him).

You can recognize Cosmo by the big yellow *C* on the front of his red sweatshirt, his red boots, blue tights, yellow gloves, and green cape. (He is supercolorful.)

Between 1946 and 1947 Cosmo starred in his own comic book. He appeared in about twenty-three more comic books before retirement in 1947.

The Cornish rex, pictured here, has the same curly coat but more angular features, than the Devon rex. (PHOTOGRAPH BY ISABELLE FRANCAIS.)

Courageous Cat ～ This television cartoon cat hero was created in 1961 by Bob Kane, who is no doubt better remembered for creating Batman. Courageous and his sidekick, Minute Mouse, do their good deeds through superior deductive skills and plain old good luck.

They live in Cat Cave in the hills overlooking Empire City. When police flash the "cat signal" on television, the heroes jump into their sleek, sporty red Catmobile, a vehicle that could have been owned by James Bond. With the flick of a switch it can turn into a Catplane or Submobile and is equipped with skindiving equipment, spyglasses, a loudspeaker, and of course a car phone. Courageous Cat carries with him a balloon gun (by holding on to it he can fly); a refrigerated-air gun; a flashlight gun; a rope gun; a magnet gun (it shoots a stream of magnets); a cannonball-interrupter (it stops cannonballs); a shark-repellent gun; a sword gun; a can-opener gun; an umbrella gun; a rivet gun; and a "bum's rush" gun (this one has two hands that catch the villains and get rid of them). And if all else fails, Courageous Cat keeps a feather with which to tickle the villains.

Courageous Cat is immediately identifiable in his red bodysuit with a star on the chest, black trunks, yellow belt and cape, and white gloves. Eighty-five episodes were produced by Trans-Artist. Courageous Cat was syndicated in 1991.

Cozy Cat Cottage ～ The Cozy Cat Cottage, a bed-and-breakfast, is located in Whitianga, New Zealand, a small, quiet town on the coast. As you can imagine, the cottage is chock-full of cat mementos collected by owners Gordon and Janet Pearce. And if you're lonesome for your cats while visiting New Zealand, you should find many new feline friends at the Cozy Cat Cottage, as the Pearces also breed Siamese. Although the Pearces do not breed dolphins, you can see wild dolphins nearby where they reside in Whitianga's safe harbor. The address of the Cozy Cat Cottage is 41 South Highway, Whitianga, New Zealand. The telephone number is 0843/64-488.

Cymric (*KIM-rick*) ～ This breed is also referred to as the long-haired Manx. It was developed during the 1930s, when the Manx cat was bred with Persians to produce cats with a greater conformation and thickness in their short-hair coats. The result was the Cymric, which has longer hair than the Manx.

PERSONALITY: The Cymric tends to be a true companion. It is very playful.

da Vinci, Leonardo ∿ (1452–1519)
This brilliant Italian artist, sculptor, architect, musician, engineer, mathematician, and scientist once declared that "the small feline is a masterpiece." Coincidentally, that is how his own painting, the Mona Lisa, is referred to. Da Vinci made many sketches and drawings of cats in all kinds of positions.

Day, Doris ∿ (b. 1924) This actress who has long been devoted to the plight of abandoned pets says, "You haven't lived until you've lived with a cat. They are the most interesting little beings, and I get the biggest kick out of them."

In 1971 Doris Day cofounded the organization ACTORS AND OTHERS FOR ANIMALS. In 1977 she founded the Doris Day Pet Foundation in Los Angeles for animals that are hungry, homeless, or hurt. The foundation finds foster homes for neglected or stray cats and dogs, provides care by a veterinarian, and organizes programs for free spaying and neutering of pets.

A third organization, the Doris Day Animal League, is a national, nonprofit advocacy group that draws the attention of the public to the plight of animals being used in laboratory testing. The league lobbies lawmakers and encourages members to write to their legislators as well.

Doris Day shares her Carmel, California, home with more than ten cats and several dogs. They are, of course, all rescued pets. One of her favorite cats was an all black cat named Punky-Kitty.

If you're going to be visiting Carmel with your cats, you may want to book a room at the Cypress Inn, which is owned by Day. Before she bought it, pets were persona non grata. She has changed that. Although the inn does not prepare food for people, there's plenty available for four-legged guests.

The Cypress Inn has just thirty-four rooms, which are usually booked very far in advance. You can contact the Cypress Inn at P.O. Box Y, Carmel, CA, 93921. Phone: 408/624-3871.

Delta Society ∿ This nonprofit organization founded in 1977, promotes beneficial relationships between animals and people. One of its most successful programs, Pet Partners, was started in 1990 and now has over 600 teams (owner and pet) registered. The animals are mostly pet cats and dogs, but other animals in the program include a pot belly pig, some rabbits, and two hens. The pets visit people in nursing homes, rehabilitation centers, crisis centers, day care centers, correctional facilities, schools and hospitals. In 1992 Oscar Ray Leonard, a big black and white cat rescued from the streets of Richland Hills, Texas, was given the Spirit of Jingles for most social animal of the year. (The award is named after Jingles, the dog of the late Dr. Boris Levinson, a psychologist who pioneered animal-assisted therapy.) Oscar, who was an abandoned, flea-bitten, battle-scarred street fighter, is now the mascot at the North Richland Hills Animal Care and Control Center. He makes regular visits to nursing homes as part of the center's "Warm Hugs on Wheels" program. Oscar's daily visits have been credited with sparking a 99-year-old woman's will to recover following a bout with pneumonia. In 1993, George, another rescued stray from Chicago, received the Jingles Award. Besides Pet Partners, the Delta Society promotes studies on how animals affect the mental and physical well-being of people and publishes a newsletter. The Delta Society is at 321 Burnett Avenue South, Third Floor, Renton Washington 98055-2569. The telephone number is 206/226-7357.

Devon rex ～ In the early to mid 1960s, a kitten with wavy hair was discovered in Devonshire, England. Its owner, Beryl Cox, called it Kirlee and it soon became her favorite. The De-

Cats like this rescued stray, George, winner of the Spirit of Jingles Award for sociability, play an important role in the Delta Society's outreach programs. (PHOTO BY DAVID E. KAY, COURTESY THE TREE HOUSE ANIMAL FOUNDATION, INC.)

von rex arrived in the United States in the late 1960s.

The Devon rex differs from the CORNISH REX in several ways: it has a shorter, less plushy, and less wavy coat, and a decided top to its nose, whereas the nose of the Cornish rex is more Roman.

Among the varieties of the Devon rex are the silver tabby Devon and the white Devon rex.

PERSONALITY: The Devon rex is usually playful and affectionate. (*See also* REX.)

Dickens, Charles ~ (1812–1870) The

English author of many classics, including *A Tale of Two Cities*, *David Copperfield*, and *Bleak House*, knew about cats from personal experience. He had a white cat named William which he renamed Williamina when she produced a litter of kittens. His writing was interrupted when Williamina brought the kittens, one by one, from the kitchen to Dickens's study and dropped them at his feet. One of the kittens Dickens kept figured out a different way to get his attention. This cat, known as "the master's cat," would snuff out the candle that Dickens was using for light to divert his attention from the books to him.

In *David Copperfield*, written in 1849 and 1850, Dickens gives some indication of his attitude toward cats:

> Mrs. Crupp had indignantly assured him that there wasn't room to swing a cat there; but, as Mr. Dick justly observed to me, sitting down on the foot of the bed, nursing his leg, "You know, Trotwood, I don't want to swing a cat. I never do swing a cat. Therefore, what does that signify to *me!*"

In *Bleak House*, a cat who belongs to one of the central characters plays an important role in one part of the book.

I'm Whittington's Cat as you plainly may see.
That famous Lord Mayor got his Fortune by me.
Then keep me with care as a Friend ought to do
And I may perhaps get a Fortune for you.

Printed for & Sold by CARINGTON BOWLES, No 69 in St Pauls Church Yard, LONDON.

Dick Whittington's cat brought his poor master fame and fortune. Engraving published by Carrington Bowles, 1777.

Dick Whittington *and His Cat* ~ This

oft-told English fable recounts the story of a poor young man who goes to London to seek his fortune and ends up becoming mayor of the city. Dick Whittington, orphaned at an early age and nearly starved, is found by Mr. Fitzwarren, a rich merchant who takes him in and gives him a job helping his mean and vindictive cook. Dick's garret room is filled with mice and rats, and when he earns a penny for cleaning a man's shoes he buys a cat, said by its owner to be a good mouser. He always shares part of his dinner with the cat, and soon his garret is mouse-free.

Shortly after this, one of Mr. Fitzwarren's trading

ships is ready to sail. It is his custom always to let his servants share in the profits of the voyage—each can give him something to be traded. But Dick is so poor that he has no possessions to trade—only his loyal and much loved cat. With great reluctance he turns over his cat, Puss.

The ship travels to the Barbary coast where a king invites the captain to come to the palace for dinner. When the food appears, so do many rats and mice, who consume the meal in an instant, and the captain learns that the king would give half his treasure to be freed of rodents. When the king sees firsthand what Puss can do to the rats and mice, he gives the captain ten times as much for the cat as for all the rest of the cargo. The boat returns to England and Dick is given the rich gifts for which his cat was traded.

In another version of the story, Dick himself goes to sea with his sole possession, the cat.

Richard Whittington actually was the mayor of London in 1397, 1406, and 1420. When you visit London, be sure to visit the Whittington Stone on Highgate Hill, with the famous cat perched on top.

The most domestic cat, which has lain on a rug all her days, appears quite at home in the woods, and, by her sly and stealthy behaviour, proves herself more native there than the regular inhabitants.

HENRY DAVID THOREAU, American writer and naturalist (1817–1862)

The most domesticated of cats somehow contrives to lead an outside life of its own.

KATHERINE BRIGGS, writer, twentieth century

The phrase "domestic cat" is an oxymoron.

GEORGE WILL, American columnist and author, twentieth century

Once cats were all wild, but afterward they retired to houses.

EDWARD TOPSELL, seventeenth-century English writer

That Cat

The cat that comes to my window-sill
When the moon looks cold and the night is still
He comes in a frenzied state alone
With a tail that stands like a pine tree cone,
And says, "I have finished my evening lark,
And I think I can hear a hound-dog bark.
My whiskers are froze'nd stuck to my chin—
I wish you'd git up and let me in."
That cat gits in.

But if in the solitude of the night
He doesn't appear to be feeling right,
And rises and stretches and seeks the floor,
and some remote corner he would explore,
And doesn't feel satisfied just because
There's no good spot for to sharpen his claws,
And meows and canters uneasy about
Beyond the least shadow of any doubt
That cat gits out.

BEN KING, *Verses*, 1894

> You, domestic Pinkie-Nose,
> Keep inside, and warm your toes.
>
> "Cat's Meat," HAROLD MONRO, British poet
> (1879–1932)

Dr. Seuss ～ (1904–1992) His real name was Theodore Seuss Geisel, but to millions of children and their parents, he was Dr. Seuss, the pseudonym he used on the hilarious, illustrated rhyming books he wrote for children (and adults). One of his most famous books is *The Cat in the Hat*, in which a mischief-making cat is bound to stir up trouble, as he tempts here:

> "I know some new tricks,"
> Said the Cat in the Hat.
> "A lot of good tricks.
> I will show them to you.
> Your mother
> Will not mind at all if I do."

All is generally put aright in the end.

Domestic cat ～ This refers to a non-pedigreed cat, usually a shorthair, which is native to that country. *See also* AMERICAN SHORTHAIR.

> Cats have intercepted my footsteps at the ankle for so long that my gait, both at home and on tour, has been compared to that of a man wading through a low surf.
>
> ROY BLOUNT, JR., American writer and humorist, twentieth century

Ears ⮑ Your cat's ears are very sensitive to sound, far more sensitive than your ears are. Cats can hear high-pitched sounds, like the squeak of a mouse, that we cannot hear. For example, in the prime of life humans can hear sounds up to about 20,000 cycles per second; when your cat is in his prime, he can hear sounds as high as 100,000 cycles per second. (If you want to get a cat's attention, speak in a falsetto voice.)

A cat's ears turn ten times quicker in the direction of sound than those of the best watchdog. Cats have some forty thousand fibers in their au-ral nerve while we have thirty thousand; and about thirty muscles while we have scarcely half a dozen. It can turn the ear a full 180 degrees.

Cats are capable of making very fine musical tone discriminations. In one series of experiments, Dr. Richard Zeliony trained cats to run in from the next room whenever he blew a whistle pitched at middle C. The cats would not come into the room when he blew a whistle as close in pitch as half a tone.

A cat's ears can also indicate its mood. The position of the cat's ears can reveal that the cat is

The position of a cat's ears may reveal his mood. When he is at rest (left), the ears are relaxed and point forward. When alert, they stand erect. When the cat is in an aggressive posture (right), the ears are flattened and turned so that the backs can be seen from the front. (DRAWINGS BY CHRISTINA DUNSTAN.)

alert, relaxed, agitated, defensive, or aggressive. When your cat's ears are twitching he may be in a state of conflict, frustration, or apprehension. When a cat is resting his ears point forward. When a cat becomes alerted to something, the cat stares at the point of interest and his ears become fully erect with the openings pointing directly forward. A cat on the defense flattens it ears by pressing them against his head to protect them. When a cat is aggressive, the ears turn so that the backs can be seen from the front. This position can also quickly be changed to flattened ears for protection.

Egypt

I am the Cat which fought near the Persea Tree in Heliopolis on the night when the foes of Neb-er-tcher were destroyed.

The Egyptian Book of the Dead

Although there is some evidence suggesting that small, wild feline species may have been tamed in different parts of the world some 8000 years ago, and that the remains of a cat may have been excavated in 6700 B.C., most evidence points to ancient Egypt as the place where the first domestic cats widely made their appearance some four thousand years ago. Wall paintings in tombs in Egypt which date back to around 2000 B.C. show the cat in scenes from daily life. Some cat "historians" say you can tell from the artwork of that era that there were two types of domestic cats—shorthaired and ginger-colored, and tawny with black markings. One type had short ears and a blunt nose and the other had a foxlike face with a sharp nose and pointy ears.

At that time, cats were very well regarded in Egypt, and for a very good reason. From looking at art produced at that time, it appears that the cats first entered farming villages along the Nile River hunting for river rats, and the cats endeared themselves to the Egyptians by eating the rats that were destroying the farmer's granaries.

The first written mention of cats appears in the ancient religious tome, Book of the Dead, in 3500 B.C. It refers to "the great cat at the pool of the Persea in Heliopolis," which appears to be a symbol for the sun god Ra (also called Re, Horus, or Ptah). According to legend, the great sun god took the form of a cat in his battle with the powers of darkness, which was symbolized by a gigantic serpent. Each day at dawn

(continued)

Cats enjoyed a privileged status in ancient Egypt and often represented deities. In this wall painting from 1300 B.C., the sun god Ra, in the form of a cat, triumphs over the serpent Apophis, god of darkness and chaos. (COURTESY EGYPTIAN EXPEDITION OF THE METROPOLITAN MUSEUM OF ART, ROGERS FUND, 1930.)

the sun god-cat would cut off the head of the serpent to force the night out and the light of day in. The Egyptians called the cat "mau," meaning light.

The goddess Bastet (also called Mut, Bast, Pasht, Ubastet, or Bubastis), was a descendant of the sun god Ra, or Ra's sister or wife. She was depicted as a woman with a cat's head. The deity of motherhood, fertility, and sex, she was also associated with Sekhnet, the lion-headed goddess of war, death, and sickness. Among her other duties were supervising good health, music and dancing, crops, hunting, wisdom, and happiness.

A great stone temple was built in Bastet's honor in the ancient Egyptian city of Bubastis between 2050 and 1400 B.C. The image of Bast was kept in a sanctuary in the center of the temple complex, and priests in the temple watched over the sacred cats who resided there. In 1890 archaeologists discovered more than three hundred thousand cat mummies buried in the temple. The cats were embalmed, mummified, and placed in sarcophagi. According to two Egyptologists, the arrangement of the mummies suggests that a strict hierarchy was adhered to. Some of the cat mummies were wrapped in strips of cloth covered with hieroglyphic praise and buried alone. Others were embalmed together and wrapped together in a single covering. Also found were mummified mice, food for the beloved cat. (The significance of the discovery of these cat mummies eluded the archaeologists, who had the twenty-four tons of cat remains destroyed.) Many ancient Egyptian tombs and burial chambers are filled with references to cats.

In ancient Egypt, domestic cats also held a distinguished place in the home. Virtually every Egyptian house displayed a small cat statue. Some Egyptians put gold rings in their cat's ears. Parents dedicated their newborn babies to Bastet by hanging a pendant with Bastet's image around their babies' necks. Teenagers had their arms tatooed with the silhouette of Bastet to improve their chances of receiving gifts from the goddess. When a child became seriously ill, family members shaved their heads, sold the hair, and used the proceeds to buy offerings for the sacred cat. The responsibility of caring for the household cat was passed from father to son.

When fires broke out there was more concern about rescuing a cat than putting out the blaze and saving the house. When a cat perished in a house fire, those who lived there would cover themselves with ashes and run through the streets, beating their breasts and tearing their clothes. When a cat died, it was the custom for those in the household to shave off their eyebrows, for a magical reason—the eyebrows resembled the soft fur of the cat and were shaped like crescents, the ancient symbol of the moon.

Egyptian laws were made to protect the cat, and killing a cat was a crime punishable by death. In 30 B.C., the Roman historian Diodorus Siculus wrote that whoever killed a cat in Egypt would be condemned to death, regardless of whether

(continued)

the act was done intentionally or by accident. In the first century B.C., a Roman soldier accidentally killed a cat in Egypt. He was mobbed by bystanders who killed him and dragged his body through the streets.

This law, legend has it, also led to a major military defeat for the Egyptians. In 522 B.C. Cambyses II, the king of Persia, invaded Egypt. Knowing the law against killing cats, each soldier carried a cat on his shield. The Egyptians, loathe to kill or even harm a cat, threw down their arms. In another version, the Persians threw live cats over the walls of the city Pelusium. The Egyptians were so panicked by this blasphemy that they became distracted and the city fell.

Although a law was enacted that forbade the export of cats from Egypt, they did eventually end up in faraway places with the help of some entrepreneurs who knew a good thing when they saw it.

In ancient Egypt they were worshipped as critics of the frail and erring human beings whose lot they share.

P. G. WODEHOUSE, English writer and humorist (1881–1975)

Egyptian Mau ~ The Mau is named for the cats worshiped in Egypt in ancient times. Mau or miw was the name for a divine household cat in ancient Egypt. The first Egyptian Maus were brought to the United States in 1956 by Princess Nathalie Troubetskoy, a member of one of the oldest Russian families. She was born in Poland in 1897, and while she was living in Rome, a child gave her a spotted silver kitten. She named the kitten Baba and when Baba was four years old, the princess brought Baba and two other Egyptian Maus to the United States. (The princess tried unsuccessfully to book passage on the ill-fated *Andrea Doria*, which sank in the Atlantic Ocean.)

The Egyptian Mau is a spotted cat and comes in five varieties: silver with black markings, brown with light brown markings, pewter with black or brown markings, smoke with black markings, and black.

PERSONALITY: Early on, Maus were unpredictable, fiery, and wild-natured. However, as a result of selective breeding, Maus today are active, intelligent, and affectionate. They are good at learning tricks and are also one of the few breeds that seems to enjoy walking on a leash.

I have an Egyptian cat. He leaves a pyramid in every room.

RODNEY DANGERFIELD, contemporary American comedian

Eliot, T[homas] S[tearns] ~ (1888–1965) Though some readers may know this poet, playwright, and critic for his "literary" poems like "The Wasteland" and "The Lovesong of J. Alfred Prufrock," cat lovers probably remember him best for his *Old Possum's Book of Practical Cats*, a book of lyrical, amusing poems about felines. Depicting a world inhabited by cats with very striking personalities—like The Old Gumbie Cat, Growltiger, Rum Tum Tugger, Old Deuteronomy, Mr. Mistoffelees, Bustopher Jones, Skimbleshanks, and others—the book has appeared in many editions since it was first published in 1939. And it was the inspiration for composer Andrew Lloyd Webber's phenomenally popular musical, *CATS*. (See NAMES for his charming poem, "Naming of the Cats.")

The naming of a cat is a serious business indeed. Illustration by Edward Gorey, from Old Possum's Book of Practical Cats. (ILLUSTRATION © 1982 BY EDWARD GOREY, COURTESY HARCOURT BRACE JOVANOVICH.)

Exotic shorthair ～ This cat is a combination of Persian, Abyssinian, American shorthair, Burmese, and other breeds. It made its appearance in the United States in the late 1960s. As a result of all the interbreeding, there are over fifty varieties of exotic shorthairs, including the color-point exotic shorthair, the blue exotic shorthair, and the blue tabby exotic shorthair, to name just a few. They are popular with people who love Persians but don't want the bother of all the grooming Persians require.

PERSONALITY: Exotic shorthairs are gentle, alert, playful, and intelligent.

Eyes ～ Contrary to popular myth, cats cannot see in the dark. However, they can see six times better in the dark than humans with any light available. A "mirrored" layer of glittering cells lies behind the retina, gathering and bouncing back rays of light in the eye and increasing the amount of light the rods and cones are exposed to. This mirror causes cat's eyes to shine reflectively at night when light hits them.

The vertical alignment of the cat's pupil also allows it to respond more quickly to change in light than a round pupil does. The darker it is outside, the wider the cat's pupils enlarge to let in as much light as possible. In bright light the pupil gets smaller, becoming just a slit. The cat has a wider field of vision than humans do, 285 degrees to our 210, and cats have the biggest eyes of all mammals. Cats also possess a "third eyelid," a membrane which extends from the inner corner near the nose toward the outer edge. It is generally not visible but will begin to extend if the surface of the eye is abraded by dust or other irritants and if extended or inflamed can be a sign of illness.

The shape and color of a cat's eyes may vary by

breed and is determined genetically. The three basic eye shapes are round (commonly found in Persians and Himalayans), almond-shaped (as in the Abyssinian), or slanted (like the Siamese). All of the pigment in a cat's iris is flecked with black, brown, or yellow coloring, but because of the way it scatters light the eyes may appear to range from deep golden yellows and ambers to tranquil, hypnotic hazel, green and blue-green, to piercing blues. Eye color and shape can be exacting criteria when judging a pedigreed cat.

Some cats may have two different colored eyes—one blue and one orange. Generally these are white pedigreed cats, shorthair or longhair, although domestic cats can have the different colored eyes as well. The parents of these cats may both have blue eyes, both have orange eyes, or one may have blue eyes and the other orange eyes.

It was once thought that cats could not distinguish colors, that they could only see in shades of gray. Research has now proven this to be untrue. Studies have shown that cats can distinguish between a number of colors, though exactly how many and what effect this has on how they perceive the world is not yet known.

Cats' eyes can reflect different moods. Narrowed pupils may be an indication of tension and the threat of attack. Wide open pupils indicate fear and a readiness to fight. However, veterinarian Michael W. Fox says that, "When a cat looks at you and then half closes its eyes, it's not that he is ignoring you." Fox says the cat does this when she is relaxed in your presence.

There are many myths surrounding cats' eyes. One is that you can tell the tide from the size of the cat's pupils. When the pupils are narrow, it is low tide and when they are wide, it is high tide. Another is that you can tell the time of day by looking at the shape of a cat's pupils. The French poet and critic, CHARLES BAUDELAIRE, spoke of the cat as a timepiece. In 1861 in the *Revue Fantaisiste*, he relates a story about a missionary walking in a Nanking suburb who asks a little boy the time. The boy goes to find out the time and when he returns he carries a big cat. The boy looks straight in the eyes of the cat and says without any hesitation that it is not quite midday. He was correct.

Another myth is that the cat's eyes shine at night because they are casting out the light they gathered during the day. In ancient Egypt, cats were called *Mau*, the Egyptian word for light, because their eyes "glowed" in the dark. Their eyes were thought to hold the light of the sun and keep away evil spirits during the night. And it was thought at various times in history that the shining of the cat's eyes at night represented the fires of hell.

Because of the cat's supposedly good eyesight, in his *Alphabetical Book of Physical Secrets*, written in 1639, Owen Wood relates a way to treat bad eyesight fostered by the occultist Mrs. Beeton. The head of a black cat is burnt to ashes. The ashes are then blown into the eyes three times a day and oak leaves wetted with rosewater are placed on the eyes.

In the years before the Civil War, African-American slaves believed that cats could see ghosts and that ghost visions were reflected in their eyes. They killed cats and used their eyes in voodoo ceremonies and also used the cat's whiskers in voodoo.

There is no doubt that cat's eyes are special, as Algernon Swinburne notes in his poem *To a Cat*:

Glorious eyes that smile and burn,
Golden eyes, love's lustrous meed . . .

See also CAT'S-EYE.

Familiar ~ This term was used to describe a cat believed to be the embodiment of Satan or the companions of witches. *See* WITCHCRAFT.

Felix the Cat ~ Felix was the first true animated film star. Felix debuted in the three-minute-long "Feline Follies" in 1919. Although Australian Pat Sullivan is frequently given credit for creating Felix, according to Jeff Rovin's *The Illustrated Encyclopedia of Cartoon Animals*, it was really artist Otto Messmer who came up with the black and white cartoon cat. Messmer created Felix at Sullivan's animation studio in New York City. The cat's name came from a combination of *felicity* (happiness) and *feline*, and was chosen specifically to counteract cruel suspicions about cats.

Many of Felix's antics were based on Charlie Chaplin's adventures. Between 1921 and 1928, Felix starred in 150 silent cartoons. In 1923 his Sunday newspaper comic strip debuted and began appearing daily four years later. Felix the Cat also appeared in his own comic book. At one time, his popularity was so great that even the hugely suc-

Felix the Cat. (COURTESY MUSEUM OF MODERN ART/FILM STILLS ARCHIVE.)

cessful Walt Disney, who was thinking of creating a cat character, decided to feature another animal, a mouse named Mickey. (We all know how popular *he* became.)

Felix eventually ended up on TV. As a matter of fact, Felix was the first still image broadcast on television when WNBC inaugurated its experimental transmitter in 1930! Felix appeared in some 260 four-minute cartoons starting in 1960.

Felix has also been featured on a lot of merchandise, more than two hundred items including dolls, toys, clothing, and sporting goods, and in popular songs such as "Felix Kept on Walking" in Britain and "Felix the Cat" in the United States. Felix has also appeared, in large floating balloon form, in the Macy's Thanksgiving Day Parade in New York City since 1927.

Felix Gallery, The ～ In Lewes, England, an hour and a half from London by train, this gallery is filled with every kind of cat item imaginable. Lewes is a typical old English town in Sussex with narrow, winding cobblestone streets. The Felix Gallery is in the home of Bill and Melva Whitehead, who have two live cats in addition to the hundreds of cat statues, paintings, trays, prints, dolls, and so on for sale. The Felix Gallery is also a bed-and-breakfast. It is at 2 Sun Street, Lewes, Sussex BN7 2QB England. And if you are in Sussex you may also want to visit the CAT HOUSE in Henfield.

> The cat is the only animal without visible means of support who still manages to find a living in the city.
>
> CARL VAN VECHTEN, American writer
> (1880–1964)

Feral ～ This term refers to a domestic cat (or any other domesticated animal) that has returned to living in a wild state. *Feral* can also be used for wild animals or flowers that have never been domesticated.

Figaro ～ The cartoon cat Figaro made his debut in the Walt Disney film *Pinocchio* in 1940 as a small friendly black cat with a stripe of white. When Figaro appeared in subsequent roles he was not nearly so sweet. In the short cartoon "Figaro and Cleo," in 1943, Figaro is no longer Mr. Nice Guy, but is out to do in Cleo the goldfish, also one of Pinocchio's pets. And did you know that at one point, Figaro *lived* with Minnie Mouse? Figaro made his last appearance in 1949 in "Pluto's Sweater." Clarence Nash, better known for being the voice of Donald Duck, was the voice of Figaro.

First cat, the ～ There are a number of different legends which explain how cats made their entrance into the world. According to Hebrew folklore, Noah was concerned that rats might be a problem on the ark—eating all the provisions—and prayed to God for help. God responded by making the lion, who was sleeping, unleash a giant sneeze from which emerged a little cat.

In an Arabic legend, Noah's sons and daughters are worried about their safety on the ark because of the presence of the lion. Noah prayed to God for help and God afflicted the lion with a fever. But not too much later another dangerous creature emerged—the mouse. Again, Noah prayed and this time God caused the lion to sneeze and the cat issued forth.

In a medieval legend the Devil plays a role in the creation of the cat. Trying to copy God and create a man, the evil Devil manages only to produce a small, pathetic skinless animal—the cat. St. Peter felt sorry for the creature and gave it a fur coat, which is the cat's only valuable possession. See also HISTORY OF THE CAT.

French folktale ~ In one charming French fable, a king sends his three sons out and tells them the one who returns with the most perfect dog will be the next king. The princes, who find this a little puzzling, nevertheless go on their way. They agree to meet in twelve months and go together to their father with the dogs they have found. The youngest prince, who is the handsomest, most amiable, and accomplished in the world, becomes lost in a forest during a thunder-and-lightning rainstorm. Finally he spots a light. He goes toward it and comes upon the most magnificent palace he has ever seen, with a golden door covered with sapphires. He pulls the chain of diamonds on the door and hears an exquisite bell. Soon the door opens. He sees twelve hands in the air, each holding a torch. He is guided into a vestibule where he hears a beautiful voice chanting the following words:

"Welcome, Prince, no danger fear,
Mirth and love attend you here;
You shall break the magic spell,
That on a beauteous lady fell."

The hands guide him through the palace to a room with a fireplace, where they remove his wet clothes and give him the finest linen imaginable. They take him to another room where a table is spread for supper for two and suddenly sees a small figure less than a foot high with a long black veil. The figure removes the veil and before him stands a beautiful white cat who tells him that his presence gives her the greatest pleasure. They dine together on exquisite food, the White Cat

assuring him that there are special dishes for him that did not contain rat or mouse.

The prince stays on and on at the luxurious palace, conversing with the White Cat and partaking in different amusements until he nearly forgets his mission. He says to the White Cat, who he now loves dearly, "Either make yourself a lady or make me a cat." A few days before it is time for the prince to leave, the White Cat gives him an acorn that she says contains the perfect dog and a wooden horse to take him home.

By this time the prince's two brothers have indeed found beautiful dogs, but when the youngest prince takes out his acorn a most perfect dog, so small that it could fit through a ring, emerges. But the king really doesn't want to give up his crown, so he again sends the brothers off, this time to find a piece of cloth so fine that it could fit through the eye of a needle. Again, they all take different roads. The youngest prince gets on his wooden horse and in a short time is back at the palace with his beloved White Cat. The twelve months pass quickly and when it is time to leave, the White Cat gives the Prince a nut containing, she says, the fabric that would fit through the eye of a needle and she cautions him not to open it until he is with his father, the king. And she gives him a carriage of gold, silver, pearls, and diamonds drawn by twelve horses white as snow to take him home.

The other two brothers have found the finest and most exquisite fabrics—but neither can go through the eye of the needle. The youngest prince takes out the walnut and cracks it open. Inside is a filbert. When he cracks that there is a cherrystone. In the cherrystone is a kernel, in that a grain of wheat, in that a grain of millet seed (the youngest brother is getting a bit annoyed and thinks he's been deceived by his dear White Cat), but he opens the grain of millet seed and finds a piece of fabric four hundred yards long that easily goes through the eye of the needle. But the king is still not ready to relinquish his crown. This time he tells his sons that the one who returns in one year with the most beautiful lady will marry her and receive his crown.

The princes set out again. The youngest prince arrives quickly at the palace of his beloved White Cat. On the day he is to leave the White Cat tells the prince that he must cut off her head and tail and throw them in the fire. With great reluctance, great love, and many tears the Prince honors her request. No sooner is this done, than the most beautiful woman ever seen in the world stands before him. And the White Cat/Princess explains to the astonished and joyful Prince that she was turned into a white cat by the Fairy Violent when her parents, who ruled six kingdoms, reneged on an agreement with the fairies. The only way she could be restored to herself was if a young prince cut off her head and tail.

When the king learns that his sons have returned with what he requested, he starts thinking of other things to send them for so he could hold on to his crown. But the White Cat/Princess knows what he is thinking and tells him she possesses six kingdoms—and that one can go to each of the elder sons, she and the youngest prince would rule over the other four, and the king could keep his own. This, she explained, would keep the king from having to decide which of his daughter-in-laws-to-be was the most beautiful. And they all live happily ever after (of course).

Friends of Cats ～ This organization
was founded in 1927 near San Diego, California, by a group of residents who chipped in and bought every animal from the local pound. Calling themselves the Animal Rescue League, they were determined that every unwanted or abandoned animal would have a home.

Two years later, Maude Erwin came on the scene. She cared for the twenty cats who were living in the makeshift shelter, and helped raise additional funds to care for the growing number of abandoned pets.

In 1954 a board of directors was formed and The Maude Erwin Foundation for Cats received its first charter. Three years later, while caring for some three hundred cats, Maude Erwin died. In 1966 the foundation changed its name to Friends of Cats and moved to a six-acre site twenty miles from San Diego.

Friends of Cats has nineteen miniature cottages. There is a timid ward for cats who are fearful of people, a cottage for wild cats, and a hospice for cats diagnosed with feline leukemia. The cats are available for adoption but prospective owners are carefully screened. Cats who are not adopted need not worry. They receive full room, board, and love until the end of their lives. Friends of Cats can be reached at 619/561-0361.

Fritz the Cat ～ Created by 16-year-old
Robert Crumb in 1959, Fritz, a tabby, started out as an "underground" cat—on the sleazy side, crude, sex-driven, and drug-loving.

The first professional appearance of Fritz was five years later in a comic strip in *Help* magazine. Fritz may be best known for his starring role in the first X-rated full-length cartoon feature, Ralph Bakshi's *Fritz the Cat*, produced in 1972. Fritz weaves his way through police chases, group sex encounters, black ghettos, motorcycle revolutionaries, and the destruction of property. Did the public like this sleazy cat? You bet! The film was a financial success although Bob Crumb disowned it.

Its sequel, *The Nine Lives of Fritz the Cat*, produced two years later, was not a success.

Galle cat ~ French artist Emile Galle made many of these ceramic cats in the late 1800s. The pale yellow cats with blue hearts were placed in the windows of houses of ill repute in seaports. If the cat was in the window looking out, it meant the house was open. If the cat was looking out, but had two red cats-eye marbles at her feet, it meant that everyone in the house was "busy" and to come back. If the cat was facing inside the house, it meant that the establishment was closed. Could this be where the term *cathouse* comes from? Or is it the other way around?

Garfield ~ This very well-known cartoon cat, created by Jim Davis, first appeared in June of 1978. He now runs in over two thousand newspapers and has been translated into a dozen different languages. He has even had a French marigold named for him—it matches his golden color, has more profuse flowers than ordinary marigolds, and grows about ten inches tall. And in 1985 he debuted as a hot-air balloon in the Macy's Thanksgiving Day Parade.

Garfield has also had specials on TV, as well as a Saturday morning cartoon show, and has more than one Emmy sitting on his mantel. And it is doubtful that you could find a bookstore which does not carry at least one Garfield paperback book chock-full of his adventures. Garfield is self-ish, hedonistic, and fat. To quote Jim Davis, "Way down deep, we're all motivated by the same urges. Cats have the courage to live by them." To quote Garfield, "They say a cat always lands on his feet, but they don't say how painful it is."

Just to keep you on your toes, here are a few Garfield trivia questions (although it's hard to believe any cat lover wouldn't know *every* answer, for the one or two who might not, the answers are found below:

a. What is Garfield's favorite food?
b. With whom does Garfield reside?
c. What does Garfield weigh?
d. What is the name of Garfield's girlfriend?
e. What is Garfield's favorite expression?

a. lasagna (he also has a fondness for fern, as a snack)
b. Jon Arbuckle (who happens to be a [human] cartoonist)
c. 15 pounds! (At birth Garfield weighed in at five pounds six ounces!)
d. Arlene (Garfield does try to avoid her when

possible because staying a bachelor is one of his deepest desires)

e. "big, fat, hairy deal" Another of his more famous quotes is, "I'm fat, lazy, and proud of it!" Ah, a typical cat.

> The cat is a dilettante in fur.
>
> THÉOPHILE GAUTIER

Gautier, Théophile ～ (1811–1872)

The French poet, novelist, and critic owned several cats. Madame Théophile was a reddish cat with a white breast and blue eyes. She would sleep on Gautier's bed, follow him on his walks, and sometimes at meals intercept a tidbit that he was about to eat. Another cat, black, was named Eponine after a character in Victor Hugo's *Les Misérables*.

Gautier said his cat hated high notes, especially high A, although Eponine generally enjoyed listening to female singers. It is said that whenever Gautier dined alone, he would have a place set for Eponine at his table. When he arrived she would already be there, "Her paws folded on the tablecloth, her smooth forehead held up to be kissed . . . like a well-bred little girl who is politely affectionate to relatives and other older people." They would then proceed to dine together.

The French composer Frédéric Massenet had begged Gautier on more than one occasion to write a libretto for him. He finally met with success when Gautier entered his salon, where Massenet was waiting, and found him engaged in a long and friendly conversation with Eponine. Gautier started and quickly finished *Le Preneur de Rats* (*The Ratcatcher*), but after all that, the opera was never performed.

Perhaps Gautier's motivation to treat his cat with such high regard can be explained, in part, from some of his writings, which follow:

To gain the friendship of a cat is a difficult thing. The cat is a philosophical, methodical, quiet animal, tenacious of his own habits, fond of order and cleanliness, and does not lightly confer his friendship. If you are worthy of his affection, a cat will be your friend but never your slave. He keeps his free will though he loves, and will not do for you what he thinks unreasonable; but if he once gives himself to you, it is with absolute confidence and fidelity of affection. He makes himself the companion of your hours of solitude, melancholy, and toil. He will remain for whole evenings on your knee, uttering a contented purr, happy to be with you. Put him down and he will jump up again with a sort of cooing sound that is like a gentle reproach; and sometimes he will sit upon the carpet in front of you looking at you with eyes so melting, so caressing, and so human that they almost frighten you, for it is impossible to believe that a soul is not there.

> With a cat you stand on much the same footing that you stand with a fine and dignified friend; if you forfeit his respect and confidence the relationship suffers.
>
> CARL VAN VECHTEN, American writer
> (1880–1964)

Gay Purr-ee ～ This animated feature

film appeared in 1962 and starred Mewsette, a bushy-tailed cat who has become bored with her life on the farm. Jumping on a train to Paris with her tom friend, Robespierre, she encounters numerous fur-raising adventures and is eventually rescued by Robespierre.

It wouldn't have hurt the movie one bit if Mewsette had done more singing. Her voice was provided by none other than Judy Garland! Among the other notable voices in the film were Robert Goulet, Red Buttons, and Hermione Gingold.

Gay Purr-ee was produced by Warner Brothers. A comic book adaptation was published by Gold Key.

I am as melancholy as a gib-cat.

WILLIAM SHAKESPEARE, 1564–1616,
from *Henry IV*

Gib cat ∽ This is the old English name for a tomcat. It was used in parts of England and Scotland, usually for old, bedraggled male cats.

Glendale Central Library ∽ This library in Glendale, California, has what may be the largest collection in the world of cat publications. Librarian Barbara Boyd is in charge of the twenty thousand publications and other items. If you cannot find what you're looking for about cats here, you'll probably have to write it yourself.

There are books on cat history, cat fiction, cat zodiac signs, cat poetry, cat posters, greeting cards, oil paintings, and cat curios. There are also how-to books on subjects such as how to photograph cats, how to paint them, how to psychoanalyze them, how to toilet train them, and so on. The cat collection is not for children. It is strictly for the serious cat person—one who is doing research or perhaps is a breeder, and nothing can be removed from this library.

Gotham Book Mart and Gallery ∽ This marvelous bookstore, located in the heart of the diamond district in midtown Manhattan, is indeed a gem. It is home to three cats— Thornton (Wilder), Mitchell (Kennerley), and Christopher (Morley). Owner Andreas Brown says each cat has his own personality—one likes to jump in peoples' laps (most customers don't mind); another is shy; and the third prefers to sleep in the window of the store. One cat with grace can navigate over books with ease, while another, just slightly clumsy, knocks things over regularly.

So what do these cats do to earn their room and board? "Not much," says Brown. "While there is an occasional mouse, the cats mainly attract attention [and some publicity, like appearing in this book]." He adds that there are customers who he knows come just to see the cats.

Frances Steloff, who opened the Gotham in 1920, died in 1986 at the age of one hundred and one. She helped numerous writers who went on to become some of the century's leading writers. Andreas Brown, whom she chose to be her successor, says the cats currently in residence were owned by Frances Steloff and that there were virtually always cats living at the Gotham. The Gotham Book Mart is at 41 West 47th St., New York, NY 10036. 212/719-4448.

Thomas Gray

This English poet (1716–1761) is best known for his poem "Elegy Written in a Country Churchyard." In the following poem, "On the Death of a Favourite Cat Drowned in a Tub of Goldfish," the cat Selima unfortunately goes after some goldfish she sees in a lake:

'Twas on a lofty vase's side,
Where China's gayest art had dy'd
   The azure flowers, that blow;
Demurest of the tabby kind,
The pensive Selima reclin'd,
   Gazed on the lake below.

Her conscious tail her joy declar'd;
The fair round fact, the snowy beard,
   The velvet of her paws,
Her coat, that with the tortoise vies,
Her ears of jet, and emerald eyes,
   She saw; and purr'd applause.

Still had she gaz'd; but 'midst the tide
Two angel forms were seen to glide,
   The Genii of the stream:
Their scaly armour's Tyrian hue
Thro' richest purple to the view
   Betray'd a golden gleam.

The hapless Nymph with wonder saw:
A whisker first and then a claw,
   With many an ardent wish,
She stretch'd in vain to reach the prize.
What female heart can gold despise?
   What Cat's averse to fish?

Presumptuous Maid! with looks intent
Again she stretch'd, again she bent,
   Nor knew the gulf between.
(Malignant Fate sat by, and smil'd)
The slipp'ry verge her feet beguil'd,
   She tumbled headlong in.

Eight times emerging from the flood
She mew'd to ev'ry watry God,
   Some speedy aid to send.
No Dolphin came, no Nereid* stirr'd:
Nor cruel Tom, nor Susan heard.
   A Fav'rite has no friend!

From hence, ye Beauties, undeceiv'd
Know, one false step is ne'er retriev'd,
   And be with caution bold.
Not all that tempts your wandering eyes
And heedless hearts, is lawful prize;
   Nor all, that glitters, gold.

* a sea nymph

Great Cat Massacre, The ~ In *The Great Cat Massacre and Other Episodes in French Cultural History*, history professor Robert Darnton describes a terrible massacre of cats in the eighteenth century from the point of view of the laborer Nicolas Contat, who supposedly witnessed the devastating feline destruction. The massacre was performed by men who worked for the printer Jacques Vincent in Paris in the 1730s. At the time, cats were looked upon with great favor by the print shop owners, who were known as "masters." One master kept twenty-five cats, had their portraits painted, and fed them roast fowl. The printers, including Vincent, took far better care of their pet cats than they did of their workers. Meanwhile, their employees were ill fed, overworked, and poorly housed. Two apprentices who worked for Vincent rarely slept because of the common alley cats who howled all night on the roof over their dingy bedroom.

To get even, the apprentices devised a plan. One, who was a good mimic, crawled along the roof until he reached a section which he knew to be the master's bedroom and howled and meowed loudly. After several sleepless nights, the mistress gave the order that the cats be destroyed with the enjoinder that her own favorite cat not be frightened. The apprentices along with the journeymen went out and bludgeoned every cat in sight, with the first one being the mistress's favorite. They chased cats over rooftops and trapped them in bags. Sackloads of half-dead cats were dumped in the courtyard. Then the workers staged a mock trial. The cats were declared guilty and strung from an improvised gallows.

At the time, the torture of animals, especially cats, was a popular amusement. In France, when Carnival came to an end on Shrove Tuesday, or Mardi Gras, a straw mannequin, King Carnival or Caramantran, was given a ritual trial and executed. In Burgundy, the crowd also tortured cats.

Youths passed around a cat, tearing its fur to make it howl. Cats also suffered ill effects during the cycle of Saint John the Baptist on June 24. Crowds made bonfires, jumped over them, danced around them, and threw objects with magical power into them to avoid disaster and gain fortune during the coming year. A favorite object was the cat, tied in bags, suspended from ropes, or burned at the stake. In Paris they burned cats by the sackful. In parts of Burgundy and Lorraine they danced around a burning pole with a cat tied to it. In the Metz region, a dozen cats at a time were burned in a basket on top of a bonfire on the eve of St. John's day. (The practice was abolished in Metz in 1765.)

Grimm Brothers ~ The German brothers Jakob (1785–1863) and Wilhelm (1786–1859) Grimm researched and recorded hundreds of folk- and fairy tales, including "The Companionship of the Cat and the Mouse." In this tale, a cat meets a mouse, and convinces the mouse to live with him, professing his great love for her. As winter approaches, the cat recommends that they stock up their supplies, so they buy a little jar of fat and hide it in church. As winter gets nearer, the cat thinks more and more about that very tempting jar of fat. Telling the mouse that he has to leave for a day to go to a christening, he goes, instead, to the church and eats some of the fat. He does this two more times using various excuses, and finally finishes the fat. When winter comes, and there is no longer any food to be found outside, the mouse says, "Come, cat, let's go to our jar that we've been saving. It'll taste good." Of course, when they get there the jar is empty. The mouse suspects and accuses the cat of the theft. "You'd better be quiet," the cat retorts. "One more word, and I'll eat you up." When the mouse does speak, the cat jumps and devours her. The moral of this little tale is "You see, that's the way of the world."

In the Grimm tale "The Miller's Drudge and the Cat," a miller, who has lived with only his three helpers for many years, tells them that he will give his mill to the one who brings him the best horse he can find. When they come to the first town, two older men urge Hans, the youngest, to stay there, saying he'll never find a horse; but he follows along. At nightfall they all find shelter in a cave. When Hans is fast asleep, the other two slip away. Hans is stunned to find himself alone in the cave when he awakes, thinking himself doomed to failure.

Suddenly, a little Tabby cat appears and tells Hans she knows what he is looking for. "Come with me and serve me faithfully for seven years," she says, "and I will give you the finest horse you've ever seen." So Hans, who figures he has nothing to lose, follows the cat to her enchanted castle, where they have a delicious dinner and then some of the cats' servants (all kittens) take Hans to his bedroom and help him undress and bed down. But with all the fine meals he enjoys, this would not prove to be a life of luxury for Hans. Each day he has to cut firewood and perform other tasks.

One day the cat asks him to mow the meadow and bring in the hay when it is dry. When Hans returns he asks the cat if it isn't time for his reward, for he'd served her faithfully. "Not yet," she replies, and tells him he must now build her a small silver house. When the house is finished and Hans again asks about his reward, the cat takes him to the house he has just finished and shows him her horses inside, the finest Hans has ever seen. Then she tells Hans to return to the miller, and she will bring him a horse in three days.

When Hans gets back to the mill, the other two workers are already there—one with a black

Drawing by Arthur Rackham, the British artist who illustrated numerous children's books and fairy tales.

horse that is blind and the other with a black horse that is lame. "Where's your horse, Hans?" they ask, laughing. "It will be here in three days," he says. And they laugh some more.

Three days later, a carriage drawn by six magnificent horses pulls up to the gate. A beautiful princess emerges from the carriage—the cat who Hans had faithfully served for seven years. The princess asks the whereabouts of Hans and learns that he is in the goosehouse because he was too dirty and his clothes were too bedraggled to allow him to sleep inside with the others. When Hans comes out, the servant washes him and dresses him in splendid clothes. Then the princess asks for a seventh horse, intended for the miller, to be brought in. The miller gasps when he sees the magnificent horse and decides that the mill will go to Hans. Instead, the princess tells the miller to keep both the horse and the mill, and she and Hans ride off together to the little silver house, which has become a huge castle filled with silver and gold. There they are married, and of course, live happily ever after.

Grooming ～ While other animals groom themselves, including dogs, horses, and even

cows, their grooming habits are definitely inferior to that of the cat. The cat grooms itself from top to bottom. Though a cat spends a lot of time licking its fur, it is doing more than just cleaning. The saliva contains both cleaning and deodorizing elements, and grooming helps maintain healthy skin and removes dead hair. At the same time the cat is smoothing its fur to make it a more efficient insulator. In warm weather licking the fur is a way for a cat to cool off, since cats do not have sweat glands and licking puts moisture on the fur. Cats will also groom when they are agitated to reduce stress. Constant licking and scratching may also be a sign of injury.

A cat will also groom when you have been holding it. A cat is very sensitive to smell and licks itself to get rid of your smell, which has somewhat masked its own scent.

A cat may spend as much as one-third to one-half its waking life grooming itself, other cats, or you!

When a cat grooms itself it is *autogrooming*, or self-grooming. When a cat grooms another cat it is called *allogrooming*. Allogrooming is done more as a friendly gesture, a way to strengthen the tie with another cat (or person), than as a way to clean the other cat.

It is not known who wrote the following poem, but it gives what might be, after all, the perfect explanation for at least one of the cat's grooming habits:

Why Cats Wash After Eating

Some years ago a famous cat,
The pangs of hunger feeling,
Had chanced to catch a fine young mouse,
Who said, as he ceased squawling:
"All genteel folk their faces wash
Before they think of eating!"
And wishing to be thought well-bred
Puss heeded his entreating.

But when she raised her paw to wash,
Chance for escape affording,
The sly young mouse said his good-bye
Without respect to wording.
A feline council met that day
And passed, in solemn meeting,
A law forbidding any cat
To wash till after eating!

In addition to its role in cleaning, grooming can make the fur a better insulator, mask a scent, or be a friendly gesture used to strengthen a bond between a mother cat and her kittens or cats and people. (DRAWINGS BY CHRISTINA DUNSTAN.)

Guffey ～ This small town in Colorado, with twenty-five residents and about three hundred in the surrounding area, has elected a very special mayor. Wiffy La Gone, an abandoned tabby, was elected mayor in the early 1990s. Wiffy's office is in the Guffey General store, where besides performing her mayoral duties, she catches an occasional mouse. When asked what Wiffy's mayoral duties consist of, Laurie Smith, who works at the store, said, "Oh, she just oversees everything. She really doesn't have any official duties."

Wiffy is not the first cat to be mayor of Guffey. He succeeded Smudge (who met his demise at the jaws of a coyote) and Paisley, who died of old age. Besides being mayor, Wiffy is also a bit of a tourist attraction. Smith says people from all over the United States have dropped in to say hello to Wiffy.

There is, indeed, no single quality of the cat that man could not emulate to his advantage.

CARL VAN VECHTEN, American writer (1880–1964)

Harry and Tonto ∼ This 1974 movie stars Art Carney as Harry and his trained cat Tonto. When Harry is evicted from his New York apartment, he goes cross-country and of course takes Tonto along. On the way, they pick up a young female hitchhiker. They wind up in Los Angeles, where the hitchhiker ends up with Harry's grandson.

Tonto won a Patsy (Picture Animal Top Star Award) for his role in *Harry and Tonto*.

Havana ∼ The Havana was developed in Great Britain in the 1950s by the crossbreeding of a seal-point Siamese and black shorthair with a Siamese ancestry. Not surprisingly, this cat's coat is a rich brown, resembling the color of the expensive tobacco in the Havana cigar. Some say the cat was named for the cigar. Others say the cat was named for the rabbit of the same color.

The Havana has the long, narrow face of the Oriental type and a long, svelte body. The breed was recognized for championship competition in 1958. The first Havana browns arrived in the United States in the mid-1950s. The American variety of the breed, the Havana Brown, has a less Oriental look, a sturdier physique, and a quiet disposition.

PERSONALITY: The Havana Brown is active, affectionate, and highly intelligent.

Health ∼ There are many ways to make sure your cat stays as healthy as possible. That includes protecting your cat from accidents as well. Before going into all the things that can go wrong with your cat, however, let me say that in general cats are tough, resilient, and more resistant to illness than many other animals. With those attributes and your efforts, your cats have an excellent prospect of living long and healthy lives.

Of obvious effect on your cat's health is the food your feline eats. Make sure he gets a good, well-balanced diet. Pound for pound, cats need six times as much protein and calcium as humans. Canned cat food has been available since the 1950s. It's hard to believe, but there are now close to a hundred different brands of cat food in the United States. Cat food must meet standards set up by the Association of American Feed Control Officials (AAFCO). Most cat foods provide 100 percent of the nutrients needed for the specified stage of a cat's life. Your cats should be fed a varied menu to prevent their becoming addicted to one particular food. That is important because if at some point if a cat has to go on a special diet for health reasons, a cat who eats only one kind of food could actually starve to death.

If you are making fresh food for your cat, it's also important to vary the menu—chicken, beef, fish, and so on—so that the cat gets all the nutrients he needs. For example, too much liver will cause vitamin A poisoning. If you are making your cat's meals, it might be a good idea to run your menus by your vet at some point. Fresh water should always be available.

According to Richard Gebhardt, author of *The Complete Cat Book*, kittens should be fed three times a day until they are six months old. Then they should be fed twice a day. At one year of age they can be fed once a day. However, dry food for the cat to nibble on should also be available. The particular advantage of dry foods is that they provide exercise of your cat's teeth and gums.

When you put down the food, any that is left after half an hour should be thrown out. Cats have a great sense of timing, and when your cat realizes that the food will not be there all day, he will learn to eat what he needs during that half hour. Food dishes should be washed after every meal. The water bowl should be washed daily.

When you get a new cat you should ask the previous owners what the cat was being fed. If you want to change the diet, you should do it gradually so that it is easier for the cat to adjust. Your cat's appetite can be affected by various factors such as a move to a new location, your absence, or being boarded while you are away. Clean the litter box daily or whenever soiled. Groom your cat regularly to prevent matting and hairballs. This is also a good way to observe your cat and check for any possible problems.

When you get a new cat, the first thing you should do is have him examined by a veterinarian. Find out if your vet is available twenty-four hours, and if not, where you can get help in an emergency. Today, there are more and more

vets who treat only cats and if you have access to a cats-only vet, that is whom you might want to use. Your vet will also tell you what vaccinations your cat should get and how often.

Once your pet is established in your home, you will know your cat well enough to know when he is out of sorts, and possibly needs a visit to the vet. Following are some symptoms or conditions which may require medical attention:

· eyes—sore or runny; a blue or white film over the eye; the eyeball has a blue or white area on it; the lids are swollen; protruding "third eyelids"

· mouth—salivating; pawing at the mouth; exaggerated chewing motions; tentative chewing as if chewing a hot potato

· nose—running, watery nostrils, snuffling, and sneezing

· ears—scratching the ear, shaking the head, tilting the head to one side; sudden ballooning of the ear flap; tiny white insects moving around inside the ear; a bad-smelling, chocolate-colored, or purulent discharge

· Chest—coughing, gasping, labored breathing

· digestion—vomiting, diarrhea, constipation, blood in the stool

· urinary system—difficulty passing urine, blood in the urine; loss of weight, excessive thirst

· female genitalia—white, yellow, pink, or brown purulent discharge from the vagina

· skin—thin or bald patches in the fur; scratching; wet or dry sores; orange specks in the fur of the head and ears or between the toes

You should take your cat to the vet immediately if he has a deep wound, or a wound that will not stop bleeding even after pressure has been applied; if he seems drowsy after eating a foreign substance; if he eats a poisonous plant; if his temperature is higher than 105; if he has a sudden weakness in his hindquarters; a red ulcerated sore on the mouth or other part of the body; runny nose accompanied by an elevated temperature, pale gums and weakness; evidence of trauma accompanied by shortness of breath, elevated temperature, pale gums, and lethargy; vomiting accompanied by lethargy; lethargy, frequent attempts to urinate, elevated temperature, bloody stools; diarrhea accompanied by bloody stools, elevated temperature and vomiting; or constipation accompanied by straining and failure to defecate. If you are not sure, if you have observed any of these symptoms it's better to give the vet a call.

If your cat has an infectious disease he should probably be isolated from any other cats until he is recovered, although by the time he is diagnosed, there is a good possibility that he will have already infected other cats.

There is a wide variety of illnesses that can afflict your cat, some of which are preventable with a yearly vaccination. Some of the medical disorders which can occur in cats include:

· feline infectious enteritis (FIE panleukopenia)—inflammation of the lining of the intestine; very poor prognosis, but can be *prevented with yearly vaccinations*

· gastroenteritis (food poisoning)

· hairballs—formed by cat's swallowing hair during grooming; can be prevented if you regularly comb your feline's fur

· respiratory virus infection (RVI), aka feline respiratory disease (FRD) and commonly referred to as the cat flu—caused primarily by feline viral rhinotracheitis or feline calicivirus (FCV); serious; very contagious; *prevented by yearly inoculation*

· feline infectious anaemia (FIA)—caused by fleas and other bloodsucking insects; may require blood transfusion; poor prognosis

· feline leukemia virus (FeLV)—highly contagious among cats; suppresses immune system (like AIDS does in humans); prognosis poor, no real treatment; *yearly vaccination approximately 65 percent effective*

· feline immunodeficiency virus (FIV)—similar to FeLV and AIDS in humans; highly contagious among cats; suppresses immune system; prognosis poor, no real treatment

· feline infectious peritonitis (FIP); pyothorax—fatal disease, highly contagious, which usually affects young cats; inflammation of the lining of the abdomen

· feline urinary syndrome (FUS) aka cystitis—formation of stones in the bladder which can block urination; can be caused by consumption of too much dried food

· kidney disease—kidney tissue is destroyed; occurs frequently in older cats

· heart disease

· tumor (cancer)—as in humans, can be treatable; early detection and treatment offers best prognosis; generally affects older cats

· worms: roundworms, tapeworms, heartworms, hookworms, lungworms, whipworms and treadworms—these can occasionally spread to humans; treatable

· toxoplasmosis—mild flulike common illness caused by eating infected meats (humans can get this as well from eating bad meat)

· fleas, mites, ticks, lice—most common in the summer; treatable; generally not serious but can pass on disease; easily preventable; can pose possible health hazard to humans

· rabies—usually fatal (unless discovered very early before symptoms appear); *preventable with a yearly inoculation*

The prognosis of all of these diseases improves with early detection and treatment, so a visit to the vet at the first sign of ill health is advised.

There are things you can do to prevent injury to your cat at home and elsewhere. There is a well-known saying—"curiosity killed the cat." Unfortunately, that has occurred with some frequency. Curious cats can slip through very small spaces. Be sure secure screens are in place before you open windows. Cover unused electrical outlets and make sure that no electrical cords are frayed. If your cats like to chew on the cords wrap them in heavy tape or plastic tubing. As you would for a child, keep all chemicals and cleaners in a secure cabinet which your cat is unable to open! Another problem can be poisonous plants. Some of the more common house plants that are poisonous to cats are: poinsettia, philodendron, caladium, dieffenbachia, English ivy, hydrangea, Jerusalem cherry, mistletoe, daffodils, Easter lily, iris, oleander, rhododendron and holly. If you are not sure what plants you have, describe them to the staff at a local plant store. If you have a rare plant, check with the vet to see if it is known to be hazardous to cats. Make sure any harmful plants are unreachable to your cats. Never share your chocolate ice cream, chocolate bar, or any chocolate item with your cat. Chocolate is poisonous to cats.

Heathcliff ∽ Heathcliff is a chubby cartoon cat whose favorite pastime is spilling garbage cans. He is owned by the Nutmeg family; his girlfriend is Sonja; and his nemesis is the bulldog Spike, who has his own problems standing up to Heathcliff.

Created by George Gately in 1973, the Heathcliff comic strip has appeared in more than one thousand newspapers, and more than three dozen Heathcliff paperbacks have been published. In addition, Heathcliff has appeared on television in ABC's *Heathcliff and Dingbat*, in 1980, and *Heathcliff and Marmaduke*, in 1981.

Heathcliff the Movie was released in 1986 with Mel Blanc doing the voice of the cat. In 1986,

Marvel Comics' *Heathcliff* comic book began publication.

Hemingway, Ernest ∽ (1898–1961)
The American journalist, novelist, and short story writer lived in Key West, Florida, with some fifty cats. (The number changed regularly.) As he put it, "One cat just leads to another." He also had cats in his winter home in Cuba. He would talk about his cats in letters to his wife and sons, mentioning the growth and fortitude of these "marvelous" cats. He described one of the cats as "strong as a bear and built like a wolverine," and another as "a fine, slow, friendly, good cat." Among the names Hemingway gave his cats are Dillinger, Thruster, Furhouse, Fats, Friendless, Friendless's Brother, Willy, and Nuisance Value. (I would not think less of you for borrowing some of those names for your cats.) He enjoyed spending time with his cats and training them. He taught several of them to "make a pyramid like lions at the circus." His stories about cats include "Cat in the Rain" and "Killers," both written in the 1920s.

When Hemingway committed suicide in 1961, he left behind a reputation for award-winning writing, sons, and many cats. Today, his home is a museum and visitors can see descendants of those cats. The staff has given the cats celebrity names. Marilyn Monroe appeared in a movie with Timothy Dalton; Frank Sinatra appeared on television in *Lifestyles of the Rich and Famous*: And several of the cats had roles in a movie about Hemingway starring Stacy Keach.

There is a waiting list of people who want to buy "Hemingway" kittens. Many of the Hemingway cats are born with extra toes—some as many as seven toes on each paw. The price of the kittens that are sold depends on how many toes each has—the more toes, the higher the pricetag. The Hemingway museum is at 907 Whitehead

Street in Key West, Florida 33040. It is open daily from nine to four and has an entrance fee which includes a guided tour. 305/294-1575.

Herbert Hoover Presidential Library ∼

Besides housing books, this library is also home to Herbie the cat. Herbie—named after Hoover, of course—showed up one day at the library wet, shivering, and hungry. A sympathetic employee fed him and the rest is history. One of the library guards built a house for Herbie and he never left. The small, white-shingled cottage is a mini-replica of the house in which President Hoover was born. In addition to the chimney, windows, and covered entrance, it has wall-to-wall carpeting and a gazebo for Herbie's food dish. The cottage is located on the porch of the library. Its floor is warmed by under-the-surface heating rods to keep the chill out.

During the day Herbie generally sits by the entrance waiting to greet the steady stream of tourists, about 150,000 a year. Many visitors say that Herbie was the highlight of their visit.

Hero cats ∼

Cats have been credited with performing many heroic deeds. Many people alive today owe their lives to their faithful felines. In Washington, D.C., a cat saved the lives of six sleeping people when fire broke out. He scratched the face of the head of the household until he woke up. And in Wisconsin, Pat, a twenty-pound cat, woke her owner and made so much noise when burglars entered the house that the burglars fled.

In Dora, Alabama, Teresa Harper had just let her pet poodle, Lacy Jane, into the yard when she heard a cry. She rushed out and saw a huge pit bull who had Lacy Jane pinned to the ground, tearing at her throat. Sparky, Harper's cat and a pal of Lacy Jane, jumped twelve feet from the top of the porch onto the dog's head and raked her claws along the dog's muzzle. Though critically injured, Lacy Jane survived (as did Sparky). Teresa Harper calls Sparky a "real heroine," adding, "Another moment or two and Lacy Jane would have been dead."

In her book *Secrets of the Cat*, Barbara Holland describes how a Doberman sprang to attack a small kitten. At that instant, a neighboring gray cat, who had become the kitten's friend, pounced on the Doberman, scratching and clawing at him. The Doberman released the kitten, and the cat released the Doberman. The Doberman's owner checked him for any serious injuries then declared that cats should not be let loose on the streets in a dog's world. The courageous cat had saved the life of the small, defenseless kitten.

In a pub in London, the mistress of the establishment found her cat in a state of great excitement. Stroking the cat did not help. The cat ran wildly to and fro between her mistress and the fireplace until the woman became alarmed and called for help. A robber was found hiding in the chimney. At his trial it was discovered that he'd robbed several places in exactly the same way—remaining in the tap room then concealing himself in a similar manner.

The *Kansas City Star* reports a story about the cat Duke, who saved his family members in a fire. First he wakened nine-year-old Jessica Mugrove, then he woke her thirteen-year-old sister, Felicia. Although he was unable to rouse the girls' parents, Jessica and Felicia did, and Duke continued meowing until everyone was out of the blazing house. In the end, everyone was saved except Duke, who lost his way and died in the fire.

Poor eleven-year-old Puff faced the same fate. When a fire started in the home of the Briemon family in Waubeka, Wisconsin, early one morning, Puff raced upstairs and scratched frantically on the bedroom door. When Carolann Briemon realized that Puff was alerting her to a fire, she and her husband woke their three children and a niece and then fled. Puff, who had saved their lives, perished in the blaze.

Boo Boo was more fortunate than Duke and Puff, as was his owner, Luther Criswell. Luther and his wife had considered giving Boo Boo away when they moved to their new home in New Albany, Indiana. Fortunately, they didn't. Luther, who had been in an accident and was heavily sedated, was fast asleep when the smoke alarm went off. He didn't hear it, but eight-year-old Boo Boo sprang into action, jumping on Luther and scratching and biting him. Luther's anger at being wakened turned quickly to fear when he saw the smoke. He and his wife managed to open a window and escape with Boo Boo. When members of the local Animal Rescue League read about Boo Boo in the *New Albany Tribune*, they presented him with a basket of toys and a certificate of commendation. Since then Boo Boo has had his own medical problems costing the Criswells several hundred dollars. Luther says, "He's worth every penny."

And then there's Walt Hutching, whose life was saved by his cat, Mi-Kitten. It was only about six o'clock in the evening when he was hit on the head from behind as he walked to his apartment in Richmond, Virginia. He fell flat on his face on the pavement and heard the bone above his left eye crunch. The attacker fled when two men nearby ran to Walt's aid. Walt insisted that he was all right. At home he passed out on the dining-room floor. When Mi-Kitten came home through the open kitchen window, he started screaming. He screamed until a downstairs neighbor came up to investigate. He found Walt lying unconscious on the floor with Mi-Kitten sitting on his chest, still screaming. Walt was rushed to the hospital. The doctor who treated him for his double

concussion told Walt he'd probably have been dead by morning if he'd remained on the floor. That was in 1980. Walt and Mi-Kitten are still together on *very good terms*!

Frances Martin's cat Mouse was so named because he was a neutral shade of gray, shy, and mousy, venturing outside only when necessary. His name didn't change, but his demeanor surely did when he became the unexpected hero in Frances's life. One night Frances suddenly woke to find a shadowy figure, smelling of alcohol, looming over her. She was terrified when he started to speak. Suddenly, a gray form screamed and sprang, attaching itself to the intruder's face, scratching and biting it. It was Mouse. The man ran out the front door, with Mouse still attached to his face. Suddenly there was a sickening thud and Mouse stopped screaming. Frances ran out and found a small shapeless mound on the ground. She picked Mouse up, praying he was not dead. For a while Mouse hung limp and unmoving. Finally, Mouse flexed her body, stretched, and emitted a weak "Perrow." Because of the damage done to the intruder's face, it was easy for the police to find the would-be attacker and arrest him. He was charged with the rape and robbery of another solitary woman who lived in a nearby town. Today, Frances has a sign on her gate that says, "Beware, Watch Cat on Duty."

Perhaps the sign at John Graham's house in Charleston, South Carolina, should read, "Beware, Detective Cat on Duty." When Pumpkin, his orange tabby, slipped outside one night, John went looking for her. He found Pumpkin by the family's overturned boat. Underneath the boat slept an escaped convict who had been convicted of three murders. John notified authorities, and he and Pumpkin received the three thousand–dollar reward that was being offered for the arrest. (I imagine Pumpkin had some pretty fancy meals after that!)

Debra Blume's black and white stray cat, Casper, is yet another cat hero. Debra, who had lost 85 percent of her hearing, had just put her new baby, Shannon, down for a nap. She was washing the dishes when Casper suddenly came running to her, screaming. When Casper started clawing the back of her leg, she lost her patience and went to boot him out of the house. But Casper ran into the room where little Shannon was sleeping. Debra followed and found Shannon choking on some mucus. Casper was no longer the annoying feline; he was the hero. A very grateful Debra says that Shannon might have died if Casper had not alerted her.

Charlie Jones of San Diego, California, had as his companion Samantha, a gray cat with white spots on her forehead. Samantha fell in love with seven-year-old Jennifer, who lived across the street. Samantha waited every day for Jennifer to come home from school. One day, well after the time that Jennifer usually came home, Samantha went inside and started pulling Charlie's trousers. Samantha led Charlie outside and across the street to Jennifer's house. The girl's mother was frantic. Jennifer had never returned home, and the police were on their way. When they arrived, Charlie, a retired cop, went along on the search, following the cops in his own car, with Samantha on the seat beside him. One officer told him that they'd heard about a child molester who had kidnapped a seven-year-old in Arizona. Finally, the police helicopter reported seeing something that looked like a car in the woods about ten miles away. When Charlie reached the spot, Samantha jumped from the car. A shot was heard, and a moment later Samantha came out of the underbrush. Although the sergeant was annoyed at the cat's interference, it was Samantha who found the car. When the police got to the car, little Jennifer was being held by the kidnapper, who had his gun to her head. He threatened to shoot her unless they threw down their guns and let him use their cars for a getaway. They threw their guns down. As the kidnapper backed away, dragging Jennifer with him, Samantha sprang from behind him and sank her teeth into his neck. The kidnapper screamed in fear and dropped his gun. The police moved in quickly and rescued Jennifer and arrested the kidnapper.

Finally, Mourka, the hero-cat of Stalingrad, carried messages about enemy gun emplacements from a group of Russian scouts to a house across the street.

High-rise syndrome ～ As cats have become more popular among urban city dwellers and have taken up residence in tall apartment buildings, the incidence of cats falling or leaping from upper-floor windows has increased to such an extent that it has prompted the identification of a "high-rise syndrome." Studies of these falls have revealed that while initially falls from greater heights do often result in greater injuries, at a certain point the level of injury actually *decreases* with greater height.

Cats are notoriously flexible and have a tremendous ability to right themselves, using their inner ear system to restore their balance during a fall. When they fall from great heights, the inner ear system is disturbed by their acceleration; however, after falling about five stories, the cat reaches a constant "falling speed," allowing the inner ear system to stabilize and assist the cat in twisting into an upright position with limbs spread to create drag and break the fall. Thus, the cat may be more vulnerable if it falls from a lower height that does not allow the cat sufficient time to assume this position.

Nonetheless, any fall presents enormous risks, and even a cat that survives a fall from a lower floor in populated areas may not survive encounters with cars, trucks, and buses on a busy street. Falls are more common in summer when windows are likely to be open; a cat may spot a moth or firefly and attempt to catch it, and fall from the window. Or the cat, being curious, may simply be a bit too zealous in his investigation. This tragedy is preventable. If you open a window, be sure you have a screen that is securely in place, one that cannot be pushed out. Despite the old saying that "cats always land on their feet," unfortunately, for the cat, this is not always the case.

Hillbilly Cat ～ This nickname was given to the late great rock-and-roller, Elvis Presley, in the mid 1950s, when there was some question as to just what his music was. That name was soon replaced by the King of Rock and Roll, which he may very well have preferred.

Himalayan ～ What could be better than a Siamese or a Persian? There are some people who would say, without hesitation, the Himalayan. The Himalayan is a combination of the two, bred to have a Siamese-patterned cat with the coat and body of a Persian.

Cat owners in both Sweden and the United States started breeding the Himalayan in the 1920s. In the 1930s it took two Harvard Medical School workers five years to produce the first pointed longhair, whom they called Debutante. In the mid-1930s Britain got into the act with the formation of an experimental breeders' club, and by the 1940s the Himalayan really came into its own. In Britain and most other countries, the breed is known as the colourpoint longhair. For a short time the cat was called a Khmer in Europe.

The Himalayan has Siamese markings—a mask, ears, feet, and tail that are a different color than the rest of the body. He has a round, massive head, short thick neck, small ears, large round bright blue eyes, short thick legs, large round paws, and a long thick coat.

The varieties of Himalayans include seal, blue, chocolate, lilac, flame, cream, tortoise, blue-cream, lilac-cream, chocolate-tortoise, and lynx.

PERSONALITY: The Himalayan has the gentle nature of the Persian with a touch of Siamese curiosity.

> For he will not do destruction if he is well-fed, neither will he spit without provocation.
>
> CHRISTOPHER SMART, English poet
> (1722–1771)

Hissing ～ A cat makes a hissing sound when he feels threatened, upset, pushed too far, or when his territory has been invaded. The hiss is to frighten and warn the possible attacker in the same way a snake hisses. It has been suggested that the cat makes the sounds in imitation of the snake, but I'd be more inclined to believe that the snake copied the cat's hiss.

> Everything that moves serves to interest and amuse a cat.
>
> F. A. PARADIS DE MONCRIF, French writer (1687–1779)

History of the cat

*What sort of philosophers are we, who know
nothing of the origin and destiny of cats?*

HENRY DAVID THOREAU, American writer
and naturalist (1817–1862)

It is not really known when and where the domestic cat first appeared. There are various theories. Some fossil remains similar to those of the typical house cat survive from the Pliocene era, some 10 million years ago. But it is thought that the earliest wild cats became domesticated only eight thousand years ago. And there are historians who do not believe that wild cats themselves became domestic, but that a mutation resulted in the domestic cat.

The remains of a cat excavated at Jericho, in Jordan, appear to date back to 6700 B.C. In 1983 Alain le Brun found a cat jawbone while excavating at the neolithic settlement of Khirokitia in southern Cyprus, dating from 6000 B.C. Since Cyprus had no wild cats, the animal must have been brought over to the island by its early human settlers. And since it is unlikely that they would have taken a wild cat with them to the island, it is possible that the domestic cat was around as long ago as eight thousand years ago.

Other cat remains, thought to be of the Asiatic desert cat, were found in Pakistan by archaeologists. The remains appear to date back some four thousand years. There are some scientists who believe that today's domestic cat is a descendant of the Asiatic wildcat. But there is really nothing to indicate that these were domestic cats. Thus, the origin of the cat remains as much a mystery as the mysterious beast herself. Here is a brief account of the origin of the domestic cat and her history around the world:

EGYPT—Of all the ancient cultures, Egypt showed the most reverence for the cat. Most historians believe that the domestic cat originated in Egypt about 2000 B.C., though there is mention of cats even earlier in the Book of the Dead. The cat continued to play a prominent role in both everyday life and religious ceremonies, where it was seen as the embodiment of the goddess Bastet. Cats were mummified and cat motifs appear frequently on tombs and in burial chambers. There were also strict laws

(continued)

105

regarding the treatment of cats; a person harming a cat was severely punished. (*See* EGYPT for much more detail.)

ASIA—Some theories hold that the first domestic cats were kept in China and India. Though that is doubtful, Chinese and Sanskrit writings show that the cat was present in India and China over two thousand years ago. The Chinese philosopher Confucius owned a cat around 500 B.C. MOHAMMED, who founded the Islamic faith in the seventh century, described the cat as a pure animal in the holy book, the Koran. Dogs were described as unpure. Mohammed kept cats and his followers were cat lovers as well.

A characteristic cat image from ancient Egypt, where cats were associated with the goddess Bastet. (DRAWING BY MARGARET BUNSON.)

During the same period the Japanese used cats as guards in Buddhist temples to protect sacred manuscripts. The Japanese considered it good luck if a cat crossed their path. For several centuries from the tenth onward, owning a cat was restricted to members of the nobility and cats were kept on silk leashes. The early Japanese Emperor Ichijo had a dog exiled and its master imprisoned when the dog dared to chase his beloved cat Myobo no Omoto (Omoto means lady-in-waiting). A tortoiseshell cat is considered lucky in Japan, though in China the oldest and ugliest cat is the luckiest. To Buddhists, all cats are lucky. Light-colored cats bring their owners silver; dark cats bring gold. In China, a black cat with white throat patches is known as "dark cloud over snow." In the seventeenth century, a decree was issued that allowed them to run free to help catch mice that were infesting the silk warehouses, and they are credited with helping to save the silk industry. Some believe that the souls of those who have achieved a higher spiritual state next dwell in the bodies of cats. But although cats in Japan, Persia, Burma, and Siam were very popular, they never did achieve the status they had in Egypt.

AFRICA—Another theory on the origin of the domestic cat is that they came from Ethiopia and were brought to Egypt by Sesotris after he conquered Nubia. And finally there is a theory that the domestic cat has no true wild ancestors—that the Egyptians discovered a mutation and were interested enough to make it into a pet and breed it.

WESTERN EUROPE—How domestic cats arrived in the Mediterranean is not really known. The most likely possibility is that in 2000 B.C. the Phoenicians traded with Egypt for cats which they used on their ships as mousers and then sold as exotic creatures in Greece and Italy. But according to legend, the Greeks, who had the same rodent problems as the Egyptians, traveled to Egypt to buy cats. When the Egyptians refused to sell them, the Greeks simply stole six pair. Back in Greece, the cats, as is their wont, multiplied and wandered, eventually inhabiting Europe. There is evidence in works of art that by the fifth century B.C. the cat was frequently treated by Greeks as a domesticated animal. The Greeks (very wise indeed) came to care for the cats more as companions than mousers.

Cat with fish, from an Indian painting (DATE UNKNOWN).

The cat plays a significant role in Greek myth. The sun god Apollo created the lion; while his sister Artemis, who personified the moon, created the cat, originating the legend that the cat came from the moon. (The Greeks identified Artemis with the Egyptian goddess Bastet, herself a catlike deity.)

Roman legions always brought their pet cats with them and it is thought that is how the first cats were introduced in Britain, in the tenth century. The cats were quite rare and highly prized for protecting grain from rodents with their mouser talents. Domesticated cats were supposed to have arrived in Northern Europe as late as the twelfth century. However, images of domestic cats are found at the base of a Celtic cross and in eighth- or ninth-century Celtic illuminations.

AMERICA—Though an archeologist in Peru is convinced that the cat was the supreme god of the Mochiacas Indians who lived in the Andes, the first domestic cats in America were reportedly brought

(continued)

107

by a French missionary. When he found himself amongst the Huron Indians in the Great Lakes area in North America, as a token of friendship, he presented the Huron chief with what he perceived as a generous and valuable gift—two large French mousers. The chief accepted the cats, but assumed the cats were like the wild and dangerous cats they knew so well. And so the cats were left to fend for themselves. Left on their own, they soon perished. In 1749, when entire colonies were overrun with black rats, it was decided to import domestic cats, no matter what the price. The cats arrived, stayed, and multiplied.

Our fascination with cats dates to ancient times. This cat image appeared on a Roman floor mosaic from Orange, France.

FATE OF THE CAT—During the beginning of the Middle Ages in Europe, cats enjoyed the protection of the church, where cat images could be found in architectural features as well as decoration on church furniture. Farmers also appreciated cats who would protect barns and granaries from mice. But their privileged status was not to last.

Starting in the tenth century, the fortunes of cats took a decided turn for the worse. In 1231 Pope Gregory XI launched the Inquisition, in which people who owned or helped a cat paid with their lives. In the Roman Catholic world, and a large part of the protestant world, men and women were tortured and even hanged just for aiding or giving shelter to a sick or injured cat. In orchestrating and encouraging persecution of the cat, the Church relied on long-held suspicions of the cat, one being that sorcerers could turn themselves into cats. The horror of cats and their persecution increased over time. (If what you just read is all you want to know about those times, I would suggest skipping ahead, though the following information is historically significant, neither researching nor writing it was pleasant!)

During the Middle Ages, millions of cats were tortured, burned, and destroyed. On All Saints Day, baskets, barrels, and sacks of live cats were publicly burned as sacrifices. The Druids came up with wicker cages in which cats would be placed and then held over flames. Later, more durable iron cages came into existence. Cats were burned alive at the beginning of spring (Lent) or buried alive to protect a crop from evil

(continued)

A cat cavorts on this mola *(textile panel), crafted by the Kuna Indians of the San Blas Islands in Panama in the 1920s.* (COURTESY OF THE ART INSTITUTE OF CHICAGO, GIFT OF F. LOUIS HOOVER, 1970.)

spirits. In southern France kittens would be buried alive to get rid of the weeds. In Russia, Poland, and Bohemia cats were buried alive to increase the yield of apple trees.

In Denmark on the eve of Shrove Tuesday, a live cat was put in a barrel and horsemen ran spears through it. In some parts of England on Shrove Tuesday, a cat was whipped to death. In France, Cat Wednesday was held on the second Wednesday of Lent. There would be a huge bonfire that the governor and chief magistrate would attend. Thirteen cats would be put in a wooden cage over the fire while people danced.

The Eve of St. John was another very dangerous time for cats. In Paris cats were packed in barrels or baskets and swung from a pole over a fire. Ashes and pieces of charred bone would be taken home for good luck and as protection from lightning. The king would attend the event and in 1648, King Louis XIV, wearing a wreath of roses, started the fire himself. (The king then abolished the practice—maybe he found it just a bit too distasteful. However, it continued in other parts of France.)

At Aix-en-Provence, the very finest tomcat would be wrapped in swaddling clothes to represent the baby Jesus. He would be adored at a special shrine, taken on procession with flowers thrown in his path and finally put in a basket and thrown into a huge bonfire. This practice continued until 1757.

All Saints Day was yet another day for cats to avoid. In France and Germany, a

Woodcut from the Copendium Maleficarum, *by Brother Francesco Maria Guazzo, published 1608. The book recounts the evil deeds committed by people who had assumed the shape of cats.*

Woodcut from The Historie of Four-Footed Beastes, *by Edward Topsall, 1658.*

(continued)

This study of a cat was painted by Italian artist Ulissi Aldovrandi in the late sixteenth century.

cat would be decorated with garlands at the beginning of the planting season and pampered till the harvest, when he would be eaten. Harvesting the last of the crops is still called "killing the cat" in some countries.

During the eleventh, twelfth, and thirteenth centuries, the persecution of cats escalated. It wasn't enough to just kill the cat. It was important that the cat suffer. Cats were tortured—burned, boiled, skinned alive, buried alive, dropped from towers, and so on. (*See also* GREAT CAT MASSACRE.)

Cats may very well have its prey, the rat, to thank for its survival. In the eleventh and twelfth centuries, returning Crusaders brought back a new, smarter, and hungrier rat in their ships. The black

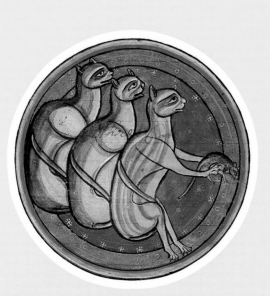

Three cats and a rat from a thirteenth-century English bestiary.

rat multiplied quickly, destroying harvested grain and spreading the plague. Cats were badly needed by farmers to combat the rats and save the food supply. Some cats who surely would have met ritualistic, horrendous deaths were now spared. But when the bubonic plague, known as the Black Death, swept through Europe in the fourteenth century, there simply were not enough cats left to destroy the plague-spreading black rats. As a result, a quarter of the population of Europe perished.

France is credited with reviving modern interest in cats in Europe in the seventeenth century. Cardinal Richelieu kept dozens of cats at court. In the early eighteenth century, the French queen of Louis XV had cats. Many women followed her example and it became *très* fashionable to have a pampered cat as a companion. The fortunes of cats had finally been reversed.

Not only were cats held in high regard and dearly loved by some wealthy women, but some of these women actually included them in their wills. In 1678, Madame Dupuis, a famous French harpist, left most of her fortune to her cats. However, her angry relatives protested the will, and won.

Conditions were improving in England as well. The British Parliament passed the first anticruelty law in 1822. Just two years later the first organization was created to protect animals. In 1837, that organization became the Royal Society for the Prevention of Cruelty to Animals, thanks to cat lover Queen Victoria, who became its patron.

During the time cats were being tortured and massacred in Europe, felines fared far better in the Far East, particularly white ones. In Japan, when a white cat gave birth to five white kittens on the tenth day of the fifth moon in the year 999 at the Imperial Palace, a cat cult developed. The birth was perceived as very mystical and for centuries thereafter cats were spoiled. They were kept inside or taken out on leashes and given special treats to eat and special treatment.

When mice were making mincemeat of the silkworm cocoons, upsetting Japan's traditional industry, the Japanese tried to frighten off the rats with pictures and statues of cats. It didn't work, and in 1602 cats were ordered back to the streets to perform the job that only a real cat is capable of. All cats had to be let loose and it was against the law to buy, sell, or even make a gift of a cat. However, cats were still respected for the services they performed. Though the Japanese thought some cats possessed magical and sinister powers—for example, it was thought that cats with long tails could take on a human shape and cast spells on innocent people—there is no evidence that cats were tortured and killed as they were in Europe.

In Japan, the cat took on religious significance after death. In Tokyo a small but correctly proportioned temple called Go-To-Ku-Ji was built for cats some two hundred years ago. Guardians of duty remind human visitors to the temple that the death of a cat is, as much as the death of a person, an event requiring gravity and respect. On the altar there is a huge assemblage of cats—paintings, statues, in porcelain and bronze, and carved in relief. Each has a paw raised as if in greeting. This is the way the cat for good luck and happiness, Maneki Neko, is represented. The cemetery for cats stretches out around the altar. When a Japanese cat is buried there, her owner deposits a likeness of the cat on the crowded altar.

In China cats were not actually worshiped, but they were held in very high esteem. As living assistants to the Hearth God (the household protector whose image was displayed in every home), cats were bringers of good fortune—and one cat was collared and kept inside the home. The older the cat got, the more venerated it was—the Chinese treated the aging cat the way they did with their elders—with great respect.

Thus, the cat has had a long distinguished history, one that has seen the rise and fall of numerous great civilizations while it has suffered its own turns at the hands of fate. With its current status as the most popular pet in the United States and other countries, the future of the domestic cat seems well secured.

> Cruel, but composed and bland,
> Dumb, inscrutable and grand
> So Tiberius might have sat,
> had Tiberius been a cat.
>
> MATTHEW ARNOLD, English writer and
> literary critic (1822–1888)

> Through all my exemplary life,
> So well did I in constant strife
> Employ my claws and curses,
> That even now though I am dead,
> Those nibbling wretches dare not tread,
> On one of Petrarch's verses.
>
> "Petrarch's Cat," ANTONIOUS QUAERINGUS,
> Latin author

> Thou art the Great Cat, the avenger of the Gods, and the judge of words, and the president of the sovereign chiefs and the governor of the holy Circle, thou art indeed . . . the Great Cat.
>
> Inscription on the royal tombs at Thebes

> To respect the cat is the beginning of the aesthetic sense.
>
> ERASMUS DARWIN, English poet and naturalist (1731–1802)

The Old English Cat

The catte is a beaste of uncertain heare and colour, for some catte is white, some rede, some black, some skewed and speckled in the fete and in the face and in the eares. And he is . . . in youth swyfte, plyante and mery and lepeth and reseth on all thynge that is tofore him; and is led by a strawe and playeth therwith. And is a right hevy beast in age, and ful slepy, and lieth slily in wait for myce. . . . And he maketh a rutefull noyse and gustful when one proffereth to fythte with another.

from *De Rerum Natura*, 1398,
BARTHOLOMEW GLANVIL

Hodori ～ This cartoon tiger cat was the mascot of the 1988 Olympics, which took place in September and October in Korea. But Hodori was certainly not a new figure to the Koreans; he'd been appearing in Korean legends and folktales for years. His reputation was that of a dignified, brave, strong, energetic, noble, and friendly cat. The Hodori used as the Olympian mascot was designed by artist Kim Hyun. Hodori could be seen doing all kinds of "olympic" activities, such as playing ball, riding horseback, boxing, boating, and carrying a flag. He could also be found on numerous souvenirs—including T-shirts, banners, coins, buttons, towels and so on.

Homeward Bound: The Incredible Journey ～ This 1993 Walt Disney movie is based on the 1963 animated Disney movie *The Incredible Journey.* In this film, Sassy the cat and two dogs cross the Sierra Nevada on their own to rejoin their human family after having been mistakenly left behind. Sassy, a Himalayan whose real name is Tiki, was chosen by talent scouts from Walt Disney studios who auditioned dozens of cats. Tiki was trained by Joe Camp and Tammy Maples of Jungle Exotics, and during the filming Tiki enjoyed the services of a full-time chef who prepared gourmet meals from beef heart, kidney, stew meat, and liver. Tiki's favorite food, pre–star treatment, was canned chicken.

Hugo, Victor ~ (1805–1885) This French poet, novelist, and playwright, who lived in exile until the fall of the Napoleonic empire, was a great fan of the cat. First there was Canoine, who sat on a dais of crimson satin. On his granddaughter's birthday, he brought to her another of his favorite cats Gavroche, who held in his paws a huge bouquet of flowers. The note pinned to it said, "From Gavroche, Boulevard de la Mère-Michel." Although Hugo is a well-known and highly esteemed writer, I have no doubt that Gavroche pawed the note himself. I'm not entirely sure about the acquisition of the flowers.

> O cat of churlish kind
> The fiend was in thy mind
> When thou my bird untwin'd
>
> John Skelton, "A Curse
> on a Cat," 1560

Hunting ~ It's a natural instinct for the carnivorous cat to hunt, but cats pursue the activity with varying degrees of enthusiasm and skill. Cats possess only the rudiments of hunting skill by instinct and learn the refinements of technique by watching other cats. Mother cats teach their kittens to hunt by bringing live prey back to the den and then allowing the kittens to kill it. Cats that do not grow up in a hunting environment often show less interest in the activity later.

Being independent, cats generally hunt alone. After locating prey by using their keen senses, they will approach stealthily, with body pressed close to the ground. As the cat narrows in on its subject, eyes fixed, it will wiggle its hind paws and tail as if getting ready to accelerate. The cat will then leap forward in the air, planting the rear feet squarely and pinning the prey in the front paws. If the animal struggles, the cat may turn on its side and rake over the animal with the back claws. Or the cat may release the prey—in a game of cat and mouse—before renewing the attack. Once the prey is in exactly the right position in its mouth, the cat kills it with a dislocating blow to the neck.

She Sights a Bird

She sights a Bird—she chuckles—
She flattens—then she crawls—
She runs without the look of feet—
Her eyes increase to Balls—

Her Jaws stir—twitching—hungry—
Her Teeth can hardly stand—
She leaps, but Robin leaped the first—
Ah, Pussy, of the Sand,

The Hopes so juicy ripening—
You almost bathed your Tongue—
When Bliss disclosed a hundred Toes—
And fled with every one—

Emily Dickinson, American poet
(1830–1886)

The Cat, *by an unknown American artist from the late nineteenth century.* (© 1994 NATIONAL GALLERY OF ART, WASHINGTON, GIFT OF EDGAR WILLIAM AND BERNICE CHRYSLER GARBISCH.)

Cats will often present their masters with their hunting trophies as a social gesture and there is little point in scolding the cat for doing what comes naturally. In fact, its keen hunting ability is probably responsible for the early domestication of the cat as dead mice were indeed a cause for reward. *See also* MOUSER.

> Only those who do not like cats know all about them.
>
> JEAN BURDEN, twentieth century
> American poet

Incredible Journey, The ⌇ This Walt Disney animated picture, based on the children's book of the same name by Sheila Burnford, was produced in 1963. It features a Siamese cat, bull terrier, and a Labrador retriever. The three pals embark together on a two hundred–mile trip over the treacherous Canadian terrain. They encounter many obstacles and survive all kinds of crisis as they make their way home. In 1993, Disney released *Homeward Bound: The Incredible Journey*, a live-action film based on this animated feature.

> A cat is nobody's fool.
>
> HEYWOOD BROUN, American writer
> (1888–1939)

> I've met many thinkers and many cats, but the wisdom of cats is infinitely superior.
>
> HIPPOLYTE TAINE, French philosopher
> (1828–1893)

Ingres, Jean Auguste Dominique ⌇ (1780–1867) This well-known French painter loved his cats dearly. He spent some years in Italy and was the head of the Ecole de France in Rome. One New Year's Day when he was preparing to be presented to the Prince Borghese, he received the news that his favorite cat, Patrocle, had suddenly died and he was overcome with grief. He missed seeing the prince and all his other appointments. He locked himself in his bedroom and spent the day weeping for his beloved friend.

> Cats are a mysterious kind of folk. There is more passing in their mind than we are aware of.
>
> SIR WALTER SCOTT, Scottish poet and
> novelist (1771–1832)

Intelligence ⌇ If you are a cat owner, chances are you think your cat is very smart. You are right! In general, cats possess an IQ far superior to that of dogs. The only animals allegedly smarter than cats are monkeys and chimpanzees,

and primates are the only other animal proven to have the ability to learn by observing others. As an American naturalist and writer puts it, "Cats virtually always underestimate human intelligence just as we, perhaps, underestimate theirs." And maybe H. G. Frommer has an explanation for that. He says, "The smart cat doesn't let on that he is."

Psychologists have done many experiments and studies to assess the intelligence of the cat— and how it compares with other animals. Dr. Donald Adams at Wesleyan University placed cats in boxes that were difficult to get out of. When first placed in the box, a cat would try to get out by brute force—pushing against the sides of the box or scratching at the lid. When this didn't work the cat would investigate other strategies to get out. When the cat finally figured out how to get out

and did so, Adams put it back in the box to see if it would remember how it had gotten out before. He found that the cats no longer needed their previous trial-and-error approach, but simply did what had worked before. Adams said that his cats had been using thinking of a high order: they understood how they had gotten out and remembered exactly what had to be done to solve the problem again. As a result of his research, Adams concluded that cats possess almost the same level of problem-solving ability as monkeys.

In another study, biology professor V. Dethier at Princeton University and physiological psychology professor Eliot Stellar at the University of Pennsylvania used a device called the "triple plate problem" to study feline intelligence. The cats had to learn to press a number of plates in a specific order. They could correctly recall combinations involving up to seven separate presses. Monkeys were the only animals who performed better than cats.

The IQs of cats and dogs were directly compared by doctors N. Maier at the University of Michigan and T. Schneirla at the American Museum of Natural History in New York. The animals were shown a great number of boxes and taught that food could be found only under the box with a lit lamp on top. When the training was finished, the identification light was turned on briefly and the animal was prevented for various amounts of time from approaching the box. They found that dogs could remember for up to five minutes which box had the food; cats went to the correct box as long as sixteen hours later.

> What fun to be a cat!
>
> CHRISTOPHER MORLEY, British writer
> (1890–1957)

So in peace our tasks we ply,
Panguar Bán, my cat, and I;
In our arts we find our bliss,
I have mine and he has his.

from *Panguar Bán*,
Anonymous Celtic monk,
eighth or ninth century

The Cats of Kilkenny

There once were two cats of Kilkenny,
Each thought there was one cat too many;
So they fought and they fit,
And they scratched and they bit,
Till, excepting their nails
And the tips of their tails,
Instead of two cats, there weren't any.

TRADITIONAL

Irish folktales ∽ Like other cultures, the Irish have recorded numerous tales about cats. In her book *Children of the Salmon*, Eileen O'Faolain includes the tale "The Cat's Place by the Fire," which explains why cats get to snooze by a warm fireplace and dogs are left out in the cold. Long ago, cats were always allowed to stay by the fire. One day, the family dog came in from the cold and started an argument with the warm, comfy cat, telling her he would see to it that she stayed indoors no longer. The man of the house heard them arguing and told them that they would race five miles and the winner would get to stay in the house. When they raced the next day, the dog had a healthy lead until he came across a tramp who gave him a blow with his stick. The dog started barking at the tramp and tried to bite him. Mean-while, the cat was quietly making her way home and when the dog finally arrived she was sitting in front of the fire. And she said to the dog, "Now I've won the race, and the place inside by the fire is mine forever more."

In "The Cat and the Mouse," a cat and mouse are playing when the cat bites off the mouse's tail. "I'll only return it if you bring me a drop of milk," the cat says. So the mouse goes to the cow and asks for a drop of milk. The cow demands a wisp from the barn, the barn demands a key from the smith, the smith demands a cake from the bread-woman, and the breadwoman demands water from the river. So the mouse gives water from the river to the breadwoman; the breadwoman gives a cake to the mouse who gives it to the smith; the smith gives a key to the mouse and the mouse gives it to the barn; the barn gives a wisp to the mouse and the mouse gives it to the cow; the cow gives the mouse a drop of milk and the mouse gives it to the cat. And when the cat has drunk the drop, she eats the mouse.

Another tale goes like this: there was a farmer who every night cooked up turnips and beets, for his cows in an old heavy cast iron pot. But in the morning, he found the heavy lid moved and a lot of what he'd cooked for the cows gone. So, one night, he hid in the kitchen and saw the ginger tom go up to the pot, shift the lid, and help himself to the food. The farmer gave him a fierce welt with his stick and the cat ran off with a yelp, while the farmer went to bed. But no sooner was he comfortable than a long line of cats filed in and sat in a court circle. Then a big black cat called the court to order. The terrified farmer's guilt or "just cause" was argued back and forth all night. Finally, the black tom judge held up his paw and announced his verdict—"Not guilty"— and the farmer fainted with relief. And so the farmer was spared the fate of so many others who have lost their case in the court of cats, only to have their eyes scratched out.

Italian folktales ～

According to one charming Italian folktale, cats are heaven sent. The story goes like this: The Devil who was sick and tired of the holier-than-thou St. Francis, sent one hundred mice trained in the arts of spiritual subversion and demoralization to take up residence in St. Francis's cell in Assissi. Once there, the mice set about distracting the saint and destroying his piety. They nibbled his toenails, used his bed as a trampoline when he tried to sleep, and gnawed on the food of his plate as St. Francis tried to eat. Within a week, the poor saint was hungry, irritable, and tired from lack of sleep and a good meal. It wasn't long before the Exterminating Angel told God what was happening and a plan was formulated. A very good mouser, a tom named Felix, was sent down to save St. Francis. Felix told St. Francis his plan, and that night, as St. Francis sat at his table and the mice did all they could to torment him, Felix suddenly shot out from the monk's brown habit. He scratched, swiped, pawed, and bit until every mouse but two were destroyed. The lucky two managed to escape into the cracks in the walls of St. Francis's cell. And that is why today, all cats who are descendants of the heavenly cat will spend hours waiting by a crack in the wall so that they can finish the job and get back to heaven.

Ivory, Lesley Anne ～

This contemporary English artist is no doubt one of the most popular painters of cats in the world. Her realistic cats are frequently placed in a beautiful and ornate background containing a lush oriental rug or colorful flowers or any other decorative setting. Her paintings have appeared in an extensive range of cards, calendars, gift stationery, and books.

Lesley Anne Ivory studied textile design and typography, taught art, and eventually started doing commissioned work. Although she painted all kinds of wildlife, cats became her favorite, at least in part because she loved them and always had them around. Many of her own cats appear in her paintings. Her cat Chesterton, the only son of her cats Twiglet and Gabrielle, appears in the painting "Chesterton in the City," looking out the window at New York.

She calls the subjects of her painting "Christie, Posky and Zelly on Art Deco Rug" "three of the loveliest kittens imaginable." The kittens were adopted by her son Julian, who bought the first in a pet store, then went and bought the second so that the first would have a companion, and then, realizing that the third kitten would be alone in the pet shop, returned and bought him too. Ivory says, "I feel we have brought him up in the right way of thinking."

Lesley Anne Ivory had her first one-person show in London in 1988. Her first one-person show outside of Britain was in New York in 1993. Her books include *Cats Know Best, Meet My Cats, Cats in the Sun, Glorious Cats*, and the forthcoming *Cats Among Toys*.

A kitten is in the animal world what a rosebud is in the garden.

ROBERT SOUTHEY, British poet (1774–1842)

James Russell Webster Mansion
Inn ᵔ This inn, in scenic upstate New York, belongs to antique dealer Barbara Cohen and her husband, Leonard. Besides elegant accommodations, you will find a huge collection of cat figures, everywhere, including musical cats, mom cat and kittens, art deco cats, devil cats, and some outstanding antique cats. In addition, you'll find live cats. The Cohens' cat household includes Radcliffe Worthington (a butterscotch tabby), Alexandra Tatiana (a Himalayan sealpoint), Nicolas Alexie (a black angora/Persian), Sherwood Louise (a Russian blue/sealpoint), and Shiraz (a Balinese sealpoint). The Greek Revival Webster Mansion was built in 1845 by James Russell Webster, a relative of Daniel Webster and a friend of Abraham Lincoln (who was also a cat lover). The address is 115 East Main Street, Waterloo, New York 13165; 315/539-3032.

Japanese bobtail
ᵔ Instead of a typical tail, the bobtail cat has a bushy tail fanning out to form a small pompon. He can be traced back to the seventh century in the Far East. For hundreds of years the Japanese bobtail was highly valued and guarded. That changed in 1602 when Japanese authorities decreed that *all* cats should be set free to cope with vermin which were threatening silkworms. It was forbidden to buy or sell a

This red and white Van male, Hoseki, was the CFA's first Longhair Japanese Bobtail Grand Champion. Like most Japanese bobtails, Hoseki has a very friendly disposition. (PHOTOGRAPH BY MARILYN LEHRFELD, COURTESY MARILYN KNOPP, MARI CHO CATTERY, POMONA, NEW JERSEY.)

cat, and the bobtail went from being highly re-vered to being just another cat living on the street or the farm.

The Japanese bobtail came to the United States after the World War II, when soldiers stationed in Japan returned with their families and pets. It wasn't until 1971 that the Japanese bobtail was recognized as a pedigree and granted provisional status by the Cat Fanciers Association. Five years later they were competing in cat shows.

The traditional varieties of the Japanese bob-tail are the red and white, black and white, and tortoiseshell and white.

PERSONALITY: The Japanese bobtail is active, eats ravenously, has a sunny disposition, and is ex-tremely vocal. He is a very personable cat full of curiosity.

*J*apanese *folktales* ～ The Japanese have created their share of stories about the popu-lar cat. One tale features a rich lord who likes to collect fine carvings of animals but lacks a carving of a mouse. He called in two skilled carvers and told them that the one who carved the most life-like mouse would be given a bag of gold. The decision would be made by the lord's cat. Which-ever carving the cat pounced on would obviously be the most lifelike. When the artists returned, one of their carvings looked exactly like a mouse while the other one, made from some rough material that flaked, hardly looked like a mouse at all. When the cat was brought into the room, however,

Opposite: Cat in Window, *from the series "Famous Sites of Edo: One Hundred Views," by the 19th cen-tury Japanese artist Ando Hiroshige.* (COURTESY THE METROPOLITAN MUSEUM OF ART, ROGERS FUND 1914.)

he went immediately to the badly carved mouse. The lord was surprised but gave the bag of gold to the carver who'd done such a poor job. He then asked him how he'd made a mouse that, so un-mouselike, had still attracted the cat. "It was easy," said the man. "I carved the mouse out of dried fish." The lord couldn't help laughing when he heard how the cat and everyone else had been fooled. So the lord said he'd have to hand out two bags of gold, one to the man who carved so well, and one to the man who carved so cleverly. The lord kept the wooden mouse for himself and gave the other one to his appreciative cat.

In her children's book *The Cat Who Went to Heaven*, Elizabeth Coatsworth tells the story of a poor painter in Japan who can hardly afford food for himself, much less for his cat. Yet, he allows a little cat named Good Fortune into his life, and through his painting Good Fortune is blessed and welcomed into heaven by none other than the great Buddha.

Another story tells how when the great Buddha artist Cho-Densu was painting the Nirvana pic-ture, his famous masterpiece, a little cat sat pa-tiently by his side watching. The cat asked the artist why the picture showed humans, spirits, animals, trees, and plants surrounding the Bud-dha but no cats. Cho-Densu told him that the cat was not on the list of animals protected by the Buddha and never seen in a Nirvana picture be-cause of all the animals at the Buddha's funeral the cat was the only one to fall asleep. What could the cat say? But he stayed by Cho-Densu's side and watched him paint. One day he could not find the ultramarine mineral he needed for his coloring. The next day the little cat brought the ultramarine mineral to Cho-Densu and then showed him where he could get it. As a reward, the grateful Cho-Densu painted the little cat into the picture—and if you travel to the great Nirvana painting, in the Tofukuji monastery in Kyoto, you will see the little cat in the painting. In another

The Javanese is a breed that is both lovely and devoted. (PHOTOGRAPH BY ISABELLE FRANCAIS.)

version, when animals were called to the bedside of the dying Buddha, the cat was sleeping and couldn't be bothered making the trip. Buddha said the first twelve animals to reach his bedside would be selected for immortality. Needless to say, the cat was not one of those selected. In another variation, the cat was forbidden to attend the mourning at Buddha's deathbed because it had killed the rat that had been sent as medicine by Buddha's mother.

See also MANEKI NEKO.

Javanese ～ The Javanese was a result of breeding American shorthairs with Siamese to produce new colors; when some of the cats had long hair, a new breed was born. (Some people consider the Javanese to be the same breed as the Balinese.) They have the look and appeal of the native dancers for whom they are named. Javanese are dainty and fine boned, with a coat like silk chiffon. Their longhaired coat comes in many colors. Javanese were accepted for championship competition in 1987. Like Siamese, Javanese are quite talkative but their voice tone is easier on the ear.

PERSONALITY: They are highly trainable, easy to care for, and an excellent cat for children. Javanese are very devoted and tend to follow the humans they own around.

Johnson, Dr. Samuel ∼ (1709–1784)

The English lexicographer, critic, poet, and conversationalist took great care to provide his cat Hodge with every creature comfort. In his 1791 biography, *Life of Johnson*, James Boswell (1740–1795) commented on just how much Johnson pampered Hodge:

I never shall forget the indulgence with which Dr. Johnson treated Hodge, his cat; for whom he himself used to go out and buy oysters lest the servants, having that trouble, should take a dislike to the poor creature. I am unluckily one of those who have an antipathy to a cat, and I own I frequently suffered a good deal from the presence of the same Hodge.

I recollect him one day scrambling up Dr. Johnson's breast apparently with much satisfaction while my friend, smiling and half-whistling, rubbed down his back and pulled him by the tail; and when I observed he was a fine cat, saying, "Why yes, sir, but I have had cats that I liked better than this"; and then, as if perceiving Hodge to be out of countenance, adding, "but he is a very fine cat, a very fine cat indeed."

The Life of Samuel Johnson, JAMES BOSWELL, British diarist and biographer, (1740–1795)

Just Cats

∼ Owned by disc jockey Alison Steele, Just Cats is probably the only totally feline boutique in the world. Many shops featuring cat supplies and items with cat motifs have sprung up around the country in the last few years. In fact there is one in England near Windsor Castle, one in France on the left bank, and even one in Tokyo. Just Cats remains unique as the only feline boutique to also feature actual cats.

Since 1988 Just Cats has specialized in breeding and selling fine pedigreed show/breeding and pet-quality Persian and Himalayan kittens. They have recently added a breeding program for Oriental Short Hairs, Color Point Short Hairs, and Siamese. Their association with a vast network of cat fanciers of all breeds has enabled them to accommodate clients around the world seeking unusual breeds. Their kittens have traveled to new homes in Brazil, Argentina, Japan, Italy, France, Switzerland, Puerto Rico, and Mexico. They refuse to compromise the privacy of their celebrity clientele by naming names, but the list is indeed impressive.

Just Cats' merchandise includes jewelry, housewares, wearing apparel, lamps, pictures, linens, stationery, books, collectible plates, toys, dolls, and statues. Items for Monsieur le Chat include plain and fancy collars, T shirts, sweaters, hats and even costumes for special occasions. There are also beds and bowls of every description and a huge collection of unique and original toys. Just Cats is located at 244 E. 60th St. New York City 10022, phone 212/888-CATS.

Cats are intended to teach us that not everything in nature has a function.

GARRISON KEILLOR, American writer and humorist, twentieth century

K

Katten Kabinet ~ This cat museum in Amsterdam, Holland, was started by Dutch financier Boy Meijer as a tribute to his cat, J. P. Morgan, who died at the age of eighteen. Meijer had already paid a lot of tribute to his beloved feline friend when it was alive. When J. P. was five, Meijer commissioned a portrait of the cat; he had a bronze sculpture made in his honor; J. P.'s face appeared on the guilder; and a volume of poetry dedicated to him was published. Katten Kabinet opened in December 1990 and includes catifacts from as long ago as ancient Egypt, when cats were worshiped. Among those on the board of directors of the museum is the Spanish ambassador, who owns seventeen cats.

Katzen Museum ~ This museum, with a collection of over ten thousand cat items on display, is located in Switzerland, in the small town of Riehen, near Basel. Here you can find paintings, stuffed cats, porcelain, bronze, plastic, wooden, and glass cats. There are also cat games, tableware, and clocks. One of the most valuable items on display is a three thousand–year-old bronze cat from Egypt. The museum was opened in 1982 by Rosemarie Muller, who had been collecting cats for some twenty years. When her collection threatened to force her out of her home, she created the museum. The Katzen Museum is located at Baselstrasse 101, 4125 Riehen/Basel, 61-672694.

Keats, John ~ (1795–1821) The British romantic poet was just twenty-six when he died of tuberculosis in Rome, where he had gone for a cure. He had given up the study of medicine to pursue poetry. His poem "To Mrs. Reynolds' Cat" is a tribute to an aging tom.

Cat! who hast pass'd thy grand climacteric,
    How many mice and rats hast in thy days
    Destroy'd?—How many tit bits stolen? Gaze
With those bright, languid segments green, and
    prick
Those velvet ears—but pr'ythee do not stick
    Thy latent talons in me—and upraise
    Thy gentle mew—and tell me all thy frays
Of fish and mice, and rats and tender chick.
Nay, look not down, nor lick; thy dainty
    wrists—

For all the Wheezy asthma,—and for all
Thy tail's tip is nick'd off—and though the fists
   Of many a maid have given thee many a
   maul,
Still is that fur soft as when the lists
   In youth thou enter'dst on glass bottled wall.

Kennedy, John F. ～ (1917–1963)

Tom Kitten, a blue-gray shorthair kitten, lived with the Kennedy family in the White House for a very short time. Tom was Caroline Kennedy's kitten, and he moved into the White House when Jack Kennedy became the thirty-fifth president in 1960. Tom's stay was brief because, according to a story in the *Washington Daily News*, Tom had "too much privacy and not enough cats around." So Tom took up residence at the Georgetown home of Mary Gallagher, personal secretary to First Lady Jackie Kennedy. Tom died just two years later of cirrhosis of the liver. Of his untimely death, *The Alexandria Gazette* said that Tom was worth remembering because, "Unlike many humans in the same position, he never wrote his memoirs of his days in the White House and never discussed them for quotation, though he was privy to many official secrets."

See WHITE HOUSE CATS.

You walk as a king scorning his subjects.

"To Winky," AMY LOWELL, American poet
(1874–1925)

King of the Cats ～ Several versions of

the legendary tale of the king of the cats survive from Europe, and may have originated in Ireland, where the mighty cat Irusan was said to rule over

---

Sir Walter Scott's Cat

The cat assumed a kind of ascendancy among the quadrupeds—sitting in state in Scott's arm-chair, and occasionally stationing himself on a chair beside the door, as if to review his subjects as they passed, giving each dog a cuff beside the ears as he went by. This clapper-clawing was always taken in good part; it appeared to be, in fact, a mere act of sovereignty on the part of grimalkin, to remind the others of their vassalage; which they acknowledged by the most perfect acquiescence. A general harmony prevailed between sovereign and subjects, and they would all sleep together in the sunshine.

"Abbotsford," WASHINGTON IRVING, American
author (1783–1859)

---

all of the other cats on the heath. In William Baldwin's *Beware the Cat*, published in 1553, the sovereign cat is named Grimalkin and news of his death is passed along by talking cats to humans, who in turn are overheard by their cats, and thus the news spread. In all versions of the tale, the demise of the king causes a new pretender to appear, as recounted by Sir Walter Scott in Washington Irving's 1835 essay, "Abbotsford":

He went on to tell a little story about a gude man who was returning to his cottage one night, when, in a lonely out-of-the-way place, he met with a funeral procession of cats all in mourning, bearing one of their race to the grave in a coffin covered with a black velvet pall. The worthy man, astonished and half frightened at so strange a pageant, hastened home and told what he had seen to his wife and children. Scarce had he finished, when a great black cat that sat beside the fire raised himself up, exclaimed "Then I am king of the cats!" and vanished up the chimney. The funeral seen by the gude man was one of the cat dynasty.

"Our grimalkin here," added Scott, "sometimes reminds me of the story, by the airs of sovereignty which he assumes; and I am apt to treat him with respect from the idea that he may be a great prince incog., and may some time or other come to the throne."

Rudyard Kipling

The English writer (1856–1936), who was born in India, is famous for numerous books for children and adults, such as *The Jungle Books* and *Kim*. In "The Cat That Walked by Himself," one of the tales in the *Just So Stories*, published in 1902, the cat makes an agreement that he will be kind to babies (as long as they don't pull his tail) if he will be allowed to sit by the fire and drink milk thrice daily. As you can see in the following line, the cat made it quite known that he was still independent: "I am the cat that walks by himself, and all places are alike to me."

The Cat That Walked by Himself

Hear and attend and listen; for this befell and behappened and became and was, O my Best Beloved, when the Tame animals were wild. The Dog was wild, and the Horse was wild, and the Pig was wild—as wild as wild could be—and they walked in the Wet Wild Woods by their wild lones. But the wildest of all the wild animals was the Cat. He walked by himself, and all places were alike to him.

Of course the Man was wild too. He was dreadfully wild. He didn't even begin to be tame till he met the Woman, and she told him that she did not like living in his wild ways. She picked out a nice dry Cave, instead of a heap of wet leaves, to lie down in; and she strewed clean sand on the floor; and she lit a nice fire of wood at the back of the Cave; and she hung a dried wild-horse skin, tail-down, across the opening of the Cave; and she said, "Wipe your feet, dear, when you come in, and now we'll keep house."

That night, Best Beloved, they ate wild sheep roasted on the hot stones, and flavored with wild garlic and wild pepper; and wild duck stuffed with wild rice and wild fenugreek and wild coriander; and marrow-bones of wild oxen; and wild cherries, and wild grenadillas. Then the Man went to sleep in front of the fire ever so happy; but the Woman sat up, combing her hair. She took the bone of the shoulder of mutton—the big fat blade-bone—and she looked at the wonderful marks on it, and she threw more wood on the fire, and she made a Magic. She made the First Singing Magic in the world.

Out in the Wet Wild Woods all the wild animals gathered together where they could see the light of the fire a long way off, and they wondered what it meant.

Then Wild Horse stamped with his wild foot and said, "O my Friends and O my Enemies, why have the Man and the Woman made that great light in that great Cave, and what harm will it do us?"

Wild Dog lifted up his wild nose and smelled the smell of roast mutton, and said, "I will go up and see and look, and say; for I think it is good. Cat, come with me."

"Nenni!" said the Cat. "I am the Cat who walks by himself, and all places are alike to me. I will not come."

Illustration by Rudyard Kipling, from "The Cat that Walked by Himself," Just So Stories, 1902.

"Then we can never be friends again," said Wild Dog, and he trotted off to the Cave. But when he had gone a little way the Cat said to himself, "All places are alike to me. Why should I not go too and see and look and come away at my own liking." So he slipped after Wild Dog softly, very softly, and hid himself where he could hear everything.

When Wild Dog reached the mouth of the Cave he lifted up the dried horse-skin with his nose and sniffed the beautiful smell of the roast mutton, and the Woman, looking at the blade-bone, heard him, and laughed, and said, "Here comes the first. Wild Thing out of the Wild Woods, what do you want?"

Wild Dog said, "O my Enemy and Wife of my Enemy, what is this that smells so good in the Wild Woods?"

Then the Woman picked up a roasted mutton-bone and threw it to Wild Dog, and said, "Wild Thing out of the Wild Woods, taste and try." Wild Dog gnawed the bone, and it was more delicious than anything he had ever tasted, and he said, "O my Enemy and Wife of my Enemy, give me another."

(continued)

The Woman said, "Wild Thing out of the Wild Woods, help my Man to hunt through the day and guard this Cave at night, and I will give you as many roast bones as you need."

"Ah!" said the Cat, listening. "This is a very wise Woman, but she is not so wise as I am."

Wild Dog crawled into the Cave and laid his head on the Woman's lap, and said, "O my Friend and Wife of my Friend, I will help your Man to hunt through the day, and at night I will guard your Cave."

"Ah!" said the Cat, listening. "That is a very foolish Dog." And he went back through the Wet Wild Woods waving his wild tail, and walking by his wild lone. But he never told anybody.

When the Man waked up he said, "What is Wild Dog doing here?" And the Woman said, "His name is not Wild Dog any more but the First Friend, because he will be our friend for always and always and always. Take him with you when you go hunting."

Next night the Woman cut great green armfuls of fresh grass from the water-meadows, and dried it before the fire, so that it smelt like new-mown hay, and she sat at the mouth of the Cave and plaited a halter out of horse-hide, and she looked at the shoulder of mutton-bone—at the big broad blade-bone—and she made a Magic. She made the Second Singing Magic in the world.

Out in the Wild Woods all the wild animals wondered what had happened to Wild Dog, and at last Wild Horse stamped with his foot and said, "I will go and see and say why Wild Dog has not returned. Cat, come with me."

"Nenni!" said the Cat. "I am the Cat who walks by himself, and all places are alike to me. I will not come." But all the same he followed Wild Horse softly, very softly, and hid himself where he could hear everything.

When the Woman heard Wild Horse tripping and stumbling on his long mane, she laughed and said, "Here comes the second. Wild Thing out of the Wild Woods, what do you want?"

Wild Horse said, "O my Enemy and Wife of my Enemy, where is Wild Dog?"

The Woman laughed, and picked up the blade-bone and looked at it, and said, "Wild Thing out of the Wild Woods, you did not come here for Wild Dog, but for the sake of this good grass."

And Wild Horse, tripping and stumbling on his long mane, said, "That is true; give it me to eat."

The Woman said, "Wild Thing out of the Wild Woods, bend your wild head and wear what I give you, and you shall eat the wonderful grass three times a day."

"Ah," said the Cat, listening, "this is a clever Woman, but she is not so clever as I am."

Wild Horse bent his wild head, and the Woman slipped the plaited hide halter over it, and Wild Horse breathed on the Woman's feet and said, "O my Mistress, and Wife of my Master, I will be your servant for the sake of the wonderful grass."

"Ah," said the Cat, listening, "that is a very foolish Horse." And he went back through the Wet Wild Woods, waving his wild tail and walking by his wild lone. But he never told anybody.

When the Man and the Dog came back from hunting, the Man said, "What is Wild Horse doing here?" And the Woman said, "His name is not Wild Horse any more, but the First Servant, because he will carry us from place to place for always and always and always. Ride on his back when you go hunting."

Next day, holding her wild head high that her wild horns should not catch in the wild trees, Wild Cow came up to the Cave, and the Cat followed, and hid himself just the same as before; and everything happened just the same as before; and the Cat said the same things as before, and when Wild Cow had promised to give her milk to the Woman every day in exchange for the wonderful grass, the Cat went back through the Wet Wild Woods waving his wild tail and walking by his wild lone, just the same as before. But he never told anybody. And when the Man and the Horse and the Dog came home from hunting and asked the same questions same as before, the Woman said, "Her name is not Wild Cow any more, but the Giver of Good Food. She will give us the warm white milk for always and always and always, and I will take care of her while you and the First Friend and the First Servant go hunting."

Next day the Cat waited to see if any other Wild Thing would go up to the Cave, but no one moved in the Wet Wild Woods, so the Cat walked there by himself; and he saw the Woman milking the Cow, and he saw the light of the fire in the Cave, and he smelt the smell of the warm white milk.

Cat said, "O my Enemy and Wife of my Enemy, where did Wild Cow go?"

The Woman laughed and said, "Wild Thing out of the Wild Woods, go back to the Woods again, for I have braided up my hair, and I have put away the magic blade-bone, and we have no more need of either friends or servants in our Cave."

Cat said, "I am not a friend, and I am not a servant. I am the Cat who walks by himself, and I wish to come into your cave."

Woman said, "Then why did you not come with First Friend on the first night?"

Cat grew very angry and said, "Has Wild Dog told tales of me?"

Then the Woman laughed and said, "You are the Cat who walks by himself, and all places are alike to you. You are neither a friend nor a servant. You have said it yourself. Go away and walk by yourself in all places alike."

Then Cat pretended to be sorry and said, "Must I never come into the Cave? Must I never sit by the warm fire? Must I never drink the warm white milk? You are very wise and very beautiful. You should not be cruel even to a Cat."

(continued)

131

Woman said, "I knew I was wise, but I did not know I was beautiful. So I will make a bargain with you. If ever I say one word in your praise you may come into the Cave."

"And if you say two words in my praise?" said the Cat.

"I never shall," said the Woman, "but if I say two words in your praise, you may sit by the fire in the Cave."

"And if you say three words?" said the Cat.

"I never shall," said the Woman, "but if I say three words in your praise, you may drink the warm white milk three times a day for always and always and always."

Then the Cat arched his back and said, "Now let the Curtain at the mouth of the Cave, and the Fire at the back of the Cave, and the Milk-pots that stand beside the Fire, remember what my Enemy and the Wife of my Enemy has said." And he went away through the Wet Wild Woods waving his wild tail and walking by his wild lone.

That night when the Man and the Horse and the Dog came home from hunting, the Woman did not tell them of the bargain that she had made with the Cat, because she was afraid that they might not like it.

Cat went far and far away and hid himself in the Wet Wild Woods by his wild lone for a long time till the Woman forgot all about him. Only the Bat—the little upside-down Bat—that hung inside the Cave, knew where Cat hid; and every evening Bat would fly to Cat with news of what was happening.

One evening Bat said, "There is a Baby in the Cave. He is new and pink and fat and small, and the Woman is very fond of him."

"Ah," said the Cat, listening, "but what is the Baby fond of?"

"He is fond of things that are soft and tickle," said the Bat. "He is fond of warm things to hold in his arms when he goes to sleep. He is fond of being played with. He is fond of all those things."

"Ah," said the Cat, listening, "then my time has come."

Next night Cat walked through the Wet Wild Woods and hid very near the Cave till morning-time, and Man and Dog and Horse went hunting. The Woman was busy cooking that morning, and the Baby cried and interrupted. So she carried him out-side the Cave and gave him a handful of pebbles to play with. But still the Baby cried.

Then the Cat put out his paddy paw and patted the Baby on the cheek, and it cooed; and the Cat rubbed against its fat knees and tickled it under its fat chin with his tail. And the Baby laughed and the Woman heard him and smiled.

Then the Bat—the little upside-down Bat—that hung in the mouth of the Cave said, "O my Hostess and Wife of my Host and Mother of my Host's Son, a Wild Thing from the Wild Woods is most beautifully playing with your Baby."

"A blessing on that Wild Thing whoever he may be," said the Woman, straightening her back, "for I was a busy woman this morning and he has done me a service."

The very minute and second, Best Beloved, the dried horse-skin Curtain that was stretched tail-down at the mouth of the Cave fell down—*woosh!*—because it remembered the bargain she had made with the Cat, and when the Woman went to pick it up—lo and behold!—the Cat was sitting quite comfy inside the Cave.

"O my Enemy and Wife of my Enemy and Mother of my Enemy," said the Cat, "it is I: for you have spoken a word in my praise, and now I can sit within the Cave for always and always and always. But still I am the Cat who walks by himself, and all places are alike to me."

The Woman was very angry, and shut her lips tight and took up her spinning-wheel and began to spin.

But the Baby cried because the Cat had gone away, and the Woman could not hush it, for it struggled and kicked and grew black in the face.

"O my Enemy and Wife of my Enemy and Mother of my Enemy," said the Cat, "take a strand of the wire that you are spinning and tie it to your spinning-whorl and drag it along the floor, and I will show you a Magic that shall make your Baby laugh as loudly as he is now crying."

"I will do so," said the Woman, "because I am at my wits' end; but I will not thank you for it."

She tied the thread to the little clay spindle-whorl and drew it across the floor, and the Cat ran after it and patted it with his paws and rolled head over heels, and tossed it backward over his shoulder and chased it between his hind-legs and pretended to lose it, and pounced down upon it again, till the Baby laughed as loudly as it had been crying, and scrambled after the Cat and frolicked all over the Cave till it grew tired and settled down to sleep with the Cat in its arms.

"Now," said the Cat, "I will sing the Baby a song that shall keep him asleep for an hour." And he began to purr, loud and low, low and loud, till the Baby fell fast asleep. The Woman smiled as she looked down upon the two of them and said, "That was wonderfully done. No question but you are very clever, O Cat."

That very minute and second, Best Beloved, the smoke of the fire at the back of the Cave came down in clouds from the roof—*puff!*—because it remembered the bargain she had made with the Cat, and when it had cleared away—lo and behold!—the Cat was sitting quite comfy close to the fire.

"O my Enemy and Wife of my Enemy and Mother of my Enemy," said the Cat, "it is I, for you have spoken a second word in my praise, and now I can sit by the warm fire at the back of the Cave for always and always and always. But still I am the Cat who walks by himself, and all places are alike to me."

Then the Woman was very very angry, and let down her hair and put more wood on the fire and brought out the broad blade-bone of the shoulder of mutton and began to

(continued)

make a Magic that should prevent her from saying a third word in praise of the Cat. It was not a Singing Magic, Best Beloved, it was a Still Magic; and by and by the Cave grew so still that a little wee-wee mouse crept out of a corner and ran across the floor.

"O my Enemy and Wife of my Enemy and Mother of my Enemy," said the Cat, "is that little mouse part of your magic?"

"Ouh! Chee! No indeed!" said the Woman, and she dropped the blade-bone and jumped upon the footstool in front of the fire and braided up her hair very quick for fear that the mouse should run up it.

"Ah," said the Cat, watching, "then the mouse will do me no harm if I eat it?"

"No," said the Woman, braiding up her hair, "eat it quickly and I will ever be grateful to you."

Cat made one jump and caught the little mouse, and the Woman said, "A hundred thanks. Even the First Friend is not quick enough to catch little mice as you have done. You must be very wise."

That very moment and second, O Best Beloved, the Milk-pot that stood by the fire cracked in two pieces—*ffft*—because it remembered the bargain she had made with the Cat, and when the Woman jumped down from the footstool—lo and behold!—the Cat was lapping up the warm white milk that lay in one of the broken pieces.

"O my Enemy and Wife of my Enemy and Mother of my Enemy," said the Cat, "it is I; for you have spoken three words in my praise, and now I can drink the warm white milk three times a day for always and always and always. But *still* I am the Cat who walks by himself, and all places are alike to me."

Then the Woman laughed and set the Cat a bowl of the warm white milk and said, "O Cat, you are as clever as a man, but remember that your bargain was not made with the Man or the Dog, and I do not know what they will do when they come home."

"What is that to me?" said the Cat. "If I have my place in the Cave by the fire and my warm white milk three times a day I do not care what the Man or the Dog can do."

That evening when the Man and the Dog came into the Cave, the Woman told them all the story of the bargain while the Cat sat by the fire and smiled. Then the Man said, "Yes, but he has not made a bargain with *me* or with all proper Men after me." Then he took off his two leather boots and he took up his little stone axe (that makes three) and he fetched a piece of wood and a hatchet (that is five altogether), and he set them out in a row and he said, "Now we will make *our* bargain. If you do not catch mice when you are in the Cave for always and always and always, I will throw these five things at you whenever I see you, and so shall all proper Men do after me."

"Ah," said the Woman, listening, "this is a very clever Cat, but he is not so clever as my Man."

The Cat counted the five things (and they looked very knobby) and he said, "I will catch mice when I am in the Cave for always and always and always; but *still* I am the Cat who walks by himself, and all places are alike to me."

"Not when I am near," said the Man. "If you had not said that last I would have put all these things away for always and always and always; but I am now going to throw my two boots and my little stone axe (that makes three) at you whenever I meet you. And so shall all proper Men do after me!"

Then the Dog said, "Wait a minute. He has not made a bargain with *me* or with all proper Dogs after me." And he showed his teeth and said, "If you are not kind to the Baby while I am in the Cave for always and always and always, I will hunt you till I catch you, and when I catch you I will bite you. And so shall all proper Dogs do after me."

"Ah," said the Woman, listening, "this is a very clever Cat, but he is not so clever as the Dog."

Cat counted the Dog's teeth (and they looked very pointed) and he said, "I will be kind to the Baby while I am in the Cave, as long as he does not pull my tail too hard, for always and always and always. But *still* I am the Cat that walks by himself, and all places are alike to me."

"Not when I am near," said the Dog. "If you had not said that last I would have shut my mouth for always and always and always; but *now* I am going to hunt you up a tree whenever I meet you. And so shall all proper Dogs do after me."

Then the Man threw his two boots and his little stone axe (that makes three) at the Cat, and the Cat ran out of the Cave, and the Dog chased him up a tree; and from that day to this, Best Beloved, three proper Men out of five will always throw things at a Cat whenever they meet him, and all proper Dogs will chase him up a tree. But the Cat keeps his side of the bargain too. He will kill mice and he will be kind to Babies when he is in the house, just as long as they do not pull his tail too hard. But when he has done that, and between times, and when the moon gets up and night comes, he is the Cat that walks by himself, and all places are alike to him. Then he goes out to the Wet Wild Woods or up the Wet Wild Trees or on the Wet Wild Roofs, waving his tail and walking by his wild lone.

Cat and Kittens, *by an unknown American artist, c. 1872.* (© 1994 NATIONAL GALLERY OF ART, WASHINGTON, GIFT OF EDGAR WILLIAM AND BERNICE CHRYSLER GARBISCH.)

> There is no more intrepid explorer than a kitten.
>
> JULES CHAMPFLEURY, French writer
> (1821–1829)

Kittens ~

If a queen, or female cat, has successfully mated, her litter of kittens will be born about nine weeks later. The average first litter of a female cat is three or four kittens. The average number of kittens in subsequent litters is four, though that number can vary according to the breed of the cat. The largest litter recorded was nineteen kittens to a Burmese, of which fifteen survived.

Since there can be a delay of about half an hour between the arrival of each kitten, the process can be quite lengthy and tiring for the mother, or dam. (Sometimes the time between births is much longer.) During the time before the next arrival, the mother attends to the newest kitten—breaking away the birth sac (the amniotic sac) in which the kitten is encased; cleaning the mouth and nose of the kitten so that it can breathe; biting through and eating the umbilical cord; eating the afterbirth—the placenta—which gives her nourishment to cope with the long hours of kitten caring she has ahead of her

Most kittens tend to be playful as well as adorable, as demonstrated in this lovely folk art painting, Four Cats Playing, *by an unknown artist.* (COURTESY COLONIAL WILLIAMSBURG FOUNDATION.)

My Little White Kitties into Mischief, *a lithograph by Currier and Ives.* (COURTESY THE METROPOLITAN MUSEUM OF ART, BEQUEST OF ADELE S. COLGAGE, 1963.)

on the first day of their lives; licking the kitten all over, helping to dry its fur; and then resting (if she is lucky!) until the next one arrives.

Newborn kittens weigh only two to five ounces and are four to six inches long. On their arrival, their eyes are closed so that they are unable to see, and they cannot hear because their ears are folded back. They can wriggle and squirm but cannot walk. The mother's maternal instincts kick in immediately and over the next two to three months the mother teaches the kittens all they need to know.

The kittens' first nourishment, milk, comes from the mother. Each kitten chooses one of the mother's teats and uses it all the time. It is very rare that kittens will use a different teat. A kitten gets milk by pushing her forepaws against the mother's body as she suckles. The pushing triggers a nerve/hormone reflex that initiates the flow of milk. A kitten who is not getting enough milk will be fretful and cry. If the mother is not able to supply enough milk for all her kittens another cat who is nursing kittens may have enough milk to help out. After birth, kittens consume as much as four times the calories per pound as adult cats. During the initial period of growth, they will usually gain about half an ounce a day, and during the first 20 weeks of life they increase in weight by 2000 percent. They begin to eat solid food at about three to four weeks, and are usually weaned by two months.

If a mother decides, after her kittens are born, that she is no longer happy with the spot she has so carefully selected for the purpose she may find

A Kitten

He's nothing much but fur
And two round eyes of blue,
He has a giant purr
And a midget mew.

He darts and pats the air,
He tarts and cocks his ear,
When there is nothing there
For him to see and hear.

He runs around in rings,
But why we cannot tell;
With sideways leaps he springs
At things invisible—

Then half-way through a leap
His startled eyeballs close,
And he drops off to sleep
With one paw on his nose.

ELEANOR FARJEON

selves. The mother and kittens bond quickly and recognize each other by their own characteristic smells.

When the kittens are five to ten days old their eyes will start to open. It takes about three weeks for the eyes to open fully. At about two and a half weeks of age the kittens will start to crawl around and their ears will straighten up. They start standing at about three weeks. And at this point the little balls of fur start to look like little cats.

By ten months of age, a kitten is considered an adult cat in the United States. It appears that kittens mature more quickly in Britain; there, a kitten becomes a cat at nine months. Domestic or non-pedigree kittens generally mature sooner than pedigrees; are litter trained earlier; wean earlier; and start to play earlier.

Kittens should receive their first vaccinations at eight weeks. Until that time they are very vulnerable and should be kept away from other cats.

Kittens are cute, adorable, and especially cuddly, and for that reason many people opt to buy or adopt a kitten. Who could give a better description of the little charmers than William Wordsworth, in his poem *The Kitten and Falling Leaves*, written in 1804:

See the Kitten on the wall,
Sporting with the leaves that fall . . .
What intenseness of desire
In her upward eye of fire!
With a tiger-leap half-way
Now she meets the coming prey,
Lets it go as fast, and then
Has it in her power again.

a new "den." She will gently carry each kitten by the scruff of the neck to the new location. She may, in fact, do this several times.

A mother licks her kittens frequently to stimulate their breathing and blood circulation. This also tones their muscles. Licking the little kittens' bottoms encourages them to defecate and urinate regularly. (Young kittens do not automatically urinate and defecate.) During this time the kittens are also learning how to groom them-

Mother cats—and others—take great care to see that kittens are kept in a safe place. (COURTESY DAILY NEWS PHOTO.)

And in his book *Walden*, written in 1854, Henry David Thoreau offers this just-as-perfect kitten description:

> A kitten is so flexible that she is almost double; the hind parts are equivalent to another kitten with which the forepart plays. She does not discover that her tail belongs to her until you tread on it.

See also MATING.

Kitty ⁓ This is a pet name for a cat of any age. How often have you heard someone calling to a cat, "Here kitty, kitty, here kitty"? (Sometimes it works and sometimes it doesn't.)

Kliban, B. ⁓ (In case you ever wondered, the B is for Bernard and Kliban is pronounced KLEE-ban). Kilban's first book, *Cat*, was published in 1975 when Kliban was 40. It became something of a phenomenon, prompting a series of cards, posters, T-shirts, and sequels, and sold close to half a million copies in three years. Ironically, Kliban was not a great cat lover, and as a matter of fact as a child was allergic to cats. He got his first cat as an adult when, while living in California, he rescued a stray cat in North Beach which he named Noko Marie. When he got a second cat it wasn't long before there were kittens. Kliban started sketching them and putting them in cartoons. The rest is history. One of his more well-known descriptions of the feline is that a cat "is a hell of a nice animal frequently mistaken for meatloaf."

Kneading ∽ This is what a cat is doing when she plops down in your lap and starts repeatedly pushing one paw, then the other, into your belly, and leaving, needless to say, *lots* of hair. (This is a lot less comfortable when a cat is not declawed, when you have just finished a large meal, or when you are wearing nothing. It is also inconvenient and annoying when you are wearing your best duds for a night on the town.)

> When I am playing with my cat, who knows whether she have more sport in dallying with me, than I have in gaming with her? We entertain one another with mutuall apish trickes. If I have my houre to begin or refuse, so hath she hers.
>
> MICHEL DE MONTAIGNE, French essayist
> (1533–1592)

This habit is begun in kittenhood, when the kneading serves a real purpose, stimulating the flow of milk to the mother's nipples—the kitten's first source of nourishment during its first weeks after birth. In later life, cats do this when they are content.

B. Kliban's famous large striped cats, playing musical instruments. (© 1992 JUDITH KAMEN KLIBAN. COURTESY WORKMAN PUBLISHING COMPANY.)

Derek Tangye finds kneading superior to purring: "I am inclined to believe that kneading is a more subtle expression of pleasure than a purr. The knead, that gentle in-and-out movement of paws and claws, is a private demonstration of serene ecstasy."

Korat ∾ The Korat is one of the oldest natural breeds, named for the province in Thailand from where it was thought to have originated. In Thailand the Korat is known as Si-Siwat. The compound words mean a mingled color with a smooth glossy shell. Among the meanings for the Thai word *sawat* are good fortune and prosperity. For that reason, the Korat is known as the good luck cat.

The first known reference to what is presumed to be the Korat appeared in the *Cat-Book Poems*, which was rescued from a Siamese city leveled by Burmese invaders in 1767. The Korat, a blue cat, is fairly rare.

PERSONALITY: She is intelligent, mild-mannered, affectionate, not very vocal, and a great cat for children.

Krazy Kat ∾ This kartoon kat first appeared in 1910 in George Herriman's comic strip *The Dingbat Family*. Krazy Kat and Ignatz (a mouse) got their own regular series in 1913. Others who appeared in the strip include Krazy Katfish, a seagoing cousin; Katbird, a winged cousin; and Mrs. Kat, who lived in Katnip Kourt, Kokonino. The popular comic strip ended with Herriman's death in 1944. In addition to the comic strip, there were three different series of silent Krazy Kat animated cartoons and seventy-three shorts.

Princess

You purr-fect playful
pet. Professional prowler
pulling corpus delecti
of robins and jays through
backyard brush. This you proudly
do for me laying them
whole at my feet.
I put a bell
around your neck and
though you jingle and jangle
through your domain
from your trophy days
you must now refrain.

ARLEEN COHEN

Lady and the Tramp

Lady and the Tramp ~ This 1955 Walt Disney film was the first animated feature in CinemaScope. It featured a lot of dogs. Also hanging around were delightfully evil Siamese cats. Among the songs in the movie is the "Siamese Cat Song." Singer Peggy Lee is one of the voices heard in this film.

Last Post, The

Last Post, The ~ Founded in 1982 by animal lover and radio personality Pegeen Fitzgerald, the Last Post is a retirement community for cats located on thirty-five acres near Falls Village, Connecticut. Over four hundred cats reside there. It is a nonprofit organization with much of its expenses paid by cat owners who leave money to The Last Post to care for their cats upon their death. New cats stay briefly in a special room with staff members to help them acclimate, easing their pain on losing a loved one and growing used to the change from family to institutional living. Some cats roam outside in five fenced-in acres; others stay inside and watch television or play with other cats or with toys. Elderly cats who prefer a quieter environment live in a special building where the music and food are softer. Contact The Last Post at 95 Belden Street, Falls Village, CT 06031; 203/824-0831.

Late Show, The

Late Show, The ~ This Robert Altman film pays homage to the private eye movie of the 1940s. After his partner is killed trying to find a stolen cat named Duff, an aging detective played by Art Carney sets out to find the killer. The cat's owner is Lily Tomlin. *The Late Show* was produced by Warner in 1977.

Law

Law ~ The late eighteenth-century English writer Robert Southey once commented, "I could have persuaded myself that the word *felonious* is derived from the feline temper." Over the years some amusing and not so amusing laws have sprung up regarding felines. Here are a few of them:

Dallas, Texas—Cats running the streets after sundown are required to wear headlights.

Lemonine, Montana—Cats are required to wear three bells as a warning to birds.

Berea, Ohio—At one time there was a law on the books in Berea that required a cat on the street after dark to display a red taillight.

Reed City, Michigan—At one time it was illegal to own both a cat and bird.

Natchez, Mississippi—Cats are prohibited from drinking beer.

California—In 1973, then–California Governor Ronald Reagan signed a law that specified prison penalties for kicking or injuring another person's cat.

Cats and their owners have ended up in courtrooms as well. In Oklahoma, in 1924, a man named Helsel shot and killed a white Persian cat named Fletcher who was after one of his prized chickens. He was sued by Fletcher's owner and had to pay $150 for the cat's death.

In Scotland, in 1887, a man whose carrier pigeon was killed by a cat sued the owner of the cat. He lost the case because the judge ruled that the owner of the pigeon had not watched over his bird carefully enough. However, he did not make him pay court costs because the owner of the cat at first said his cat was innocent—and denied that the cat had done away with the bird.

In England, the owner of Arthur, a cat who was a star in British cat-food commercials, refused to lend him to the cat-food company to make more commercials. The owner charged that the company had removed Arthur's teeth so that Arthur would have to dip his paws into the cat food while they shot the commercial. A court did rule in favor of the cat-food company, saying the company owned Arthur. However, Arthur never appeared before the cameras again because he sought asylum in the Russian Embassy. The man who claimed to be the owner placed him there to keep him out of the jurisdiction of the British courts.

One cat, named Mousam, received a notice in the mail to report for jury duty. When Mousam's owners, just the slightest bit puzzled, notified the Board of Election that Mousam was a cat, he was disqualified—because he couldn't speak English.

Lear, Edward ∼ (1812–1888)

This nineteenth-century British humorist, who wrote the well known poem THE OWL AND THE PUSSYCAT had a favorite cat named Foss. When he moved to a new house he instructed his architects to make his new home identical to his old home so that Foss's move to the new house would be as easy as possible. When Foss died at the age of seventeen, he was buried in the garden of Lear's rented villa in San Remo. An engraved headstone marks the site. Humorous sketches of Foss can be found in letters written by Lear. And Foss, of course, made his appearances in verse, such as in *The Courtship of Yonghy-Bonghy-Bó*:

> He has many friends, layman and clerical.
>   Old Foss is the name of his cat.
> His body is perfectly spherical,
>   He weareth a runcible hat.

The nineteenth-century British artist Edward Lear drew many humorous sketches of cats, such as Foss the Cat, as well as composing whimsical poems about them. (COURTESY WILLIAMS COLLEGE MUSEUM OF ART, BEQUEST OF JANE T. RITCHIE. PHOTOGRAPH BY JOSEPH SZASZFAI.)

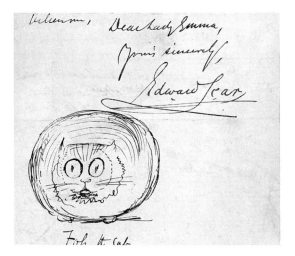

C was a lovely Pussy Cat; its eyes were large
And on its back it had some stripes, & pale;
and several on his tail.

Edward Lear's cat Foss illustrates the letter C in his Comic Alphabet, *1880.*

Lee, Robert E. ∼ (1807–1870) The commander-in-chief of the Confederate army in the Civil War was quite fond of cats. In letters home he frequently mentioned his love of cats. While fighting in the Mexican-American War, he wrote to his daughter and asked her to send him a cat for company, which she did. Lee spent the rest of the war with his cat companion.

L'enfant et les Sortilèges ∼ This opera, based on a story by Colette and written for children by Maurice Ravel, contains a duet for a male and female cat. Ravel would not let Colette make any comments on it, however, and not once did he invite her to a preliminary staging. This work, including both dancing and singing, is considered by many to be the first important lyrical fantasy on the loves of cats.

Les Animaliers ∼ This group of French artists created animal sculptures, mostly in bronze, during the reign of Britain's Queen Victo-

ria, who was partial to works of art with animal themes. The animals were portrayed realistically and were anatomically correct. Among the artists belonging to this school are Antoine Louis Barye, the son of a goldsmith who was instrumental in promoting an interest in bronze animals. In the United States, his work can be seen at the Walters Art Gallery in Baltimore, Maryland. Barye was especially known for his "big" cats—tigers and lions.

Auguste Nicholas Cain was one of the most famous sculptors of cat figures. Cats were part of many of his exhibitions and competitions.

Emanuel Frèmiet tried various art forms before settling on sculpture. His cat sculptures, charming, sweet, and playful can be seen at the Louvre in Paris as well as at the Walters Art Gallery. Frèmiet created large monuments in France and hoped to be remembered for that. But most of those are gone and it is the small bronze animals for which he is best known.

Les Chats ∼ Written in 1727 by the then unknown writer, Auguste Paradis de Moncrif, this book was the first major study of cats. While it catapulted its author to fame, he became known as "l'historiogriffe" (chronicler of the claw) and was not infrequently ridiculed. People would meow or purr at his appearance. Some would even spit at him, cat fashion, in simulated fury. He eventually was welcomed at the Académie Française, which was quite an honor. At his inauguration his speech was interrupted by half a dozen cats who were tossed in by more practical jokers. Not surprisingly, this incident drew a lot of attention. As more and more people were discussing the mysterious attractions of the cat, Moncrif would often try to educate those who derided him and his animals.

Another volume with the title *Les Chats* was written in 1870 by Jules Husson, a French journalist who used the pen name Champfleury. The French painter Edouard Manet (1832–1883) engraved a lithograph of a black cat and white cat on a roof in Paris, which became the cover piece art for all editions of the work.

> If a fish is the movement of water embodied, given shape, then a cat is a diagram and a pattern of subtle air.
>
> DORIS LESSING, twentieth century
> British writer

Doris Lessing

The British novelist and short story writer (b. 1919), well known for such works as *The Golden Notebook* and *Briefing for a Descent into Hell*, is also an avid cat lover, as she reveals in the following story.

Particularly Cats

I came to live in a house in cat country. The houses are old and they have narrow gardens with walls. Through our back windows show a dozen walls one way, a dozen walls the other, of all sizes and levels. Trees, grass, bushes. There is a little theatre that has roofs at various heights. Cats thrive here. There are always cats on the walls, roofs, and in the gardens, living a complicated secret life, like the neighbourhood lives of children that go on according to unimagined private rules the grown-ups never guess at.

I knew there would be a cat in the house. Just as one knows, if a house is too large people will come and live in it, so certain houses must have cats. But for a while I repelled the various cats that came sniffing around to see what sort of a place it was.

During the whole of that dreadful winter of 1962, the garden and the roof over the back verandah were visited by an old black-and-white tom. He sat in the slushy snow on the roof; he prowled over the frozen ground; when the back door was briefly opened, he sat just outside, looking into the warmth. He was most unbeautiful, with a white patch over one eye, a torn ear, and a jaw always a little open and drooling. But he was not a stray. He had a good home in the street, and why he didn't stay there, no one seemed able to say.

That winter was further education into the extraordinary voluntary endurances of the English.

These houses are mostly L.C.C. owned, and by the first week of the cold, the pipes

(continued)

The Cat's Rendezvous. *Cats were a favorite subject of the nineteenth-century French artist Edouard Manet.* (COURTESY MUSEUM OF FINE ARTS, BOSTON, GIFT OF W. G. RUSSELL ALLEN.)

had burst and frozen, and people were waterless. The system stayed frozen. The authorities opened a main on the street corner, and for weeks the women of the street made journeys to fetch water in jugs and cans along pavements heaped with feet of icy slush, in their house slippers. The slippers were for warmth. The slush and ice were not cleared off the pavement. They drew water from the tap, which broke down several times, and said there had been no hot water but what they boiled on the stove for one week, two weeks—then three, four and five weeks. There was, of course, no hot water for baths. When asked why they didn't complain, since after all they paid rent, they paid for water hot and cold, they replied the L.C.C. knew about their pipes, but did not do anything. The L.C.C. had pointed out there was a cold spell; they agreed with this diagnosis. Their voices were lugubrious, but they were deeply fulfilled, as this nation is when suffering entirely avoidable acts of God.

In the shop at the corner an old man, a middle-aged woman and a small child spent the days of that winter. The shop was chilled colder even than the below-zero weather nature was ordaining, by the refrigeration units; the door was always open into the iced snowdrifts outside the shop. There was no heating at all. The old man got pleurisy and went to hospital for two months. Permanently weakened, he had to sell the shop that spring. The child sat on the cement floor and cried steadily from the cold, and was slapped by its mother who stood behind the counter in a light wool dress, man's socks and a thin cardigan, saying how awful it all was, while her eyes and nose ran and her fingers swelled into chilblains. The old man next door who works as a market porter slipped on the ice outside his front door, hurt his back, and was for weeks on unemployment pay. In that house, which held nine or ten people, including two children, there was one bar of electric fire to fight the cold. Three people went to hospital, one with pneumonia.

And the pipes stayed burst, sealed in jagged stalactites of ice; the pavements remained ice slides; and the authorities did nothing. In middle-class streets, of course, snow was cleared as it fell, and the authorities responded to angry citizens demanding their rights and threatening lawsuits. In our area, people suffered it out until the spring.

Surrounded by human beings as winterbound as if they were cave dwellers of ten thousand years ago, the peculiarities of an old tomcat who chose an icy roof to spend its nights on lost their force.

In the middle of that winter, friends were offered a kitten. Friends of theirs had a Siamese cat, and she had a litter by a street cat. The hybrid kittens were being given away. Their flat is minute, and they both worked all day; but when they saw the kitten, they could not resist. During its first weekend it was fed on tinned lobster soup and chicken mousse, and it disrupted their much-married nights because it had to sleep under the chin, or at least, somewhere against the flesh, of H., the man. S., his wife, announced on the telephone that she was losing the affections of her husband to a cat, just like the wife in Colette's tale. On Monday they went off to work leaving the kitten by itself, and when they came home it was crying and sad, having been alone all day. They said they were bringing it to us. They did.

The kitten was six weeks old. It was enchanting, a delicate fairy-tale cat, whose Siamese genes showed in the shape of the face, ears, tail, and the subtle lines of its body. Her back was tabby: from above or the back, she was a pretty tabby kitten, in grey and cream. But her front and stomach were a smoky-gold, Siamese cream, with half-bars of black at the neck. Her face was pencilled with black—fine dark rings around the eyes, fine dark streaks on her cheeks, a tiny cream-coloured nose with a pink tip, outlined in black. From the front, sitting with her slender paws straight, she was an exotically beautiful beast. She sat, a tiny thing, in the middle of a yellow carpet, surrounded by five worshippers, not at all afraid of us. Then she stalked around that floor of the house, inspecting every inch of it, climbed up on to my bed, crept under the fold of a sheet, and was at home.

S. went off with H. saying: Not a moment too soon, otherwise I wouldn't have a husband at all.

And he went off groaning, saying that nothing could be as exquisite as being woken by the delicate touch of a pink tongue on his face.

The kitten went, or rather hopped, down the stairs, each of which was twice her height: first front paws, then flop, with the back; front paws, then flop with the back. She inspected the ground floor, refused the tinned food offered to her, and demanded a dirt box by mewing for it. She rejected wood shavings, but torn newspaper was acceptable, so her fastidious pose said, if there was nothing else. There wasn't: the earth outside was frozen solid.

She would not eat tinned cat food. She would not. And I was not going to feed her lobster soup and chicken. We compromised on some minced beef.

She has always been as fussy over her food as a bachelor gourmet. She gets worse as she gets older. Even as a kitten she could express annoyance, or pleasure, or a determination to sulk, by what she ate, half-ate, or chose to refuse. Her food habits are an eloquent language.

But I think it is just possible she was taken away from her mother too young. If I might respectfully suggest it to the cat experts, it is possible they are wrong when they say a kitten may leave its mother the day it turns six weeks old. This cat was six weeks, not a day more, when it was taken from its mother. The basis of her dandyism over food is the neurotic hostility and suspicion towards it of a child with food problems. She had to eat, she supposed; she did eat; but she has never eaten with enjoyment, for the sake of eating. And she shares another characteristic with people who have not had enough mother-warmth. Even now she will instinctively creep under the fold of a newspaper, or into a box or a basket—anything that shelters, anything that covers. More; she is overready to see insult; overready to sulk. And she is a frightful coward.

(continued)

Kittens who are left with their mother seven or eight weeks eat easily, and they have confidence. But of course, they are not as interesting.

As a kitten, this cat never slept on the outside of the bed. She waited until I was in it, then she walked all over me, considering possibilities. She would get right down into the bed, by my feet, or on to my shoulder, or crept under the pillow. If I moved too much, she huffily changed quarters, making her annoyance felt.

When I was making the bed, she was happy to be made into it; and stayed, visible as a tiny lump, quite happily, sometimes for hours, between the blankets. If you stroked the lump, it purred and mewed. But she would not come out until she had to.

The lump would move across the bed, hesitate at the edge. There might be a frantic mew as she slid to the floor. Dignity disturbed, she licked herself hastily, glaring yellow eyes at the viewers, who made a mistake if they laughed. Then, every hair conscious of itself, she walked to some centre stage.

Time for the fastidious pernickety eating. Time for the earth box, as exquisite a performance. Time for setting the creamy fur in order. And time for play, which never took place for its own sake, but only when she was being observed.

She was as arrogantly aware of herself as a pretty girl who has no attributes but her prettiness: body and face always posed according to some inner monitor—a pose which is as good as a mask: no, no, *this* is what I am, the aggressive breasts, the sullen hostile eyes always on the watch for admiration.

Cat, at the age when, if she were human, she would be wearing clothes and hair like weapons, but confident that any time she chose she might relapse into indulged childhood again, because the role had become too much of a burden—cat posed and princessed and preened about the house and then, tired, a little peevish, tucked herself into the fold of a newspaper or behind a cushion, and watched the world safely from there.

Her prettiest trick, used mostly for company, was to lie on her back under a sofa and pull herself along by her paws, in fast sharp rushes, stopping to turn her elegant little head sideways, yellow eyes narrowed, waiting, for applause. "Oh beautiful kitten! Delicious beast! Pretty cat!" Then on she went for another display.

Or, on the right surface, the yellow carpet, a blue cushion, she lay on her back and slowly rolled, paws tucked up, head back, so that her creamy chest and stomach were exposed, marked faintly, as if she were a delicate subspecies of leopard, with black blotches, like the roses of leopards. "Oh beautiful kitten, oh you are so beautiful." And she was prepared to go on until the compliments stopped.

Or she sat on the back verandah, not on the table, which was unadorned, but on a little stand that had narcissus and hyacinth in earthenware pots. She sat posed between spikes of blue and white flowers, until she was noticed and admired. Not only by us, of course; also by the old rheumatic tom who prowled, grim reminder of a much harder life, around the garden where the earth was still frostbound. He saw a pretty half-grown cat, behind glass. She saw him. She lifted her head, this way, that way; bit off a fragment of hyacinth, dropped it; licked her fur, negligently; then with an insolent backwards glance, leaped down and came indoors and out of his sight. Or, on the way upstairs, on an arm or a shoulder, she would glance out of the window and see the poor old beast, so still that sometimes we thought he must have died and been frozen there. When the sun warmed a little at midday and he sat licking himself, we were relieved. Sometimes she sat watching him from the window, but her life was still to be tucked into the arms, beds, cushions, and corners of human beings.

Then the spring came, the back door was opened, the dirt box, thank goodness, made unnecessary, and the back garden became her territory. She was six months old, fully grown, from the point of view of nature.

She was so pretty then, so perfect; more beautiful even than that cat who, all those years ago, I swore I could never have an equal. Well of course there hasn't been; for that cat's nature was all tact, delicacy, warmth and grace—so, as the fairy tales and the old wives say, she had to die young.

Our cat, the princess, was, still is, beautiful, but, there is no glossing it, she's a selfish beast.

The cats lined up on the garden walls. First, the sombre old winter cat, king of the back gardens. Then, a handsome black-and-white from next door, his son, from the look of it. A battle-scarred tabby. A grey-and-white cat who was so certain of defeat that he never came down from the wall. And a dashing tigerish young tom that she clearly admired. No use, the old king had not been defeated. When she strolled out, tail erect, apparently ignoring them all, but watching the handsome young tiger, he leaped down towards her, but the winter cat had only to stir where he lay on the wall, and the young cat jumped back to safety. This went on for weeks.

Meanwhile, H. and S. came to visit their lost pet. S. said how frightful and unfair it was that the princess could not have her choice; and H. said that was entirely as it should be: a princess must have a king, even if he was old and ugly. He has such dignity, said H.; he has such presence; and he had earned the pretty young cat because of his noble endurance of the long winter.

By then the ugly cat was called Mephistopheles. (In his own home, we heard, he was called Billy.) Our cat had been called various names, but none of them stuck. Melissa and Franny; Marilyn and Sappho; Circe and Ayesha and Suzette. But in conversation, in love-talk, she miaowed and purred and throated in response to the long-drawn-out syllables of adjectives—beeeooori-ful, de*lici*ous puss.

On a very hot weekend, the only one, I seem to remember, in a nasty summer, she came in heat.

H. and S. came to lunch on the Sunday, and we sat on the back verandah and watched the choices of nature. Not ours. And not our cat's, either.

(*continued*)

For two nights the fighting had gone on, awful fights, cats wailing and howling and screaming in the garden. Meanwhile grey puss had sat on the bottom of my bed, watching into the dark, ears lifting and moving, tail commenting, just slightly at the tip.

On that Sunday, there was only Mephistopheles in sight. Grey cat was rolling in ecstasy all over the garden. She came to us and rolled around our feet and bit them. She rushed up and down the tree at the bottom of the garden. She rolled and cried, and called, and invited.

"The most disgraceful exhibition of lust I've ever seen," said S. watching H., who was in love with our cat.

"Oh poor cat," said H. "If I were Mephistopheles I'd never treat you so badly."

"Oh, H.," said S., "you are disgusting, if I told people they'd never believe it. But I've always said, you're disgusting."

"So that's what you've always said," said H., caressing the ecstatic cat.

It was a very hot day, we had a lot of wine for lunch, and the love play went on all afternoon.

Finally, Mephistopheles leaped down off the wall to where grey cat was wriggling and rolling—but alas, he bungled it.

"Oh my God," said H., genuinely suffering. "It is really not forgivable, that sort of thing."

S., anguished, watched the torments of our cat, and doubted, frequently, dramatically and loudly, whether sex was worth it. "Look at it," said she, "that's us. That's what we're like."

"That's not at all what we're like," said H. "It's Mephistopheles. He should be shot."

Shoot him at once, we all said; or at least lock him up so that the young tiger from next door could have his chance.

But the handsome young cat was not visible.

We went on drinking wine; the sun went on·shining; our princess danced, rolled, rushed up and down the tree, and, when at last things went well, was clipped again and again by the old king.

"All that's wrong," said H., "is that he's too old for her."

"Oh my God," said S., "I'm going to take you home. Because if I don't, I swear you'll make love to that cat yourself."

"Oh I wish I could," said H. "What an exquisite beast, what a lovely creature, what a princess, she's wasted on a cat, I can't stand it."

Next day winter returned; the garden was cold and wet; and grey cat had returned to her fastidious disdainful ways. And the old king lay on the garden wall in the slow English rain, still victor of them all, waiting.

Library Cat Society (LCS) ~

The Library Cat Society was founded in 1987 by Phyllis Lahti, who saw her first library cat, a black and white tabby stretched out on a window box, at the Rome Public Library in Michigan. Lahti went on to become a librarian as well as a teacher, writer, and illustrator. And she never forgot the first "library cat" she'd seen. When she herself rescued a cat during a blizzard, she named him Reggie and her library in Minnesota got its own first library cat. The LCS has recognized over three dozen libraries that have cats, most of which are public libraries. But since there are more than fifteen thousand public libraries in the United States, there is no doubt that there are many other library cats who remain in various states of incognito all over the country. Baker and Taylor, official mascots for the Baker & Taylor Company, a book distributor, reside in the Douglas County Library in Minden, Nevada. They spend most of their time at the checkout counter, where they restore disorder when things get too quiet. Ann Bumstead, a librarian at the Woodbury Public Library in Woodbury, Connecticut, says that Fred, a female cat, frequently climbs into the lap of a visitor or sprawls across the notebook and papers of a student trying to do homework.

The society's worthy goals include encouraging the presence of cats in libraries, recognizing the need to respect and care for library cats, and bringing library cat advocates together. The Library Cat Society can be reached by writing to Box 274, Moorhead, MN 56560 or by calling 218/236-7205. You can get a free sample copy of the newsletter by sending a stamp with your request.

Lincoln, Abraham (1809–1865) ~

The sixteenth president of the United States (1861–1865) was quite fond of cats as a boy growing up in Kentucky. Once, on a winter trip to General Grant's headquarters during the Civil War, he heard a faint meowing sound and found three nearly frozen kittens. He rescued them, got them food and shelter, and eventually adopted them, bringing them back to the White House. There is no doubt that Lincoln was not only a cat lover but an astute cat observer, as revealed by his well-known quip: "No matter how much cats fight, there always seem to be plenty of kittens." *See* WHITE HOUSE CATS.

Longhair cats ~

Longhair cats are not as populous as cats with short or medium-length hair and their history does not go back as far as that of the shorthairs. It is believed that Longhair cats developed in cold countries such as Norway, Sweden, and so forth, where longer hair was required for survival. It seems likely that they arose from spontaneous mutations which were then selectively bred. Longhair cats arrived in Europe in the late 1500s. The most popular longhair is the PERSIAN. Among the other longhairs are the BALINESE, TURKISH ANGORA, NORWEGIAN FOREST CAT, and the MAINE COON. Longhair cats don't shed any more than shorthairs; it only *seems* that way because the hair is so visible.

I am as vigilant as a cat to steal cream.

from *Henry IV*, WILLIAM SHAKESPEARE
(1564–1616)

Cats sleep fat and walk thin.

"Catalog," ROSALIE MOORE, 20th century
American poet

Maine coon ⌁ The Maine coon is the oldest American breed. It is believed he may have roamed in Maine as well as other parts of New England during the early days of that state's history in the seventeenth century; and that his thick coat (like that of the NORWEGIAN FOREST CAT) is a result, in part, of the cold climate in New England.

There are many myths regarding the Maine coon. One is that he descended from cats sent from France to the United States by Marie Antoinette. Another story relates how a sea captain named Coon brought Persians and Angoras to this country. When Coon's cats jumped ship, they introduced the longhair cat to the United States. Others believe the Maine coon was the result of the mating of a raccoon and cat, although that is genetically impossible.

In 1860, the Maine coon was shown at the New York Cat Show for the first time and won the title at that show in 1895. However, when another longhair, the Persian, arrived in the United States, it became more popular than the Maine coon, until interest in the Maine coon revived in the 1950s.

The Maine coon is bred in virtually any color and combination of colors. It is a longhair but its coat differs in texture and quality from the Persian, and its coat requires much less grooming than the Persian's coat. The Maine coon is a big cat. Males generally weigh from 18 to 20 pounds, females 10 to 15 pounds. They have muscular bodies which make them seem even heavier.

PERSONALITY: Maine coons make a quiet chirping sound and are friendly, affectionate pets. They need space in which to exercise.

Maneki Neko ⌁ These "lucky" cats originated in Japanese folklore. According to the legend there was a temple in Japan which was very poor. The abbot was a lover of cats and no matter how poor he was, he always tried to keep some cats at the temple. One day he told his cats that he wished they could bring him some luck. Just days later, some samurais passing the temple saw a cat with its paw raised in greeting. They took the invitation and stopped for rest. When an unexpected rainstorm erupted, they found shelter in the church, and in the temple they found the abbot. They decided to make the temple their benefactor. The temple soon regained its beauty, wealth, and honor. And a cat with a raised paw became a symbol for luck and good fortune.

Father and son Brown Mackerel and Brown Classic Maine Coon cats, both Supreme Grand Champions. (COURTESY LYNNE BOROFF, ADVENT HILL CATTERY, HARTLAND, VERMONT.)

Maneki Neko cats are now often displayed in the windows of commercial establishments—restaurants and inns in particular. They come in all sizes and materials including porcelain, pottery, wood, ivory, and metals. Although they can have different colors, most often they are white with red, black, and gold markings. The cat is seated with his front left leg raised. His paw is by his ear and it is pointed outward, the traditional way that the Japanese greet people. In other countries, they are frequently spotted in Japanese shops.

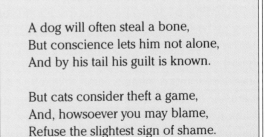

A dog will often steal a bone,
But conscience lets him not alone,
And by his tail his guilt is known.

But cats consider theft a game,
And, howsoever you may blame,
Refuse the slightest sign of shame.

"A Cat's Conscience," ANONYMOUS

In Japan, Maneki Neko brings good health and fortune. (PHOTO COURTESY BRENT THORN.)

Manx ～ The Manx is a very recognizable breed because it lacks a tail. It also has hind legs that are longer than his forelegs so that he hops somewhat like a rabbit.

According to legend, the Manx lost his tail very early on. He was out mousing in the hours right before Noah and all the animals were ready to depart on the ark. He kept saying something like, "Just a few more minutes, and I'll have gotten them all." Finally, when the rain started to fall the Manx rushed onto the boat. He was the last animal to board Noah's ark, and with the flood rising quickly, Noah slammed the door shut. The Manx's fine bushy tail was accidentally severed.

In another legend, the cat is from Tibet, where he was a temple guardian. He made his way to

Spain, was taken aboard a galleon of the Spanish Armada, which was sunk near the Isle of Man, and managed to survive the sinking and swim safely to shore. The legend continues that the Manx did have a tail when on the Isle of Man, but the kittens were stolen so often by the Irish soldiers, who used their tails as magical talismans, that mother cats were reduced to biting off the tails of their kittens to keep them alive.

The British author Aldous Huxley has written, "The tail, in cats, is the principal organ of emotional expression, and a Manx cat is the equivalent of a dumb man." In fact, the lack of a tail is caused by a serious genetic defect, which also distorts the spine and may result in many kittens who are born with problems that lead to crippling.

The Manx comes in virtually any color and coat pattern.

PERSONALITY: The Manx makes a wonderful pet. He is playful and affectionate and loves to cuddle on laps.

Marmalade ～ Once upon a time there was a starving stray cat desperately rummaging through garbage cans looking for anything at all to eat. (Many stories start this way, but this one has a happy ending.) The longhair, red tabby, now known as Marmalade, was rescued by a kind-hearted woman. Unable to keep the cat, she brought Marmalade to her veterinarian, hoping Marmalade would be adopted. And she was—by (of all people) a dog trainer named Sandi Wirth.

Sandi taught the cat a few basic tricks, and today, you'll see Marmalade in commercials for Chef's Blend Cat Food and Friskies. I don't know if Sandi is still training dogs, but at last count she had several "celebrity" cats, including Muffin, Simba's Red Sundance, and Mannix. Along with Marmalade, the four cats know sixty-seven tricks, including hissing, crying, and knocking off

Sandi's glasses. All sixty-seven tricks can be performed on cue on a movie set or the set of a TV show being taped. If you have a cat who longs to be a star, head for Hollywood (where else?) and Sandi Wirth's special training school for felines, The Animal Connection and College Fur Cats. The ten-week course is held in the San Fernando Valley. Write The Animal Connection at 5323 Colodny Drive, #110, Old Agoura Hills, CA, 91301 or call 818/597-8760.

Mating ∼ Cats generally mature sexually in about a year, although that age can vary somewhat, and they can continue to reproduce for many years. Tomcats at the very ripe old age of sixteen have been known to father kittens, and female queen cats have been known to give birth at the age of twelve. (That's equivalent to a woman having a baby in her mid-sixties.)

When a female cat goes into heat, her cries and smell are picked up by male cats in the area. In the wild, just one male cat may show up when a female is in heat; other cats may not be close enough to hear her cries or smell the scent. In more populated urban areas, many cats may respond and it is likely that a fight will break out. A less aggressive or older, more experienced tom may mount the female while the other cats are battling it out for that privilege. However, ultimately it is the choice of the female as to whom she mates with. The logistics are less complicated if only one male is present. After circling the queen, the tom utters a low-pitched cry and seizes the back of the female cat's neck with his teeth. She, in turn, raises her back end up and moves her tale to the side, enabling the tom to insert his penis. The tom ejaculates quickly and the queen shrieks and usually takes a swipe at him. Some say the scream is prompted by intense pleasure, but others speculate that it is prompted

by pain because the end of the tom's penis is covered with barbs. If the mating act is painful, it does not prevent the queen from repeating it. After mating, it takes the male cat about twenty minutes to "reload" and he may return up to seven times. During this period the female cat may shun other cats that approach or may welcome some or all of them, in which case superfecundation, the fertilization of eggs during successive sexual encounters, may occur, resulting in a litter of kittens with very different markings. While it is often assumed that different markings in the same litter are a result of gene combinations of the female and male cats, in fact, the female cat's eggs may have been fertilized by several toms with very different coat patterns.

A female cat may also go into heat when she is already pregnant. Called superfetation, this condition is fairly uncommon, affecting about one in ten cats, and generally occurring when there is a low level of the pregnancy hormone present. If the cat does become impregnated, she will carry the second litter along with the first. When she gives birth to the first litter—the second litter may emerge as well during the birthing process. The second group are usually too small and underdeveloped to survive. If the female carries the second pregnancy to full term, and a second litter of healthy kittens is born, the mother may have neither enough nipples nor milk for two litters of kittens. In a cattery, it has been observed that mothers will "share" their kittens. One mother will nurse other mother's kittens and vice versa.

Believe it or not, a cat can also experience a false or pseudopregnancy. A queen will feel like she is pregnant when she is not. For the nine weeks of her full-term "pregnancy" she will be blissfully happy. She may even find a special place to have her litter and may even produce some milk. Is this caused by wishful thinking on the part of the queen? Maybe, but a more logical explanation is that she was "impregnated" by a neutered tom. Many male cats can still go through the motions after they've been neutered and may respond to a queen in heat. In response to the penetration of the penis, ovulation will occur followed by the false pregnancy. Breeders who want to give their queen a rest between litters have been known to use a neutered tom in this way, instead of putting the queen on a contraceptive pill.

Since the average litter is four or five cats and queens are capable of reproducing many times, it would not be at all difficult for one pair of cats to add *greatly* to the cat population. Imagine a pair of domestic cats who are allowed to breed uncontrollably. If the female cat has three litters a year for a total of about fourteen kittens—and those kittens also mate and reproduce when they come of age—in five years there could conceivably be over 65,000 new cats. One cat in Bonham, Texas, reputedly delivered her 420th kitten when she was seventeen years old. Responsible cat owners should have their pets neutered or spayed to avoid adding to the problem of unwanted cats, which are ultimately destroyed.

Mau ~ *Mau* was the Egyptian word for cat in ancient times. It means "to see" and was, quite possibly, the first time that the cat was viewed as a psychic or seer. *See also* EGYPT.

Maxwell ~ Unless you visited England sometime during the first half of the 1980s, or had a friend living there, you probably are not acquainted with the cat Maxwell, who starred in a comic strip in the *Northants Post*. And that is too bad. Maxwell is as irreverent as they come. He spoofs one and all. He once stood in a field and recited an ode to a robin and then burped up feathers. Maxwell was created by Alan Moore using the pseudonym Jill de Ray. It ran from 1979 to 1986.

Mehitabel

This scruffy alley cat who claims to have at one time belonged to Cleopatra first appeared in the newspaper column of Chicago journalist and poet Don Marquis in 1916. We learn about mehitabel's adventures through archy, a poet in a previous life who has been condemned to live in the body of a cockroach. Archy writes his poetry by jumping on the keys of a typewriter, head first; since he is not able to hold down the shift key, all his work appears entirely in lowercase letters.

Mehitabel is a pretty liberated cat who has many affairs, but always demands to be treated right. When a tomcat who has lured mehitabel to his home kicks her out when his "mistress" shows up, mehitabel roughs him up then reminds him that he should be glad that she's a lady who keeps her poise. Her indomitable character is best revealed in this excerpt from "Cheerio, My Deario," from *archy and mehitabel*:

(continued)

well boss i met
mehitabel the cat
trying to dig a
frozen lamb chop
out of a snow
drift the other day

a heluva comedown
that is for me archy
she says a few
centuries
ago one of old
king
tut
ankh
amen's favourite
queens and today
the village scavenger
but wotthehell
archy wotthehell
it s cheerio
my deario that
pulls a lady through

see here mehitabel
i said i thought
you told me that
it was cleopatra
you used to be
before you
transmigrated into
the carcase of a cat
where do you get
this tut
ankh
amen stuff
question mark

i was several
ladies my little
insect says she
being cleopatra was
only an incident
in my career
and i was always getting
the rough end of it
always being
misunderstood by some
strait laced
prune faced bunch
of prissy mouthed
sisters of uncharity
the things that
have been said
about me archy
exclamation point

and all simply
because i was a
live dame
the palaces i have
been kicked out of
in my time
exclamation point
. . .
toujours gai and always
a lady in spite of hell
and transmigration
once a queen
always a queen
archy
period

Marquis's columns were collected in the volume *the lives and times of archy and mehitabel* in 1940.

Meow ～ *See* TALKING.

Miller, Karl Lewis ～ This California cat trainer provided the cats for the film *Cat's Eye*. The star was Burbank, who resides in Karl's kennel with about a dozen other cats. Karl's celeb cats are all adopted from shelters. They get good food, lots of love, and attention—things not always available at shelters. The cats have private rooms and share a spacious exercise room. Karl and his wife, Eileen, also support a colony of over a dozen feral cats.

Mind, Gottfried ～ (1768–1814) This Hungarian-born artist who lived in Berne, Switzerland, was well known for his portrayals of cats. The first painter to specialize in cat portraits, he became famous as the Raphael of Cats, or *Der Katzen Raphael*. With the exception of an occasional bear, his drawings and paintings were all of cats. His favorite cat, Minette, was always by his side when he worked.

In 1809, while Mind was living and working in Berne, Swiss authorities ordered the cats in Berne destroyed because of the detection of symptoms of madness among the cats. Although Mind managed to save Minette by hiding her, some eight hundred other cats perished. It was said that he never got over the slaughter of so many cats.

Miracles ～ There are many stories about cats who performed miracles. And there are also cat stories that are simply miraculous. Here are just a few that have been recorded.

In his book *Your Incredible Cat*, David Greene tells the story of ten-year-old Maria, a little Mexican girl who went into a coma after being hit by a drunk driver as she was riding her bike. After months in the hospital doctors sent her home saying there was nothing more they could do for her. The doctors had said that anything that reminded Maria of the past might awaken her. Willing to try anything, Maria's mother kept the

The eighteenth-century Swiss painter Glottfried Mind has been called the "Raphael of cats."

window in Maria's room open because Maria had always loved fresh air. One night—she remembers the exact day, July 27, 1976—she noticed a thin, dirty stray cat on the bed beside Maria. She was about to lift him up and toss him out the window when she noticed that as the cat patiently licked Maria's thumb, Maria's fingers started twitching, the first sign of movement since she went into the coma. Instead of being kicked out, the little cat was encouraged to sleep in Maria's room. Eight days after "Miguel's" arrival, Maria woke up and spoke for the first time in nearly seven months.

The survival of a stray black cat who traveled fifty days without food and water is told in the *National Enquirer's Special 1992 Cat* edition. The cat had wandered into a freight company in Kent, England, where employees were feeding her. She disappeared one day while workers were packing a Mercedes to be shipped to a woman in Australia. When the Mercedes finally arrived so did the inadvertent stowaway, who had become a very thin black cat. The owner of the Mercedes was so impressed by the cat's will to live that she adopted her and named her—no surprise—Mercedes.

When Sergeant Guy Jones was transferred to San Francisco, he and his wife had their two Siamese cats shipped there from Guam. One cat arrived, but the other, Sherry, didn't. The Joneses kept calling and hoping Sherry would turn up, but it finally seemed that Sherry was gone forever. Thirty-two days later a very hungry and injured Sherry was found in the hold of the giant Pan Am jet. Sherry had traveled some 225,000 miles and touched down in twelve different countries and survived. The Joneses were ecstatic when they learned Sherry had been found and nursed her back to health.

A tomcat named Timmy was exploring at a building site when he crept into a hole in the wall. As he took his afternoon nap, builders who were not aware of the cat napping bricked up the hole.

Poor Timmy was trapped for twenty-four days—until his plaintive cries were heard by one of the bricklayers. It took the local police and fire brigade to break through the wall and rescue Timmy. Timmy was a great deal thinner than he had been, but aside from that, no worse for his adventure.

Moggie ～

This slang term (also spelled *moggy*) is used to describe a non-pedigreed cat. (The correct term would probably be *mongrel*, which is used for a non-pedigreed dog—but there is no question that a non-pedigreed cat requires a more refined term.) The origin of *moggie* appears to date from the early twentieth century in London, where a local dialect pronounced it "maggie." Its original meaning was a disheveled old woman. The many scruffy alley cats wandering around in poor condition were compared to the disheveled women on the streets of London. In the 1920s and 1930s moggie was cut down to *mog*. After World War II, the more affectionate term *moggie* returned and was used for the ordinary or garden variety cat.

Mohammed ～

(570–632) The founder of Islam, the religious faith of the Moslems, was quite fond of cats. According to tradition, Mohammed's favorite cat, Muezza (which means fairest and gentlest) was sleeping on Mohammed's sleeve when the Islamic prophet wanted to get up to pray. It is said that rather than disturb the cat, Mohammed cut off that part of the sleeve on which the cat slept. During Mohammed's absence, Muezza awakened. He saw the sleeve Mohammed had cut off for him. When Mohammed returned, Muezza thanked him and to express his respect raised his tail and arched his back. As a result, Mohammed assigned a place in paradise for the saintly and heavenly cat.

He also stroked the cat's back three times, which according to legend gave the cat nine lives (3 times 3) and the ability to land on his feet after a fall. Mohammed also used water that Muezza was drinking to purify himself. It is held that Mohammed's love for his cat made the animal sacred to Moslems. Legend has it that the *M* marking that tabbies have on their forehead is in honor of the prophet.

Many followers of Mohammed were also cat-lovers. One disciple, Abuherrira, loved cats so much that he was referred to as "the father of the little cat." According to legend, Abuherrira's cat is one of four animals admitted into the Moslem paradise, as recounted in Johann von Goethe's poem, "The Favored Beasts".

> Abuherrira's cat, too, here
> Purrs round his master blest,
> For holy must the beast appear
> The Prophet hath caress'd.

(It is interesting to note that Mohammed did not like dogs; he considered them unclean.)

Morris ∽

Morris is probably the best-known cat in advertising. But he came very close to missing his calling. When animal talent scout Bob Martwick went to the Hinsdale Humane Society in Chicago in search of a cat for a mattress commercial, he found a big orange tabby who was just minutes away from being euthanized in order to make room for new arrivals. He thought the cat would do for the commercial so he paid five bucks and took the cat, who he started calling Lucky.

About six months later he got a call from a major ad agency that was holding auditions for a cat who would make a brief appearance in a commercial for 9-Lives™ cat food. Martwick brought Lucky, who was given a screen test. After the director saw the clips, he was so impressed that he called in the writers and told them to make the cat the star of the commercial. They also changed his name to Morris.

Morris's first 9-Lives commercial appeared in 1969. The cat food that the finicky Morris gobbled up on camera soon started disappearing from shelves at supermarkets around the country. Morris was given a lifetime contract and was made an honorary member of the company's board of directors. In 1973 Morris was given a special PATSY award for Outstanding Performance in a TV Commercial. In the same year he was chosen to star in the movie *Shamus* (also featuring Dyan Cannon and Burt Reynolds).

The original Morris went to cat heaven in 1978. However, he lives on in spirit in the lookalike replacements found for him. Morris—I'm not sure which one—has been quoted as saying, "Personally, I don't believe felines are a fad. We're here to stay."

Today, Morris is known worldwide. *Time* magazine once called Morris the feline Burt Reynolds. When he makes an appearance he is mobbed by human autograph seekers who want his pawprint. Among his other appearances was serving as host on the primetime TV special *A Salute to America's Pets*, which he graciously allowed Bob Hope and Lily Tomlin to cohost with him.

Morris, Desmond ∽

If you are an inquisitive cat lover/reader you will probably recognize the name Desmond Morris. The Curator of Mammals at the London Zoo has written two fascinating books about cats and their behavior: *Catwatching* and *Catlore*. He says that his cat Jambo is the inspiration for both books. A black cat with a small patch of white on his front and three white whiskers, Jambo was found in an apple tree at the Morris home crying piteously. When Morris climbed a ladder to rescue Jambo, he learned quickly that Jambo did not like being held. Though Morris was covered with scratches, by now Jambo was on the ground furiously lapping up the milk he was offered.

In *The English Cat at Home*, writer Matthew Sturgis tells about the effort made to photograph Jambo for the book. Morris told him a photograph was unlikely, as Jambo could not be held for more than three seconds. But cat photographer Toby Glanville rose to the challenge. He had his tripod set up and his camera ready when he signaled to Morris to pick up the cat. To the surprise of everyone Jambo stayed in Morris's arms for some thirty seconds as Tony shot away, finally running out of film. Unfortunately, in his excitement, he forgot to remove the lens cap so there were no pictures. (Did Jambo, one wonders, know that all along?)

In talking about the difference between cats and dogs, Desmond Morris says, "Artists like cats; soldiers like dogs."

They call me cruel. Do I know if mouse or song-
    bird feels?
I only know they make me light and salutary
    meals.
And if, as 'tis my nature to, ere I devour I tease
    'em,
Why should a low-bred gardener's boy pursue
    me with a besom?*

* broom

However we see a slightly different picture of, perhaps, a fairer cat in Christopher Smart's poem "of Jeoffry, My Cat":

For when he takes his prey he plays with it to
    give it a chance.
For one mouse in seven escapes by his dally-
    ing.

There are many FABLES and tales that explore the cat/mouse relationship. The cat/mouse theme also appears frequently in children's cartoons.

Mouser ～ This term is used to describe any animal good at catching mice and rats, but especially cats. In C. S. Calverley's 1862 poem "Sad Memories" a cat talks about how she feels in her role as mouser:

Musée du Chat ～ This cat museum opened in 1992 in the city of Ainvelle, in northwestern France. Founded by Alain Girard-Chevalier, the museum is in an old barn built at the turn of the century. You'll find exhibits depicting both love and respect for the cat as well as dislike of felines. There are seventeenth-, eighteenth-, and nineteenth-century engravings, sculptures, jewels, plates, automatons, lithographs, paintings, bronzes, porcelains, moneyboxes, and so on. The collection contains over two thousand objects. Musée du Chat is on Rue de l'Eglise, 70880 Ainvelle. The telephone number is 84-49-89-19.

Musical cats ~ Cats have long been associated with music. In ancient Egypt, for example, the sacred cat is often portrayed holding a sistrum, an instrument used in religious ceremonies and banquets as well as on other occasions. Many of these instruments also had cats portrayed on them.

In *Les Chats*, originally published in 1727, Augustin Paradis de Moncrif says that the Egyptians were more enlightened on the subject of cat music than others, who considered the cats' meowing as caterwauling. (It comes as no surprise that the Egyptians should have heard music in the cat's vocalizations since they worshiped the cat.) According to Moncrif, the first string on the violin, the most sonorous and the most moving, is best when it is of catgut. (However, I could find no confirmation that catgut—from a cat, as the name implies—was ever used. Catgut was made from sheep.) The violin is the instrument that is most frequently seen with the cat.

Cats also appear to be sensitive to music. Some cats respond to one kind of music and leave the room when another type of music is played. For example, a cat belonging to THÉOPHILE GAUTIER would listen attentively as Gautier played the piano for various singers. When a female singer sang a high A, the cat would reach up with his paw and close the singer's mouth. Whenever composer Henri Sauguet would play Debussy on the piano, his cat Cody would become ecstatic, jumping up on his lap and licking his fingers; when Saguet stopped playing, Cody would wander off. And based on a series of experiments, Dr. Richard Zeliony says that cats are capable of making very fine musical tone discriminations. When he trained cats to respond to a whistle pitched at middle C, the cats did not respond to a whistle as close as half a tone in pitch from middle C.

Several musicians have named compositions for cats. For example, the Italian composer Gioacchino Antonio Rossini wrote "Duetto Buffo di Due Gatti" ("Comic Duet for Two Cats"), in which he adapted the miaows of cats to the music of the human voice. The Italian composer Domenico Scarlatti, who spent most of his life in Spain and Portugal in the service of the queen of Spain, wrote a collection of sonatas for the harpsichord. One of them, which he dedicated to the princess of Asturias, was marked only with the indication *moderato*. It is now called the *Cat Fugue* because it sounds like Scarlatti was inspired by a cat stepping on the keyboard. Mischa Spoliansky wrote a foxtrot that was called "Wenn die Katze," which was dedicated to a cat.

A popular cat song originally published in 1893, "The Cat Came Back," includes the refrain:

But the cat came back, couldn't stay no longer
Yes, the cat came back the very next day.
The cat came back, thought he was a goner,
But the cat came back for it wouldn't stay away

Other pieces of cat music include Zez Confrey's jazz piano solo, "Kitten on the Keys" (1921); Jimmy Smith's "The Cat"; Brent Fabric's "Alley Cat"; and Al Stewart's "Year of the Cat."

Cats were used to make music in a way most unpleasant for cats in the sixteenth to eighteenth centuries. Cat organs were made by confining the cat in a narrow space in the organ with his tail sticking out through a hole. Their tails were tied to the organ keys, so that when a key was pressed a cat's tail would be pulled and the cat would yowl. This was considered very amusing. (It sounds neither amusing nor musical to me.)

The idiom of American jazz has also made use of the word cat. A jazz musician or lover of jazz referred to himself as a *cat* or a *hep cat*. African-American musicians or lovers of jazz were thus *black cats*.

Myths

Over the years many myths have been generated by the cat. You may know some of them; others no doubt will surprise you. Many have to do with the cat's ability to predict weather, and some, after all, may be true!

- Neutered male cats will become fat and lazy and won't hunt.
- Female cats will hunt only when they have a litter of cats to feed
- A cat has nine lives.
- A sty in the eye can be cured by rubbing it with a tomcat's tail.
- In the Ozarks, keeping black cats around the house means all daughters in the house will be old maids.
- Cats eat coconut meat because long ago the coconut used to be the head of a cat (a myth from the Philippines).
- You can tell the tide from the size of a cat's pupils.
- You can tell the time of day by looking at the shape of a cat's pupils.
- Cats' eyes shine at night because they are casting out the light they gathered during the day.
- For sailors, a drowned cat is the surest way to raise a favorable wind.

- If a cat washes behind its ears, it will rain.
- If a cat leaves a sunny corner and goes to sleep in the barn, it will rain.
- When a cat's whiskers droop, rain is coming.
- A cat sleeping with all four paws tucked under means cold weather.
- According to the Amish, to keep a cat at home, put a piece of food under your armpit and give it to him to eat.
- If you want to keep a cat from straying, put butter on its feet.
- If you want to keep a stray cat at your home, put some hair from her tail under the doorsill.
- When you move to a new home, let the cat in through the window instead of the door, so that she will not leave.
- Warts can be removed by rubbing them with a male tortoiseshell's tail . . . but only in May!

See also SUPERSTITIONS.

Names ∿ Just as there are books for naming newborn babies, there are entire books on naming a cat. Naming a cat is taken very seriously by many cat owners. The English poet T. S. ELIOT says all there is to say of importance about this topic in his poem "The Naming of Cats," on the facing page.

As American writer Ellen Perry Berkeley explains, many cats come to have multiple names. The cats have their "proper" names as well as more familiar monikers. For example, one of Berkeley's cats was named Turtle, because she was a tortoiseshell. When speaking about Turtle, she came to be known affectionately as Little Miss Meatloaf; and Sylvester, with his long black hair, had a second name, the Dust Mop; and Herbert became known as the Dim Bulb (with great affection, of course).

People name their cats after writers, movie stars, and flowers; objects, mythological characters, and friends and relatives. If they have more than one cat they may choose names that rhyme, like Spot and Dot; or names that go together like Bonnie and Clyde. (I once named two cats Aphro (he was black) and Desiac (she was a Siamese).

Filmmaker Julia Philips named her cat Caesar so that she could call it Julia's Caesar (you have to say that one out loud). The English actress Beryl Reid called her cat Footy because "she always sat on my foot when I was in the kitchen doing some work, and I had to walk about with her on my foot." The English writer Monica Edwards named her cat Freyni after a rock-plant, which she saw characterized in a garden manual as "forming a silvery hummock: spreading." "The first part of the description fitted her admirably," she says. "We couldn't have known in her slim young days, how well, in time, the second part would fit her." But, bear in mind, that whatever name you choose, you may never know the name the cat has chosen for herself.

If you are looking for a name for your feline, for your convenience, here are some of the many names that appear in this book. And of course, this is but a small sampling:

Rusty, Matilda, Sarah Snow, Madame Butterfly, Pyewacket, Langbourne, Binky, Kismet, Birdy, Bandit, Eponine, Black Jack, Felix, Elwood, Big Red, Tuffy, Turkey (please, don't name your cat turkey!), Sheba, Sheena, Taki, Jock, Nelson, Charmian, Fanchette, Zeverga, La Chatte, Williamina, Tonto, Damon, Pythias, Dillinger, Thruster, Furhouse (a bit peculiar), Fats (a bit

The naming of Cats is a difficult matter,
    It isn't just one of your holiday games;
You may think at first I'm as mad as a hatter
When I tell you, a cat must have THREE DIFFERENT NAMES.
First of all, there's the name that the family use daily,
    Such as Peter, Augustus, Alonzo or James,
Such as Victor or Jonathan, George or Bill Baily—
    All of them sensible everyday names.
There are fancier names if you think they sound sweeter,
    Some for the gentlemen, some for the dames:
Such as Plato, Admetus, Electra, Demeter—
    But all of them sensible everyday names.
But I tell you a cat needs a name that's particular,
    A name that's peculiar and more dignified,
Else how can he keep up his tail perpendicular,
    Or spread out his whiskers, or cherish his pride?
Of names of this kind, I can give you a quorum,
    Such as Munkustrap, Quaxo, or Coricopat,
Such as Bombalurina, or else Jellyorum—
    Names that never belong to more than one cat.
But above and beyond there's still one name left over,
    And that is the name that you never will guess;
The name that no human research can discover—
    But the CAT HIMSELF KNOWS, and will never confess.
When you notice a cat in profound meditation,
    The reason, I tell you, is always the same:
His mind is engaged in a rapt contemplation
    Of the thought, of the thought, of the thought of his name
        His ineffable effable
        Effineffable
Deep and inscrutable singular Name.

                                                T.S. Eliot

167

insulting?), Willie, Herbie, Mouse (somewhat like Birdy), Duff, Foss, Jambo, Noko Maria, Molly, and Miel.

According to *Cat Fancy*, the most popular names for cats in the United States for toms are:

Smokey	Sam
Tiger	Sammy
Max	Mickey
Charlie	Toby
Rocky	

The most popular names for female cats are:

Samantha	Pumpkin
Misty	Missy
Muffin	Tabitha
Fluffy	Tigger
Patches	

Few people have taken naming the cat as seriously as writer and naturalist Roger Caras, who called his male, blue-point Siamese Sumay. "The meaning of that name is," according to Caras, "a profoundly secret, extremely deep and personal family affair. It is known to us and the National Security Agency only. I dare not speak of it here."

Natural breed ∿ A cat which is believed to have developed on its own without any human intervention, such as the Egyptian Mau, the Japanese bobtail, the Norwegian forest cat, the Siamese, and the Maine coon. *See also* BREED.

Newton, Sir Isaac ∿ (1642–1727) The English philosopher and mathematician who lived in the early eighteenth century and formulated

the law of gravity also invented the "cat flap," so that his cats could go freely in and out the door. (I'm not sure why gravity has gotten so much more attention than the cat flap.) Newton had a cat-sized hole cut in the bottom of the door of his study. When the cat had kittens, he cut a smaller cat flap for the kittens to use.

Nightingale, Florence ∿ (1820–1910) The English nurse who was a reformer of hospital conditions and procedures was also a cat lover. (She often complained of "mysterious stains" on her paperwork.) In her *Notes on Nursing*, published in 1890, she stated, "A small pet animal is often an excellent companion for the sick, for long chronic cases especially." In his book *Cat's Company*, Michael Joseph says that Florence Nightingale would never travel without her cats. She had about sixty Persians, all named after prominent men of the day, such as Disraeli, Gladstone, and Bismarck.

> The cat has nine lives: three for playing, three for straying, three for staying.
>
> ENGLISH PROVERB

Nine lives ∿ One of the most common myths about the cat is that he has nine lives. One explanation is that nine represents the trinity of trinities and was considered a lucky number in ancient times, when the cat, too, was considered lucky. Another explanation is that MOHAMMED, who was a great lover of felines, stroked the cats back three times, which according to legend gave the cat nine lives (3 times 3) as well as the ability to land on his feet after a fall. In more modern times, John Heywood's 1546 collection of proverbs states that "No wife, no woman hath nine lives like a cat," while another old proverb claims, "It has been the providence of nature to give this creature nine lives instead of one." In Shakespeare's *Romeo and Juliet*, Mercutio replies to Tybalt, the "Good King of Cats," that he desires "nothing but one of your nine lives."

On the Death of a Cat, a Friend of Mine Aged Ten Years and a Half

Who shall tell the lady's grief
When her cat was past relief?
Who shall number the hot tears
Shed o'er her, belov'd for years?
Who shall say the dark dismay
Which her dying caused that day?

Come ye Muses, one and all,
Come obedient to my call;
Come and mourn with tuneful breath
Each one for a separate death;
And, while you in numbers sigh,
I will sing her elegy.

Of a noble race she came,
And Grimalkin was her name.
Young and old full many a mouse
Felt the prowess of her house;
Weak and strong full many a rat
Cowered beneath her crushing pat;
And the birds around the place
Shrank from her too-close embrace.
But one night, reft of her strength,
She lay down and died at length:
Lay a kitten by her side
In whose life the mother died.

Spare her life and lineage,
Guard her kitten's tender age,
And that kitten's name as wide
Shall be known as hers that died.
And whoever passes by
The poor grave where Puss doth lie,
Softly, softly let him tread,
Nor disturb her narrow bed.

CHRISTINA ROSSETTI, British poet
(1830–1894)

Non-pedigree ～ Non-pedigree cats are animals whose ancestry can't be traced. Another way of describing a non-pedigree cat is mixed breed. Non-pedigree cats come in innumerable variations with individual and unique markings and colorings. It's doubtful that you'll ever find two exactly alike.

There are thousands of non-pedigree cats to be found. The good news is that you'll have no trouble finding one—and pay little or no money for it. The bad news is that many, many non-pedigree cats are euthanized (killed) every year because they have been abandoned and/or dropped off at a humane society as kittens. Although there are some "non-kill" shelters, many simply can't afford to keep every kitten and cat that arrives on their doorstep.

You may find a stray in the woods behind your house or mewing on your doorstep, hungry and frightened in the morning. You'll definitely find many who are looking for a home at the local animal shelter. Often vets will have or know of a kitten or two available for adoption.

PERSONALITY: A non-pedigree shorthair can make a wonderful pet. It can be as loving, affectionate, and intelligent as any cat with papers. And as you read through this book, you'll find that most of the hero cats, miracle cats, and psychic cats were plain, everyday, run-of-the-mill, wonderful cats.

Norwegian forest cat ～ The Norwegian forest cat is a natural breed resembling another cold weather cat, the MAINE COON. There is little doubt that the harsh winters in Norway

This brown mackerel tabby was judged Best Norwegian Forest Cat in 1992. (COURTESY LYNNE BOROFF, ADVENT HILL CATTERY, HARTLAND, VERMONT.)

played a role in this cat's resourcefulness, hunting ability, and water-repellent coat, which can dry in about fifteen minutes after being drenched. This cat is known as the "Norsk Skaukatt" or "Skogkatt" in its homeland but is commonly referred to by its nickname, "Wegie."

The breed is centuries old in its homeland, where it may be a descendant of shorthaired cats brought from England by the Vikings and longhaired cats brought by the Crusaders. Only the fittest and most well-protected of these cats could survive the cold winters, yielding a breed that was intelligent and brave. Indeed Norse mythology refers to a cat so huge that even the god Thor could not lift it from the ground, and Freya, the goddess of love and fertility, was said to have been pulled in a carriage by two large cats.

Up until the 1930s, only Norwegian farmers appreciated this cat for its hunting abilities and after World War II, the Norwegian forest cats were in danger of becoming extinct. However, Carl-Fredrik Nordane sprang to the rescue, starting a breeding club to oversee the preservation of the Norwegian forest cat through planned breeding programs. In 1977, after Nordane persuaded the Feline International Federation of Europe to accept the cat for championship competition, he was greeted, upon his return, with music, flags, and a parade of grateful Norwegians. The first Norwegian forest cat arrived in the United States two years later.

The Norwegian forest cat is muscular and heavily boned. It has a large triangular head with fluffy ears, with lynx-like tufts. It comes in all coat colors and patterns and has long, rich fur with a wooly undercoat, but requires less grooming than some other longhaired cats. It sheds its undercoat in summer, appearing almost shorthaired, and its long, magnificent tail is carried high.

PERSONALITY: Norwegian forest cats are very intelligent, playful, affectionate, and demanding of attention. The females are especially good mothers, and the breed is not fully mature until about five years of age.

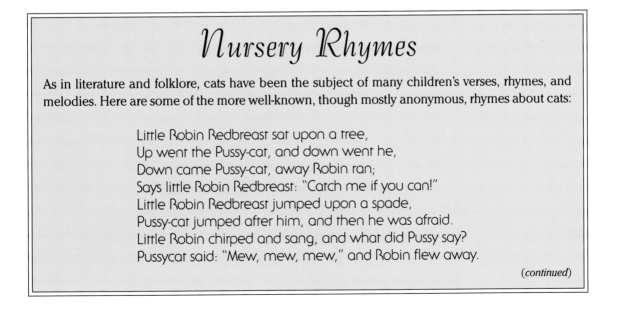

Nursery Rhymes

As in literature and folklore, cats have been the subject of many children's verses, rhymes, and melodies. Here are some of the more well-known, though mostly anonymous, rhymes about cats:

Little Robin Redbreast sat upon a tree,
Up went the Pussy-cat, and down went he,
Down came Pussy-cat, away Robin ran;
Says little Robin Redbreast: "Catch me if you can!"
Little Robin Redbreast jumped upon a spade,
Pussy-cat jumped after him, and then he was afraid.
Little Robin chirped and sang, and what did Pussy say?
Pussycat said: "Mew, mew, mew," and Robin flew away.

(continued)

Ding dong Bell,
The Cat is in the Well,
Who put her in?
Little Johnny Green,
Who pulled her out?
Little Tommy Stout.
What a naughty Boy was that,
To drown Poor Pussy Cat,
Who never did any Harm,
And Kill'd the Mice in his Father's Barn.

~

High diddle, diddle,
The Cat and the Fiddle,
   The Cow jump'd over the Moon;
The little Dog laugh'd
To see such Craft,
   And the Dish ran away with the Spoon.

~

The cat sat asleep by the side of the fire,
   The mistress snored loud as a pig:
John took up his fiddle, by Jenny's desire,
   And struck up a bit of a jig.

~

Pussy cat, pussy cat, wilt thou be mine,
Thou shalt neither wash dishes nor feed the swine
But sit on a cushion and sew a silk seam,
And eat fine strawberries, sugar, and cream.

Pussy cat, pussy cat, where have you been?
I've been to London to look at the Queen.
Pussy cat, pussy cat, what did you there?
I frightened a little mouse under her chair.

~

Diddlety, diddlety, dumpty,
The cat ran up the plum tree;
   Half a crown,
   To fetch her down,
Diddlety, diddlety, dumpty.

(continued)

172

This cat quilt was made by an unknown Kentucky artist, c. 1930–1940. (COURTESY MUSEUM OF AMERICAN FOLK ART, NEW YORK, GIFT OF LAURA FISHER, 1987.)

A cat came fiddling out of a barn,
With a pair of bag-pipes under her arm;
She could sing nothing but, Fiddle cum fee
The mouse has married the humble-bea.
Pipe, cat; dance, mouse;
We'll have a wedding at our good house.

~

Six little mice sat down to spin;
Pussy passed by and she peeped in.
What are you doing, my little men?
Weaving coats for gentlemen.
Shall I come in and cut off your threads?
No, no, Mistress Pussy, you'd bite off our heads.
Oh, no, I'll not; I'll help you to spin.
That may be so, but you can't come in.
Says Puss: You look so wondrous wise,
I like your whiskers and bright black eyes;
Your house is the nicest house I see,
I think there is room for you and for me.
The mice were so pleased that they opened the door,
And Pussy soon had them all dead on the floor.

~

Pussycat, wussicat, with a white foot,
When is your wedding, and I'll come to it.
The beer's to brew, the bread's to bake,
Pussycat, pussycat, don't be late.

~

I like little pussy,
   Her coat is so warm,
And if I don't hurt her,
   She'll do me no harm.
So I'll not pull her tail,
   Nor drive her away,
But pussy and I
   Very gently will play.
She shall sit by my side,
   And I'll give her some food;
And pussy will love me
   Because I am good.

(continued)

Cats figure prominently in nursery rhymes from Mother Goose, as well as many others. Late nineteenth-century print.

As I was going to St. Ives,
I met a man with seven wives,
Each wife had seven sacks,
Each sack had seven cats,
Each cat had seven kits:
Kits, cats, sacks, and wives,
How many were there going to St. Ives?

~

Two little kittens, one stormy night,
Began to quarrel, and then to fight;
One had a mouse, the other had none,
And that's the way the quarrel begun.

'I'll have that mouse,' said the biggest cat;
'You'll have that mouse? We'll see about that!'
'I *will* have that mouse,' said the eldest son;
'You *shan't* have the mouse,' said the little one.

I told you before 'twas a stormy night
When these two little kittens began to fight;
The old woman seized her sweeping broom,
And swept the two kittens right out of the room.

The ground was covered with frost and snow,
And the two little kittens had nowhere to go;
So they laid them down on the mat at the door,
While the old woman finished sweeping the floor.

Then they crept in, as quiet as mice,
All wet with the snow, and as cold as ice,
For they found it was better, that stormy night,
To lie down and sleep than to quarrel and fight.

ANONYMOUS (c. 1879)

(continued)

Pussy-cat sits by the fire
        How can she be fair?
In walks the little dog;
        Says: "Pussy, are you there?
How do you do, Mistress Puss?
        Mistress Pussy, how d'ye do?"
"I thank you kindly, little dog,
        I fare as well as you."

~

Three little kittens lost their mittens;
And they began to cry,
"Oh, mother dear,
We very much fear
That we have lost our mittens."
"Lost your mittens!
You naughty kittens!
Then you shall have no pie!"
"Mee-ow, mee-ow, mee-ow."
"No, you shall have no pie."
"Mee-ow, mee-ow, mee-ow."

The three little kittens found their mittens;
And they began to cry,
"Oh, mother dear,
See here, see here!
See, we have found our mittens!"
"Put on your mittens,
You silly kittens,
And you may have some pie."
"Purr-r, purr-r, purr-r,
Oh, let us have the pie!
Purr-r, purr-r, purr-r."

The three little kittens put on their mittens,
And soon ate up the pie;
"Oh, mother dear,
We greatly fear
That we have soiled our mittens!"
"Soiled your mittens!
You naughty kittens!"
Then they began to sigh,
"Mee-ow, mee-ow, mee-ow."
Then they began to sigh,
"Mee-ow, mee-ow, mee-ow."

The three little kittens washed their mittens,
And hung them out to dry,
"Oh, mother dear,
Do not you hear
That we have washed our mittens?"
"Washed your mittens!
Oh, you're good kittens!
But I smell a rat close by,
Hush, hush! Mee-ow, mee-ow."
"We smell a rat close by,
Mee-ow, mee-ow, mee-ow."

Eliza Lee Follen

177

Ocicat ∼ The ocicat is a relatively new breed, developed accidentally by a woman in Michigan named Virginia Daly in the early 1960s. She was successful in breeding an Abyssinian-pointed Siamese, but in the same litter was a large ivory cat with golden spots. Daly's daughter called the cat an "ocicat" because she thought the kitten looked like an Ocelot. The ocicat has a large, muscular body, a wedge-shaped head with a broad muzzle, and large, almond-shaped eyes.

In the mid 1960s the Cat Fanciers Association announced that the ocicat would be accepted for registration. By October 1970 only two had been registered. It was accepted for championship competition by the CFA in 1987. Between 1986 and 1989 the annual ocicat registrations jumped 292 percent.

PERSONALITY: Ocicats are known for their doglike devotion. They are very affectionate, and like other cats and dogs as well as people.

Oliver & Company ∼ The star of this 1988 Disney cartoon feature, which was loosely based on Charles Dickens's *Oliver Twist,* was Oliver the cat. When Oliver and his sibling kittens are abandoned outside a market for pass-ersby to adopt, all but Oliver are taken. It starts raining and Oliver, now wet in addition to being cold and hungry, decides to seek his own fortune. His fortunes include numerous brushes with disaster with a slew of dogs, but in the end, Oliver lives happily ever after with a little rich girl named Jenny. Among the music stars who provided songs and voices for the animals in the movie are Bette Midler and Billy Joel.

Orangey ∼ This tabby, obviously named for the color of his coat, was the first live movie star cat. Orangey won two PATSY awards—one in 1952 for his starring role in *Rhubarb* and the other for playing the role of Cat in *Breakfast at Tiffany's* in 1962. Orangey also costarred in the Jackie Gleason movie *Gigot.* He was a regular on the *Our Miss Brooks* TV show, also starring Eve Arden. To give you a little insight into Orangey's personality, one movie director called him "the world's meanest cat."

Oriental longhair ∼ This beautiful cat, and some say the best of the longhairs, is the newest descendant of a very distinguished cat family. The Oriental longhair is a result of breeding efforts with the Oriental shorthair in the late 1970s and early 1980s. Their ancestry includes Siamese, Colorpoint shorthair, Oriental shorthair, Balinese, and Javanese. Though they are difficult to breed, they display the best features of each ancestor—the style, curiousity, and intelligence of the Siamese or Colorpoint shorthair, the silky elegance and affection of the Balinese or Javanese, and the various colors, alertness, and charm of the Oriental Shorthair. They were recognized for competition in 1985 by the International Cat Association.

PERSONALITY: They are alert, intelligent, and affectionate.

Oriental shorthair ～

The Oriental shorthair is the result of the breeding of Siamese cats with other shorthairs in the 1950s at the prompting of the British Baroness von Ullman, who wanted a new variety of cat—a brown shorthair with green eyes and a Siamese body. Although she was not successful, four years later an ad and photograph of two kittens in the British journal *Our Cats* matched the description of the cats the baroness was trying to breed. The mother of the kittens was a sealpoint Siamese and the father was a brown hybrid. In the late 1950s Patricia Turner, a British cat breeder and geneticist, tried to produce the same cat but with blue eyes and a white coat. She eventually collaborated with two other

Originally the offspring a Siamese and an Abyssian, the ocicat is a relatively new breed, named after the wild ocelot which it resembles. (PHOTOGRAPH BY ISABELLE FRANCAIS.)

breeders and in the mid-1960s they developed what they called the foreign white, which received immediate and extensive publicity at its first show. Breeders working with foreign whites then started mating Siamese with a variety of shorthairs. Eventually an enormous variety of colorful and attractive Oriental shorthair cats were developed.

Oriental shorthairs come in a great variety of colors and patterns, including the ticked tabby, ebony, blue, blue tabby, tabby, chocolate tabby, and lilac.

PERSONALITY: Oriental shorthairs have the same energetic and inquisitive nature as the Siamese. They are intelligent and affectionate.

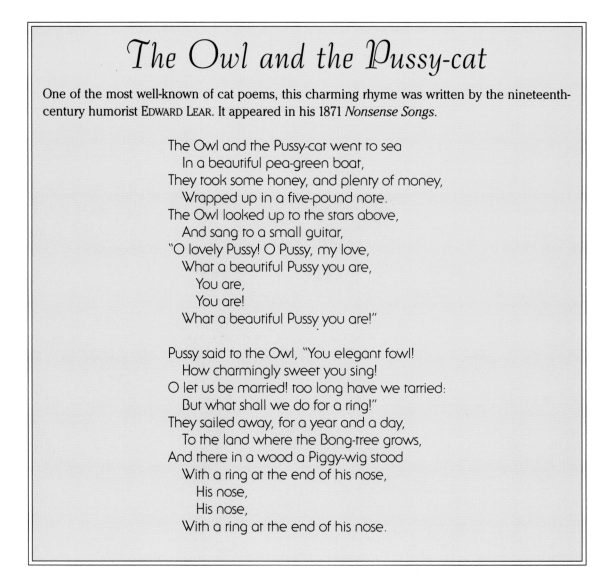

The Owl and the Pussy-cat

One of the most well-known of cat poems, this charming rhyme was written by the nineteenth-century humorist EDWARD LEAR. It appeared in his 1871 *Nonsense Songs*.

> The Owl and the Pussy-cat went to sea
>   In a beautiful pea-green boat,
> They took some honey, and plenty of money,
>   Wrapped up in a five-pound note.
> The Owl looked up to the stars above,
>   And sang to a small guitar,
> "O lovely Pussy! O Pussy, my love,
>   What a beautiful Pussy you are,
>   You are,
>   You are!
>   What a beautiful Pussy you are!"
>
> Pussy said to the Owl, "You elegant fowl!
>   How charmingly sweet you sing!
> O let us be married! too long have we tarried:
>   But what shall we do for a ring!"
> They sailed away, for a year and a day,
>   To the land where the Bong-tree grows,
> And there in a wood a Piggy-wig stood
>   With a ring at the end of his nose,
>   His nose,
>   His nose,
>   With a ring at the end of his nose.

"Dear Pig, are you willing to sell for one shilling
    Your ring?" Said the Piggy, "I will."
So they took it away, and were married next day
    By the Turkey who lives on the hill.
They dined on mince, and slices of quince,
    Which they ate with a runcible spoon;
And hand in hand, on the edge of the sand,
    They danced by the light of the moon,
        The moon,
        The moon,
    They danced by the light of the moon.

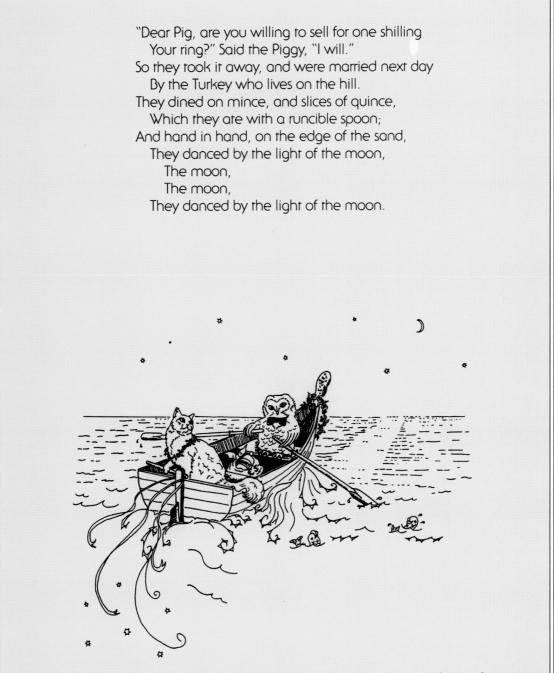

"The Owl and the Pussycat" has become one of the world's most beloved nursery rhymes. (DRAWING BY CHRISTINA DUNSTAN.)

Patsy *(Picture Animal Top Star Award)* ～ This acting award was first bestowed by the American Humane Society of Los Angeles in 1951. Begun as an award for animals in movies, its scope expanded in 1958 to include television and the first Special Commercial Award was given in 1973 to MORRIS for his work in the 9-Lives cat-food commercials. Besides cats, all kinds of animals have received rewards, including mules, lions, tigers, chimpanzees, seals, rats, dolphins, and dogs.

In the second annual awards, in 1952, the cat ORANGEY won first place for his role in the Paramount picture *Rhubarb*. In 1959, Pyewacket took first place in the movie *Bell, Book and Candle* produced by Columbia. In 1962 Orangey, who played Cat in Paramount Pictures' *Breakfast at Tiffany's* again received first place for that role. In 1966, Syn Cat was awarded first place for his role in *That Darn Cat*, produced by Walt Disney. In 1974, Midnight won top prize for appearing in the television series *Mannix*, produced by Paramount Television. In 1976 the cat Tonto, who starred in HARRY AND TONTO, received the Motion Picture Award. In 1977, the cat 17 received the top award in Category IV-Special Award for his appearance in *Dr. Shrinker*. In 1978 the Category IV-Special Award went to Amber, the cat in the movie *The Cat From Outer Space*, produced by Walt Disney. And in 1986, in Special Category IV-Award, the winner was the cats in *Alfred Hitchcock Presents*, produced by Universal. Although cats may not have received a proportionate share of awards, especially in comparison to dogs, the honors they did receive were all *the top prize*.

Pedigree ～ A pedigree cat is one that belongs to a specific breed and has papers to prove it. Registration papers list the known names of the cat's parents, grandparents, great-grandparents (and other progenitors as far back as is known), as well as these cats' titles (merit ranks earned by a cat in competition), colors, and registration numbers going back three to five generations. Pedigree cats are carefully bred for specific characteristics including color, pattern, and even personality. *See* BREEDS.

Pepper the Cat ～ Pepper is perhaps the only cat to star in silent films. One fateful day when Mack Sennett was filming a movie, a gray cat crawled up through a broken floorboard. Sennett immediately made the cat part of the scene and a star was born. Sennett named her Pepper and she got roles in many subsequent films. Pepper became very chummy with Teddy, the Great Dane who resided in the studio. When Teddy departed, Pepper was devastated and never acted in another film.

To a Persian Cat

So dear, so dainty, so demure,
So charming in whate'er position;
By race the purest of the pure,
A little cat of high condition:
Her coat lies not in trim-kept rows
Of carpet-like and vulgar sleekness:
But like a ruffled sea it grows
Of wavy grey (my special weakness):
She vexes not the night with squalls
That make one seize a boot and throw it:
She joins in no unseemly brawls
(At least she never lets me know it!);
She never burst in at the door
In manner boisterous and loud:
But silently along the floor
She passes, like a little cloud.
Then, opening wide her amber eyes,
Puts an inquiring nose up—
Sudden upon my knee she flies,
Then purrs and tucks her little toes up.

F. C. W. HILEY

Persian ∼ The Persian is the most plentiful—and prized—of all pedigree cats. It was the first longhair cat to reach Europe. Some credit Pietro della Valle, an Italian traveler, with bringing the first Persian to Europe from Persia in the 1500s.

According to Persian legend, the Persian made its first appearance on earth this way: A merchant came upon a stranger being beaten and robbed by a group of hoodlums and came to the stranger's defense, paying for his bed and board, and staying with him until he regained his strength. The next night the stranger, now recovered, thanked the merchant for coming to the rescue of someone he didn't know, and without any expectations of a reward. The stranger then revealed that he was a magician and told the merchant he could grant any wish he might have. The merchant replied that he wanted for nothing—he had a fine family and had been successful in his trading and could ask for nothing more than to sit and watch the fire, the swirling smoke, and the stars. Saying that he would make a gift of just those things, the magician took a little tongue of fire, the light of two distant stars, and a skein of swirling gray smoke to create a most wonderful little cat with gray fur, bright eyes, and fire-tipped tongue. And thus the Persian made its entrance into the world.

Persians have the longest, fullest, and woolliest hair of all the longhairs. They must be groomed (combed) regularly. There are numerous varieties, as noted below.

PERSONALITY: Persians are gentle, docile cats who don't mind just hanging out on a couch or bed and looking beautiful. Each type has its own variation of the typical Persian personality. Following are the types with their particular personalities:

· black Persian—They are affectionate and said to be more lively than the white Persian.
· white Persian—They take a great deal of pride in their appearance, cleaning themselves regularly. They are calm and affectionate and make a very good pet.
· cream Persian—They are even-tempered and friendly.
· blue Persian—They are calm and gentle.
· red Persian—They are polite, friendly, and companionable.

Persians, like Strawberry Short Legs, are one of the most popular breeds. (COURTESY GLAMOUR KATZ.)

• blue-cream Persian—They are affectionate and accommodating, though a little more outgoing than many other Persians.

• chinchilla Persian—They are generally calm and affectionate, although they do have a reputation for being more temperamental.

• cameo Persian—They are languorous and agreeable.

• smoke Persian—They are relaxed, good-natured, and gentle.

• bicolor Persian—They are placid, affectionate, and very charming.

• tabby Persian—They are more independent than the typical Persian but still friendly and agreeable.

• tortoiseshell Persian—They are affectionate, gentle, placid, and an excellent mother to their kittens.

• calico Persian—They are calm, sweet, and extremely friendly.

Persian fans may want to subscribe to the *Persian Quarterly*, 4401 Zephyr Street, Wheat Ridge, CO 80033-3299.

Personality

∼ Cats can be finicky, courageous, curious, loving, vocal, psychic, possessive, jealous, aggressive, vengeful, intelligent, and of course, independent. The personality of any cat is often a result of his or her first experiences. In the early 1930s at Temple University in Philadelphia, Eileen Karsh, Ph.D., studied the reactions of kittens to different amounts of handling. Those who were handled for as much as five minutes a day, starting at three weeks of age until they were 14 weeks old, were more attached to people than kittens who were not held until they were seven weeks of age, or not handled at all.

The personality of a cat may also vary by breed, as noted in the descriptions included in this volume, though there are many similarities. Body type frequently is an indication of personality. For example, slim, elegant cats such as the Siamese tend to be more active, vocal, and curious. Stocky breeds such as the Persian tend to be easygoing. However, as any cat owner can tell you, each cat has its own distinct personality.

> Anyone who claims that a cat cannot give a dirty look either has never kept a cat or is singularly unobservant.
>
> MAURICE BURTON, American writer,
> twentieth century

> The cat is the mirror of his human's mind, personality and attitude, just as the dog mirrors his human's physical appearance.
>
> WINIFRED CARRIERE, American writer,
> twentieth century

> Cats can be funny, and have the oddest ways of showing they're glad to see you. Rufimace always peed in our shoes.
>
> W. H. AUDEN American poet, (1907–1973)

This dilute tortoiseshell longhaired Persian, Pansy, represents the European standard. (PHOTOGRAPH BY PAUL COUGHLIN, COURTESY PAUL COUGHLIN AND JIM DRATFIELD OF PETROGRAPHY INC. AND PHYLLIS S. LEVY.)

Pussycat Sits on a Chair

Pussycat sits on a chair
Implacably with acid stare.

Those who early loved in vain
Use the cat to try again,

And test their bruised omnipotence
Against the cat's austere defense.

EDWARD NEWMAN HORN, twentieth
century American writer

To a Cat

Stately, kindly, lordly friend,
Condescend
Here to sit by me, and turn
Glorious eyes that smile and burn,
Golden eyes, love's lustrous meed,
On the golden page I read.

All your wondrous wealth of hair,
Dark and fair,
Silken-shaggy, soft and bright
As the clouds and beams of night,
Pays my reverent hand's caress
Back with friendlier gentleness.

Dogs may fawn on all and some
As they come;
You, a friend of loftier mind,
Answer friends alone in kind.
Just your foot upon my hand
Softly bids it understand.

ALGERNON CHARLES SWINBURNE, British
poet and critic (1837–1909)

Pets Are Inn ∼ This is a service which uses a computer to find a "petsitter" (or foster parent or chaperone) for a pet whose family is going to be away. Your cat stays with the caretakers and gets lots of personal attention from his fill-in parents. Most of the people taking part in the program encourage a preliminary visit so that your cat can explore his new, temporary home and meet his temporary family. It costs from about eight to fifteen dollars a day. Pets Are Inn was started in Minnesota and in 1992 had branches in thirty cities.

Pets for Patient Progress ∼

There are more and more programs being started in which pets are used therapeutically in hospitals, nursing homes, centers for abused children, and institutions for the mentally ill. One program is Pets for Patient Progress in Crystal Lake, Illinois. Volunteers take cats to visit patients in a convalescence center, or a local hospital. The cats are from the Assisi Animal Foundation, founded by Lee Linklater and her mother, Isab-

elle Yarosh. They moved to Crystal Lake in 1987 in order to start a shelter for homeless cats. The building for the cats was completed in 1988 and they now have some two hundred cats, who are cared for by the two women and volunteers. Many of those cared-for residents end up caring for others through Pets for Patient Progress. Isabelle related one incident when she brought some kittens to a convalescence home at Christmas. "There was one man in a wheelchair, the saddest person I'd ever seen. He never spoke at all. We started taking pictures of the residents holding the kittens and he rolled himself right to the front and said, 'I want a cat.' The nurses were stunned. They said they'd never heard him speak before. I still get chills when I tell that story." Pets for Patient Progress can be reached at P.O. Box 143, Crystal Lake, Ill 60039-0143; 815/455-0990

Pets for People ~ This not-for-profit

program, funded by Ralston Purina, provides healthy, loving pets to people aged sixty and over at no charge. It is run by local humane societies that help those people wanting a pet find one that is right for their life-styles. Studies indicate that pet ownership provides a sense of security and protection, as well as unqualified affection and a source of entertainment. Studies have also shown that owning a pet may actually improve health. Lowered blood pressure and reduction in stress are just two of the benefits. Pets for People has found homes for tens of thousands of cats and dogs while at the same time improving the quality of life for those senior citizens. Over 80 percent of the people getting a pet through Pets for People report feeling happier and safer. To find out where a Pets for People program is near you, call 314/982-3028. Or you can try calling animal shelters in your area.

Petting ~ See STROKING.

Phrases

The cat has entered our language in a number of colorful phrases. Though you may recognize many of them, and have used them at one time or another, do you know their origin? Here are some common cat phrases and how they evolved:

It's raining cats and dogs ~ This expression originated several centuries ago when streets in cities and towns were narrow, dirty, and poorly drained. When there was a heavy rain, large numbers of starving cats and dogs would simply drown. When the rain ended, people would find the bodies of the dead cats and dogs in the streets. Some of the people thought the bodies of the animals came from the rain, hence they said it rained "cats and dogs." In another explanation, the expression originated in Norse mythology, where cats symbolize heavy rain and dogs represent great gusts of wind. The phrase is also a slang term for highly speculative, low-priced securities or for a large, odd assortment of goods for sale; and it may be used in reference to the violence associated with fights between cats and dogs—perhaps best summed up in this quote from "The Duel," written by the American journalist and poet Eugene Field:

The Gingham dog went "Bow-wow-wow!"
And the Calico cat replied "Mee-ow!"
The air was littered, an hour or so,
With bits of gingham and calico.

(continued)

Letting the cat out of the bag ～ This phrase, now used when someone has revealed a secret, dates back to a scam practiced on market day in the eighteenth century. Piglets were often taken to market in a bag, and since a cat was worth much less than a piglet, a dishonest farmer would put a cat in the bag instead of a piglet. If the potential buyer wanted to see the piglet before paying for it, he would be told that the piglet was too feisty and it was too risky to open the bag as he might run away. However, if meows started coming from the bag, or the cat struggled so much that the seller had to let it out, his secret became common knowledge. He had, therefore, let the cat out of the bag.

A cat-in-Hell's chance ～ This is the shortened version of the original phrase which went like this: "No more chance than a cat in hell without claws." Originally it referred to being in a dangerous situation without means of defense—of being helpless.

Having kittens ～ This phrase refers to a state of great upset or anxiety. The source of this phrase goes back to medieval times when cats were thought of as witches' familiars. If a pregnant woman was suffering agonizing pain, it was believed that she was bewitched and the pain was caused by the kittens inside her womb, scratching and struggling to get out. Since witches have supernatural powers, they could supply magical potions to destroy the litter so that the woman would not give birth to kittens. As late as the seventeenth century "cats in the belly" was an accepted excuse in court for getting an abortion. It does not seem unlikely that a woman who thought she was bewitched and going to give birth to kittens would become hysterical with fear—hence the phrase "having kittens."

There is no room to swing a cat ～ In this phrase the *cat* refers to the cat-o'-nine-tails used on early naval vessels. Since the whip was too long to swing below deck, the sailor to be punished for wrongdoing had to be taken above. The whip was called a "cat" because of the scratchlike scars in left on the backs of the unfortunate sailors.

Curiosity killed the cat ～ Originally this phrase was "care killed the cat," which related to the fact that a cat has nine lives and that "care will wear them out." A woman who is spiteful and backbiting is often referred to as a cat—that woman is frequently thought of as being nosy or curious—and thus evolved the phrase "curiosity killed the cat."

Fighting like Kilkenny cats ～ This phrase refers to an Irish legend of two cats who fought so long and hard that only their tails were left. The legend may refer to a fight between two Irish towns, Kilkenny and Irishtown, which was equally destructive.

A cat may look at a king ～ This saying dates from John Heywood's collection of proverbs, published in 1546. Acknowledging the cat's air of self-reliance and superiority, it refers to someone who is unintimidated by his supposed "betters."

Belling the cat ～ This expression is derived from the fable told by Aesop and others about a council of mice who decided that in order to be aware of the cat's approach, they should put a bell around its neck. Of course, the question then became, "But who should bell the cat?" and the expression has come to refer to a plan that is the ideal solution to a problem, but is difficult to accomplish.

Like a cat on a hot tin roof ～ Derived from the older British expression "like a cat on hot bricks," this saying refers to someone who appears very ill at ease.

Grinning like a Cheshire cat ～ This is a reference to Lewis Carroll's smiling feline. *See* CHESHIRE CAT.

Looks like the cat who's swallowed the canary ～ This expression is used to describe a person who 'looks' guilty, although I'm not so sure any cat feels guilt after such an act. It's an American phrase that dates back to the 1870s.

The cat's whiskers ～ This phrase is used to refer to something that is very special. Its use probably came about because the cat's prominent whiskers are certainly remarkable. Two other phrases which are similar are: "the cat's pajama's" and "the cat's meow." All three expressions are thought to originate in the 1920s.

Pink Panther, The ～ This tall, lanky cartoon cat first appeared in the opening credits of the movie *The Pink Panther* staring Peter Sellers in 1964. In the film itself, the "pink panther" is actually a diamond which a cat burglar named the Phantom is desperately seeking. The credits featuring the cartoon Pink Panther received as many raves as the movie. As a result, the Pink Panther was featured in a series of gags in the opening credits of seven of the eight Pink Panther movies. Because of his popularity, United Artists made the Pink Panther a star of his own cartoon, *The Pink Phink,* in 1964. Animators DePatie and Freleng created the cartoon and Henry Mancini supplied the music. Among the other cartoons starring the Pink Panther were *Super Pink* in 1966, *Pink-A-Rella* in 1969 in which he played the fairy godfather to Cinderella, *Pink Plasma* in 1975, and *Pink at First Sight* in which he worked as a singing and dancing Valentine's Day messenger. DePatie-Freleng Enterprises produced ninety-five separate cartoon shorts in all. Their cartoons appeared on television. In addition, they produced cartoons specifically for television. In 1969, *The Pink Panther Show* aired on NBC. Also appearing on NBC was *The New Pink Panther Show* in 1971; *The Pink Panther Laff and a Half-Hour* in 1976; *Think Pink Panther!* in 1978; and "Pink Panther and Sons" in 1983. ABC aired "The All-New Pink Panther Show" in 1978. The Pink Panther was not confined to movie theaters and television. Gold Key published eighty-seven issues of the Pink Panther comic book from 1971 to 1984. In the comic books, the Pink Panther is a fairly middle-class cat who works as a bank teller and jogs in the park. One might say the Pink Panther rose to new heights in 1988 when he starred as one of the balloons in the Macy's Thanksgiving Day Parade.

Poe, Edgar Allan ～ (1809–1849) The

American short story writer, poet, and critic had a fondness for cats dating from early childhood and his adored Tib, a cat belonging to a distant relative. Once grown, he had his own cat, a large tortoiseshell cat named Catarina. Catarina traveled with Poe and his wife, Virginia, wherever they went and would sit on his shoulder when he was writing. When Virginia was dying of consumption and Poe was too poor to provide heat for her, a visitor to the house reported that her only source of warmth was Poe's coat and Catarina, who slept on her chest to warm her. Poe dearly loved the affectionate cat.

So, one may wonder, why did Poe write the gruesome horror story THE BLACK CAT, in which a madman, who kills and mutilates his cat, is haunted and maligned by a devil-cat who brutally avenges the pet's death? Could sweet and loyal Catarina have served, in some way, as inspiration? Poe did own a black cat, but its name is not known. Cats appear in over a dozen of Poe's stories.

A horror movie called *The Black Cat*, starring Bela Lugosi and Boris Karloff, was made in 1934. Although Poe's name was used for publicity purposes, the film bears little relationship to the original tale.

Pope Leo XII ～ (1760–1829) The Ro-

man pontiff owned a large gray and red cat with black stripes called Micetto who was born in the Vatican. When Micetto was a kitten, the Pope carried him around in the sleeve of his papal robe. Pope Leo XII was very fond of cats and in his will provided for Micetto after his demise, as noted in a a letter written by the French author and ambassador François René Chateaubriand. "I have as a companion a big grayish-red cat . . . born in the Vatican, in the Raphael Loggia. Leo XII brought it up in a fold of his robes where I had often looked at it enviously when the Pontiff gave me an audience . . . It was called 'the Pope's cat' . . . I am trying to make it forget exile, the Sistine Chapel, the sun on Michelangelo's cupola, where it used to walk, far above the earth."

Potter, Beatrix ～ (1886–1943) The En-

glish writer and artist, who was the creator of Peter Rabbit and other popular animal characters, also used cat stories and illustrations in her work. She lived a secluded life in the Lake District, where she sketched the rabbits, squirrels, hedgehogs, and cats that she observed near her home and although her most well-known animal characters assume human traits, she was equally adept at lovely naturalistic depictions. She created her first book, *The Tale of Peter Rabbit*, in 1893 to amuse a sick child and it was privately printed in 1900. She published twenty-three books in all, including *The Tale of Miss Moffet* (1906) and the cat-centered *The Tale of Tom Kitten* (1907).

Studies of a Cat, by Beatrix Potter. Though the British artist is most well known for her Peter Rabbit books, she was an accomplished naturalistic painter as well.

𝒫𝒪𝒲𝒜ℛ𝒮 *(Pet Owners with AIDS/ ARC Resource Service, Inc.)* ∽ A volunteer organization in New York City that serves the needs of pet owners with AIDS or ARC (AIDS-related complex), POWARS enables people to keep the pets even when they are too sick to care for them. Volunteers may clean the litter box, walk the dog, take the cat to the vet, bring food for the pet (patients pay on a sliding scale for food and vet care), and perform any other pet service needed.

POWARS was founded in 1988 by Steve Kohn and Howard Greenberg. Kohn says when they started POWARS there were more dogs than cats, but in 1993 there were about two cats to every dog as well as over four hundred volunteers. POWARS can be reached by writing to P.O. Box 1116, Madison Square Garden, New York, NY 10159 or calling 212/744-0842. In 1993 there were about a dozen similar organizations in different cities in the United States, and new ones were starting up.

Proverbs and Sayings

Through good times and bad times, cats have generated many myths, around the world as well as numerous proverbs and sayings. Here are some of the proverbs and sayings that have been preserved over the years, some more well known than others. I have tried to trace their origin as accurately as possible, but many of these sayings have several variations and can be heard in many different countries.

African ~

"A cat may go to a monastery, but she still remains a cat." (Ethiopia)

"When the mouse laughs at the cat, there is a hole nearby." (Nigeria)

American ~

"A cat's a cat and that's that."

"As long as a cat will play, it's okay."

"The cat is mighty dignified until the dog comes by."

Arabic ~

"A cat bitten once by a snake dreads even rope."

Chinese ~

"I gave an order to the cat, and the cat gave it to its tail."

"Happy owner, happy cat. Indifferent owner, reclusive cat."

"A lame cat is better than a swift horse when rats infest the palace."

English ~

"In a cat's eyes, all things belong to cats."

"The cat sees through shut lids."

"Dogs remember faces, cats places."

"When the cat of the house is black, the lasses of lovers will have no lack."

"A cat with a straw tail keeps away from the fire."

"Curiosity killed the cat. Satisfaction brought it back!"

"The dog for the man, the cat for the woman."

· "A cat has nine lives. For three he plays, for three he strays, and for the last three he stays."

"A half-penny cat may look at a king."

"A cat is a lion in a jungle of small bushes."

"He's as honest as the cat when the meat is out of reach."

"Wanton kittens make sober cats."

Flemish ~

"The cat is in the clock." (refers to a quarreling family)

(continued)

Detail from a carpet made in the 1830s by Vermont artist Zeruah Higley Guernsey Caswell. (COURTESY THE METRO-POLITAN MUSEUM OF ART, GIFT OF KATHERINE KEYES, IN MEMORY OF HER FATHER, HOMER EATON KEYES, 1938.)

French ~

"You will be rich or lucky in love if you find one white hair on a black cat."

"A good cat deserves a good rat."

"All cats are bad in May."

"Handsome cats and fat dung heaps are the sign of a good farmer."

"A cat with little ones has never a good mouthful."

"If a girl treads on a cat's tail, she will not find a husband before a year is out."

"The greedy cat makes the servant girl watchful."

"The tongue of a cat is poison, the tongue of the dog cures."

"A scalded cat dreads even cold water."

German ~

"To live long, eat like a cat, drink like a dog."

"Cats are everywhere at home where one feeds them."

Hindu ~

"During his lifetime, a good Hindu must feed at least one cat."

"The cat laps the moonbeams in the bowl of water, thinking them to be milk."

"The rat stops still when the eyes of the cat shine."

Irish ~

"To please himself only the cat purrs."

Indian ~

"A cat is a lion in a jungle of small bushes."

Italian ~

"Old cats mean young mice."

"The cat loves fish, but hates wet feet."

Latin ~

"The cat knows whose lips she licks."

Portuguese ~

"Wherever the mice laugh at the cat, there you will find a hole."

Russian ~

"The cat who scratches, scratches for himself."

Scottish ~

"It is weel said, but who will bell the cat?"

Spanish ~

"The cat always leaves a mark on his friend."

Western European ~

"When the cat's away, the mice will play."

"The cat-moon eats the gray mice of night."

"A borrowed cat catches no mice."

See also BLACK CAT, MYTHS.

Princess Kitty 〜 This former stray has her own fan club and newsletter. She is also the author of an advice column in *Pet Care*, a quarterly publication. (I think the rumor that her mother/owner Karen Payne occasionally gives her some help was started by other jealous cats.) Princess Kitty has mastered over seventy tricks. She can play the piano and slam-dunk a basketball. She has been called "the smartest cat in the world," and has performed throughout the United States. Princess Kitty was a neglected six-month old kitten when Karen Payne found her. In her first movie role, after just one year of training, Princess Kitty played writer Ernest Hemingway's cat Princess in the Key West segment of the six-part mini-series about the life of Hemingway.

Psi-trailing 〜 This term is used to describe the ability of a cat who has returned to his old home, which can be hundreds of miles away, after his family has moved, or a cat who, left behind when the family moved, managed to find his original owners, sometimes hundreds of miles away. The term *psi* was coined by Dr. Joseph Bank Rhine, a researcher into extrasensory perception (ESP), to describe any paranormal event.

In one of the earliest recent studies done on this phenomenon, Professor Frank Herrick drove his own cat to a spot in unfamiliar countryside some five miles away and let him go. He then followed the cat (discreetly, I presume) as the cat made her way back home, taking the shortest route. Herrick's conclusion was that cats have a navigational sense, a "direction constant" that does not rely on remembering the outward details of a trip.

In another known case, when a family in France went on a vacation to a cottage in St. Tropez on the Riviera, over three hundred miles away from home, they brought along their cat.

> Cats, even when robust, have scant liking for the boisterous society of children, and are apt to exert their utmost ingenuity to escape it.
>
> AGNES REPPLIER, American essayist
> (1855–1950)

> I allow my cats to express themselves, never interfere with their romances, and raise them with dogs to broaden their outlook.
>
> MURRAY ROBINSON, twentieth century
> American writer

And when they returned home, they were again accompanied by their cat. But not for long. Soon after the cat disappeared. Six months later, the cat was found at the St. Tropez cottage!

When Kirsten Hicks, an Australian teenager, went on a long overseas trip with his parents, his grandparents, who lived one thousand miles away, agreed to look after his Persian cat Howie. When Kirsten got home, he was heartbroken to learn that his cat had fled. A year later, Howie showed up at the door. He was filthy, sore, and bleeding, but he purred happily when he saw Kirsten.

A vet in New York gave his cat to some friends when he moved to California. About five months later a cat showed up at his door. The cat looked amazingly like the cat he'd left in New York. Inside the house, the cat went immediately to the chair he always used to sit in. The vet did a physical exam of the cat and found that sure enough, it was his cat. The cat had the same unique condition—one vertebrae larger than the other.

𝒫*sychic cats* ∾

There are all kinds of stories about cats with a "sixth sense," cats who can foretell the future and act upon it. The feats range from saving lives to predicting the weather. Here are just a few of the stories that have been reported:

It appears that cats can predict an earthquake several hours before it takes place, according to studies funded by the U.S. Geological Society. In China, cats have been used successfully for years to forecast many earthquakes. In 1975, the cat seismologists in Haicheng, a city near the Great Wall, indicated an oncoming earthquake. City officials ordered an immediate evacuation of the city, and within twenty-four hours a massive earthquake occurred, causing tremendous damage.

Just before an earthquake at Messina, Italy, a merchant noticed that his cats were in a very agitated state, running around and scratching the door to get out. When he opened the door his cats rushed out. He followed them out of the town where they scratched and tore at the grass. A short time later the earthquake occurred. The merchant's house was among many that were totally destroyed.

Before an earthquake, some female cats will carry their kittens outside. It is not known how the cat senses that an earthquake is on the way, but there are several theories. One is that cats are more sensitive to earth vibrations than even the most sophisticated instruments available.

Cats are also often considered good weather forecasters. Ancient Egyptian priests used to carefully watch the behavior of the cats in the temples for signs of the coming weather. It was thought that if the cat washed over her ear the weather would be clear. However, in Scotland it was thought that a cat passing both paws over her ears meant rain is on the way. Japanese sailors believed that a three-colored cat (white, red, and black) can foretell storms and they always had one on board.

In one famous instance, a white cat in Baltimore named Napoleon, belonging to a Mrs. de Shields, would lie prone with his front paws extended and his head tucked down on the ground between them before it rained. In 1930, when there'd been a month-long drought, Napoleon got into his "rain coming" position though the official weather forecast said, "continuing dry weather." Mrs. de Shields called the newspaper to report the change in weather, and when Napoleon's prediction came true, his forecasts were published in the press for the next six years. It is said that in all the years he was never wrong. When the cat died, "Napoleon the Weather Prophet, 1917–1936" was inscribed on his tombstone.

In another case in Lawrence, Kansas, a farm cat gave birth to a litter of kittens, caring for them

The French astronomer Joseph de Lalande detected the cat-shaped Constellation Felis *in the sky, from* Atlas Coelstis, *by J. E. Bode, 1799.*

in the barn. One day the farmer noticed that one kitten was missing. The next day another kitten had disappeared. Several days later all the kittens were missing, along with the mother. A short time after the cats had left, tornados struck the area and completely destroyed the barn. The next morning a neighbor, who lived several miles away, called to say that the cat and kittens had spent the last several days in his barn.

During World War II, many cat owners in London credited their cats for saving their lives. Their cats would become agitated and seek a place to hide *before* the sirens went off warning that a bombing mission was en route. In her book *A Passion for Cats*, English writer Beryl Reid recalls that during World War II her cat would hide whenever a German plane flew overhead, but would just ignore British planes that passed by. Many cats received "We Also Served" medals from the government in recognition of their ability to predict the air raids.

It has been observed in the past that cats had an extraordinary prescient sense. Alexandre Dumas the Elder, the French author, lived with his mother and his cat, Mysouff. Each morning when Dumas went to work, Mysouff would accompany him part of the way and then return home. He would meet Dumas at the same spot in the afternoon and accompany him home. If Dumas's mother forgot to open the door when it was time for Mysouff to meet Dumas, Mysouff would scratch the door until she released him. However, on the occasional day that Dumas was not coming home on time, Mysouff would not leave the house. The French novelist Honoré de Balzac owned a cat who asked to go out every day in time to meet him coming home from work. When Balzac unexpectedly changed his plans and wasn't coming home, his cat stayed curled in a chair and didn't ask to go out.

In his book *A Cat Is Watching*, Roger Caras tells the story of a large, black stray cat who would show up whenever his daughter, Pamela, returned from college, some two-hundred miles away. The cat, which he called Tom, would arrive just before Pamela arrived for a long weekend or holiday, and depart as soon as she left. When Pamela was away, so was Tom. He never showed up during her absence.

The French author Claude Ferrere had a cat named Kare Kedi who suddenly awoke one night howling. Her hair was rigid and she stared at the wall. Ferrere could not imagine why. The next day he learned that a neighbor who lived in the apartment next door had been murdered at the same time that Kare Kedi became so distressed.

Carol Cotter tells the story of the cat in her office named Charley. Charley gave birth to her kittens in the middle of the office and efforts to move her to a more convenient, out-of-the-way location proved unsuccessful. But suddenly, a little over a week later, Charley was frantically trying to move her babies. She chose a spot in the corner, under the table which held the coffee supplies. That night, after the office was closed, a huge rock crashed through the front window. Large pieces of glass hit the spot in the middle of the office where the kittens had been. The spot to which Charley had moved her kittens was the only protected place where the sharp flying glass did not land.

When the owner of a Persian cat dropped her off at a neighbor's to take care of while she was away, the cat moped for quite a while. Finally, the cat adjusted. About a month later, the cat suddenly got very anxious. She went into a corner and started mewing, refused to eat, and rejected any attempts to soothe her. The next day, the cat was even worse, howling mournfully. About an hour later the neighbor got a phone call telling her that the owner of the cat had died!

And finally, a not-that-remarkable story about my cat Miel—but I did promise him a bit of space in the book. There are two places my adopted orange tabby does not like to go—the vet (not too surprising?) and my house in the country. The visit to the vet is just once a year, but I go up to my house most weekends, and I used to bring Miel. I left the carrier out for days. Without exception, he was cheerful as could be welcoming me home until the day I planned to go to the country. As soon as I opened the door he ran for cover. I sat on the couch nonchalantly and read the newspaper; I made a cup of tea. Nothing worked. He knew. And he won. Eventually I relied on a cat neighbor to feed and water him over the weekend. Miel, who was born on a farm, became a true Manhattan apartment cat.

The Reverend Samuel Bishop, an English schoolmaster and poet living in the eighteenth century, has perhaps best described the uncanny psychic ability cats have revealed:

If her tail played in frolic mood,
Herself pursuing, by herself pursued;
"See!" cried my nurse, "she bids for rain
    prepare,
A storm, be sure, is gathering in the air;"
If near the fire the kitten's back was found,
Frost was at hand, and snows hung hovering
    round;
Her paw prophetic rais'd above her ear
Foretold a visit, for some friend was near.

> For he purrs in thankfulness when God tells him he is a good cat.
>
> Christopher Smart, English poet
> (1722–1771)

Purring ∾ It is commonly thought that a cat's purring is a sign of contentment. Generally, a cat purrs to indicate friendship or a need for friendship. An injured cat may purr when the vet is treating her, to express the need for help. However, a cat may also purr when it is injured, in pain, in labor, or even dying. It is not known why a cat purrs when in pain or distressed.

Purring is a continuous sound—like a low rumble or vibration. (The French call the sound a "ron ron.") A kitten can purr at the same time it is suckling. A cat can purr with its mouth closed, though it is not known exactly how it accomplishes this. It has been suggested that the purr is the result of an electrical impulse generated in the brain and carried along the central nervous system, causing certain muscles, particularly those in the throat and vocal chords, to contract and vibrate.

Cats start purring when they are kittens, sometimes when they are just a week old. Purring appears to be a primal response. They purr when they are being suckled by their mother, assuring the mother that all is well and that the milk is indeed arriving at its destination. The mother cat also purrs when she is nursing her kittens. It's her way of letting the kittens know that she too is happy and content. In later life, just as the kitten has purred when nursing, an adult cat will purr for its owner who now represents a mother figure to it.

If you listen carefully to your cat you'll hear different variations of purring. The rougher the purr and more distinct the sound of each "beat," the more intense is the cat's pleasure. When the purring is soft and smooth it is a sign that the cat is getting bored or tired. A smooth high purr usually is in response to something the cat wants that she thinks will bring pleasure. Writer Eric Gurney describes it this way: "There are a wide variety of purrs which range from the almost inaudible to the kind which can be felt through the floor. Loud purring might set up sympathetic vibrations in a building and send it crashing to the ground."

And in his poem "On a Cat Ageing," Scottish professor and poet Alexander Gray puts purring in this light:

> Louder he purrs and louder,
> In one glad hymn of praise
> For all the night's adventures,
> For quiet restful days.

Purring is just one of the characteristics that distinguishes the small, domestic cat from the large wild cats such as the tiger and lion, which do not purr. They roar.

For another insight into the origin of purring, see the BRITISH FOLKTALE in this volume, which I prefer to think of as the real explanation of this phenomenon.

Puss in the Corner ～ This is a children's game in which one player in the middle of the room tries to occupy any position along the walls as players run to change places at a signal.

Pussycat ～ This affectionate term for a cat may come from the Old English word *pusa*, meaning "bag" (something soft and sack-like) or be derived from the sound of a spitting cat. The shortened version, pussy, has unfortunately become a vulgar slang phrase.

Puss in Boots

This is probably the most famous of all cat stories and comes in a number of versions. According to Frederick Cameron Sillar and Ruth Mary Meyler, authors of the book *Cats Ancient & Modern*, "Puss in Boots" first appeared in Giovanni Francesco Straparola's book of fairy tales and fables, which was collected from many different sources and translated into French in 1585. The best-known version, however, remains Charles Perrault's retelling, published in 1696:

There was a miller who left no more estate to the three sons he had than his mill, his ass, and his cat. The partition was soon made. Neither scrivener nor attorney was sent for. They would soon have eaten up all the poor patrimony. The eldest had the mill, the second the ass, and the youngest nothing but the cat. The poor young fellow was quite comfortless at having so poor a lot.

"My brothers," said he, "may get their living handsomely enough by joining their stocks together; but for my part, when I have eaten up my cat and made me a muff of his skin, I must die of hunger."

(continued)

One of the most famous cats in all of literature, Puss in Boots. This illustration by nineteenth-century French artist Gustave Dore was published in Les Contes de Perrault *by Charles Perrault in Paris in 1899.* (COURTESY THE METRO-POLITAN MUSEUM OF ART, GIFT OF MRS. JOHN FISKE, 1960.)

The cat, who heard all this, but made as if he did not, said to him with a grave and serious air:

"Do not thus afflict yourself, my good master. Your fortunes are not so bad as you seem to think. You do not value me highly enough. You need only give me a bag and get a pair of boots made for me that I may scamper through the dirt and the brambles, and you shall see that you have not so bad a portion of me as you imagine."

The cat's master did not build very much upon what he said. He had often seen him play a great many cunning tricks to catch rats and mice, as when he used to hang by the heels, or hide himself in the meal, and make as if he were dead; so that he did not altogether despair of his affording him some help in his miserable condition. When the cat had what he asked for, he booted himself very gallantly, and putting his bag about his neck, he held the strings of it in his two fore paws and went into a warren where there was a great abundance of rabbits. He put bran and sow-thistle into his bag, and stretching out at length, as if he had been dead, he waited for some young rabbits, not yet acquainted with the deceits of the world, to come and rummage his bag for what he had put into it.

Scarce was he lain down but he had what he wanted. Two rash and foolish young rabbits jumped into his bag, and Monsieur Puss, immediately drawing close the strings, took them away without pity. Proud of his prey, he went with it to the palace and asked to speak with his majesty. He was shown upstairs into the King's apartment, and making a low reverence, said to him:

"I have brought you, sire, two rabbits of the warren, which my noble lord the Marquis of Carabas (for that was the title which Puss was pleased to give his master) has commanded me to present to your majesty from him."

"Tell your master," said the King, "that I thank him and that he does me a great deal of pleasure."

Another time he went and hid himself among some standing corn, holding still his bag open, and when a brace of partridges ran into it, he drew the strings and so caught them both. He went and made a present of these to the King, as he had done before of the rabbits which he took in the warren. The King, in like manner, received the partridges with great pleasure and ordered him some money for drink.

The cat continued for two or three months thus to carry his majesty, from time to time, game of his master's taking. One day in particular, when he knew for certain that he was to take the air along the riverside with his daughter, the most beautiful princess in the world, he said to his master:

"If you will follow my advice your fortune is made. You need only go and wash yourself in the river, in that part I shall show you, and leave the rest to me."

The Marquis of Carabas did what the cat advised him to, without knowing why or

(continued)

wherefore. While he was washing the King passed by, and the cat began to cry out:

"Help! help! My Lord Marquis of Carabas is going to be drowned."

At this noise the King put his head out of the coach-window, finding it was the cat who had so often brought him such good game, he commanded his guards to run immediately to the assistance of his lordship the Marquis of Carabas. While they were drawing the poor marquis out of the river, the cat came up to the coach and told the King that while his master was washing there came by some rogues, who went off with his clothes, though he had cried out "Thieves! thieves!" several times as loud as he could.

This cunning cat had hidden them under a great stone. The King immediately commanded the officers of his wardrobe to run and fetch one of his best suits for the Marquis of Carabas.

The King caressed him after a very extraordinary manner, and as the fine clothes he had given him extremely set off his good mien (for he was well-built and very handsome in his person), the King's daughter took a secret inclination to him, and the Marquis of Carabas had no sooner cast two or three respectful and somewhat tender glances but she fell in love with him to distraction. The King would needs have him come into the coach and take part of the airing. The cat, quite overjoyed to see his project begin to succeed, marched on before, and meeting with some countrymen who were mowing a meadow, he said to them:

"Good people, you who are mowing, if you do not tell the King that the meadow you mow belongs to my Lord Marquis of Carabas, you shall be chopped as fine as herbs for the pot."

The King did not fail to ask of the mowers to whom the meadow they were mowing belonged.

"To my Lord Marquis of Carabas," they answered all together, for the cat's threats had made them terribly afraid.

"This," said the marquis, "is a meadow which never fails to yield a plentiful harvest every year."

The master cat, who went still on before, met with some reapers and said to them:

"Good people, you who are reaping, if you do not tell the King that all this corn belongs to the Marquis of Carabas, you shall be chopped as fine as herbs for the pot."

The King, who passed by a moment after, would needs know to whom all that corn did belong.

"To my Lord Marquis of Carabas," replied the reapers, and the King was very well pleased with it, as well as with the marquis, whom he congratulated thereupon. The master cat, who went always before, said the same words to all he met, and the King was astonished at the vast estates of my Lord Marquis of Carabas. Lord Monsieur Puss came at last to a stately castle, the master of which was an ogre, the richest that had ever been known; for all the lands which the king had then gone over belonged to this castle. The cat, who had taken care to inform himself who this ogre was and what he could do, asked to speak with him, saying he could not pass so near his castle without having the honor of paying his respects to him.

The ogre admitted him and made him sit down.

"I have been assured," said the cat, "that you have the gift of being able to change yourself into all sorts of creatures you have a mind to. You can, for example, transform yourself into a lion, or an elephant."

"That is true," answered the ogre very briskly; "and to convince you, you shall see me now become a lion."

Puss was so sadly terrified at the sight of a lion so near him that he cried out loudly, and would have run away had not the ogre quickly resumed his natural form. However, he owned he had been very much frightened.

"I have been moreover informed," said the cat, "but I know not how to believe it, that you have also the power to take on you the shape of the smallest animals; for example, to change yourself into a rat or a mouse. But I must own to you I take this to be impossible."

"Impossible!" cried the ogre. "You shall see that presently."

And at the same time he changed himself into a mouse and began to run about the floor. Puss no sooner perceived this but he fell upon him and ate him up.

Meanwhile the King, who saw, as he passed, this fine castle of the ogre's, noted its beauty and marveled at its size and grandeur. He had a mind to go into it, and ordered his coach to be driven up to the entrance. Puss, who heard the noise of his majesty's coach running over the drawbridge, ran out and said to the King:

"Your majesty is welcome to this castle of my Lord Marquis of Carabas."

"What! my Lord Marquis," cried the King, "and does this castle also belong to you? There can be nothing finer than this court and all the stately buildings which surround it. Let us go into it, if you please."

The marquis gave his hand to the princess and followed the King, who went first. They passed into a spacious hall, where they found a magnificent collation, which the ogre had prepared for his friends who were that very day to visit him but dared not enter, knowing the King was there. His majesty was perfectly charmed with the good qualities of my Lord Marquis of Carabas, as was his daughter, who had fallen violently in love with him, and seeing the vast estate he possessed, said to him, after having drunk five or six glasses:

"It will be owing to yourself only, my Lord Marquis, if you are not my son-in-law."

The marquis, making several low bows, accepted the honor which his majesty conferred upon him, and forthwith that very same day, married the princess.

Puss became a great lord and never ran after mice any more but only for his diversion.

Ragdoll

Ragdoll ∼ The ragdoll breed originated in California in the mid-1960s, when Ann Baker mated a longhair, free-running cat, Josephine, with a Birman. The result was Daddy War Bucks—the father of the ragdoll.

This longhair cat has several distinctive characteristics, among them: she tends to become "limp" in a person's arms when held (hence the name ragdoll) and she is the largest of the domestic breeds of cats, with males weighing an average of fifteen to twenty pounds and females weighing in at between ten and thirteen pounds. There are three coat patterns for the ragdoll: bicolor, colorpoint, and mitted; and four colors: seal-point, chocolate-point, blue-point, and frost-point.

PERSONALITY: Ragdolls have a gentle, docile nature and become very attached to their owners.

Religion and cats

Religion and cats ∼ Cats have played a prominent and persistent role in religion all over the world. In some instances cats have been worshiped as gods. At other times, cats have been looked upon as the Devil's helpmate, or even the Devil himself. How cats have been regarded in the context of religion has played a major role in how they have been treated. For more information on the role of the cat in religion, see BIRMAN, BUDDHA (India); BURMESE, EGYPT, MOHAMMED; SIAMESE; and WITCHCRAFT.

Renoir, Pierre Auguste

Renoir, Pierre Auguste ∼ (1841–1919) This French Impressionist painter included cats in many of his pictures. Some of the most well known are *La petite fille au chat* (*Young Woman with Cat*), *Portrait de Madame Manet. Julie Manet with a Cat*, and *Sleeping Girl with Cat.* The cats in his paintings were usually content and curled up on the arm or lap of his model, emphasizing the softness and soothing pleasure of the women he loved painting.

> Of all animals, the cat alone attains to the contemplative life. He regards the wheel of existence from without, like the Buddha.
>
> ANDREW LANG, Scottish poet

Ragdolls come in a variety of colors. This one is a champion. (COURTESY SUSAN BUDGIN.)

𝕽*ex* ～ The first cat in the rex breed was one of a litter of five kittens born to a barn cat in Cornwall, England, in 1950, which became known as a Cornish Rex. When it was mated with a similar cat in Devon, England, in 1966, the kitten had straight hair, proving that the CORNISH REX and DEVON REX, although they looked alike, were actually two different cats resulting from different gene combinations. Besides the Cornish and Devon rex there is the German rex, which came on the scene in East Germany in 1951. The Cornish rex and German rex are compatible and can be successfully mated. Because rex cats lack the long guard hairs found on other cats, and shed less, they are generally better tolerated by people allergic to cats.

PERSONALITY: Rex cats are usually playful and affectionate. *See* CORNISH REX and DEVON REX.

𝕽*hubarb* ～ In this 1951 movie staring Ray Milland and Jan Sterling, a millionaire dies and leaves his baseball club to his cat, Rhubarb. Rhubarb turns out to be a wonderful manager, winning the pennant race. Rhubarb, whose real

Women with a Cat, *painted by French artist Auguste Renoir c. 1875.* (© 1994 NATIONAL GALLERY OF ART, WASHINGTON, GIFT OF MR. AND MRS. BENJAMIN E. LEVY.)

name was ORANGEY, was a big winner as well. He won the first PATSY Award (Picture Animal Top Star award) from the American Humane Society.

Richelieu, *Armand Jean du Plessis* ∾
(1585–1642) The cardinal, who was also a politician and chief minister in France from 1624 until his death, loved cats from childhood. When he became virtually head of state, he kept two servants whose only function was to take care of his cats. When he would awake in the morning, a handful of kittens would be brought to play on his bed. Among his cats were Lucifer, a beautiful black angora; Soumise, who shared his couch; Rubis, who sounded like a pot of water when he purred; Rita, whose favorite spot for a catnap were the edicts and decrees; Perruque and Racan, whose mother gave birth in the wig of the poet Marquis de Racan (I know the wigs were big then, but I didn't know they were *that* big); Gazette; Pyrame; and Thisbe, to name just a few.

Richelieu built a cattery for his cats at Versailles and provided in his will for the future care of at least fourteen of his cats who were with him when he died. Two of the cats were to get an annual income of twenty livres till the end of their lives and the other were to get ten. Two guardians were also provided for to care for the cats as long as they lived. Unfortunately for the bequested cats, however, all did not go as planned. One night Swiss regiments stormed the cattery and a massacre ensued. All that could be heard was the laughter of men and the screeching of the poor cats.

Romeo and Juliet ∾ The 1990 movie
version of Shakespeare's play *Romeo and Juliet* featured more than one hundred real cats in the starring roles. Juliet is played by a white, longhair Turkish angora. Romeo is a longhair gray. The only noncat in the movie is actor John Hurt, who plays an old Venetian bag lady, La Dame aux Chats. Voices expressing the thoughts of the leading cat characters include Maggie Smith, Ben Kingsley, Vanessa Redgrave, Francesca Annis, and Victor Spinetti. The movie took a year to make and was filmed in Belgium, Germany, Italy, and the United States, set to the music of Prokofiev's *Romeo and Juliet*, played by the London Symphony Orchestra.

Rooftop cats ∾ These life-sized ceramic
cats began appearing in the Middle Ages in Europe, mostly in France. At that time there was a superstition that a cat was a shield or guardian against evil spirits. What better way to ward off those evil spirits than having a permanent cat stationed on the roof? By the nineteenth century people were no longer that suspicious, but they retained the rooftop cats as an attractive decoration. So, the next time you are traveling in Europe, especially France, there is a reason to be looking up.

Roosevelt, Teddy ∾ (1859–1919) The
twenty-sixth president of the United States, who served between 1901 and 1909, was also a cat lover. T. R.'s gray cat Slippers had run of the White House. It's not known if his six toes helped him have fun. Slippers would often disappear then reappear. One time he reappeared as the president was leading a group of prominent guests into a state banquet. Slippers was sprawled across the carpet in the middle of the hall. As Roosevelt walked down with an ambassador's wife on his arm, he saw the cat directly in his path. He bowed to the woman as he led her around the cat. The entire procession of formally

dressed dignitaries followed the leader and made a detour around the cat, who nonchalantly ignored the whole thing. Another favorite cat, Tom Quartz, was the subject of a biography by thus, contrary to recent publishing history, establishing the tradition of presidential pet memoirs.

Rumanian folktales

Rumanian folktales ～ Have you ever wondered "Why Does a Cat Sit in the Doorstep in the Sun?" You'll find an explanation in the Rumanian tale which bears that name. Many long years ago, when Noah built the ark, he kept the door wide open so that all the animals could board, but when he called his wife to come on board she refused. Finally he said, "Oh, you devil, come in." Now this was just what the Devil himself was waiting for, an invitation. The Devil thought this would be the ideal time to put an end to all of God's creatures, so he changed himself into a mouse, followed the wife on board, and started gnawing on a plank to make a hole. When Noah saw him, he threw a fur glove at the mouse. The glove turned into a cat, who immediately seized the mouse. Wishing to end the fracas, Noah threw both overboard. The cat let the mouse go and swam back to the ark, where she lay on the doorstep to dry herself in the sun. And ever since, cats like to bask in the sun.

Russian blue

Russian blue ～ The Russian blue breed has been known by many different names over the years. She was first called the Archangel cat because it is believed that sailors brought the cats to Western Europe in the 1860s from the Russian port of Archangelsk on the White Sea, about 150 miles south of the Arctic Circle. Cat lover and artist Harrison Weir described them as having a "deeper, purer tint than the English cross-breeds, with . . . larger ears and eyes," and "larger and longer in the head."

Later this cat was known by a variety of names, including the Spanish cat, the Maltese cat, and the foreign blue.

In the late 1940s and 1950s breeders in Scandinavia and Great Britain attempted to develop the breed. This resulted in the show standards for the Russian blue being updated in 1966.

Russian blues were found in North America as early as the beginning of the twentieth century, when they were often called Maltese. In 1947, they started to be bred regularly by a Texan named C. A. Commaire, who imported two Russian blues from England. It was another twenty years before they started appearing in cat shows regularly.

The Russian blue is known for her short, fine, and very plush coat. It can be stroked both ways without exposing the skin. The dense coat protects the cats in cold weather, making them very hearty.

A Russian blue named Vashka, who belonged to Tsar Nicholas I of Russia, is probably the most well-known of the breed. It was undoubtedly one of the most pampered. Russian blues are considered a welcome omen of good luck.

PERSONALITY: The Russian blue is very quiet and has a loving temperament.

> The soul of another is darkness, and a cat's soul more than most.
>
> —ANTON CHEKHOV, Russian playwright and writer (1860–1904)

Russian folktale

Russian folktale ～ An old peasant was tired of his scarred tomcat, who was always fighting and had already lost one ear. To get rid of it he tied the cat securely in a bag and dropped it in

Probably a natural Russian breed, the elegant Russian Blue possesses a unique, plush double coat. (PHOTOGRAPH BY ISABELLE FRANCAIS.)

the middle of the forest. It took the cat some time, but he was finally able to chew a big enough hole in the bag to get out. The forest was different from the village he was used to, but he thought to himself, "I was the head cat in the village and I will be the head cat here, too." He found an old, abandoned shack which he made into his home and then went to find some mice or birds on which to dine. He remembered that in the village he had never had to forage for food for he was always fed by the villagers and decided that he should not have to hunt for food now either.

The next day, walking in the forest he saw a pretty fox. The cat had never seen such a wild beast before. The fox went up to the cat and very politely asked who he was. (She thought he was very handsome with his one ear.) He told her that his name was Cat Ivanovitch, and he'd been sent from far away to be the head forester. So the fox, whose name was Lisabeta Ivanovna, invited the cat to her home for dinner, where she fed him a tasty dish of game. When she found out that Cat Ivanovitch was not married she shyly suggested that she could be his wife. They married and soon Lisabeta was out hunting food for her lazy husband.

One day, the fox ran into an old friend, the handsome wolf, and told him she was now married to Cat Ivanovitch, who'd been sent from afar to be the head forester. The wolf asked when he could come and pay respects to the head forester, and Lisabeta told the wolf that to pay respects to her husband, he would have to bring him a sheep. As the wolf went to look for a sheep, Lisabeta thought of how smart she'd been because she would not have to hunt for food. When she next ran into the bear, she told him the same story—and that to pay respects to her husband the bear would have to bring him an ox.

When the wolf and bear arrived near the home of the fox with their prey, each was too afraid of the masterful Cat Ivanovitch to go up to the house. They found a young hare and made him go to the house to say they had arrived. Still frightened, the bear hid in a tree and the wolf, who could not climb a tree, hid under a pile of leaves. When the bear spotted Cat Ivanovitch approaching he told the wolf, "But what a little one he is for sure!" When the cat came upon the ox he started ripping it apart, purring in delight. But to the bear it sounded like the cat was saying, "Small, small, small." The bear was terrified that the cat wouldn't find the ox sufficient and come after him. Meanwhile, the wolf, as carefully and quietly as possible, moved a few leaves so that he could see what was going on. Hearing the leaves rustling, Cat Ivanovitch thought it was a mouse and pounced—landing on the wolf's nose. The wolf, terrified, ran off as fast as he could, not knowing that the cat was far more frightened of him. Screaming, Cat Ivanovitch ran up the tree for safety. The bear, who thought the cat was now coming after him, jumped from the top of the tree and landed on the ground with broken bones. He hobbled off as fast as he could. And ever since then all the wild beasts have been afraid of the cat.

> The cat went here and there
> And the moon spun round like a top,
> And the nearest kin of the moon,
> The creeping cat, looked up.
>
> "The Cat and the Moon," WILLIAM BUTLER Yeats, Irish poet (1865–1939)

Salem ∼ This extraordinary cartoon tabby made its first appearance in 1962 in "Archie's Madhouse." Salem actually belongs to Sabrina, the good witch of Riverdale, of *Archie* comics fame. Salem appeared regularly in the comic book *Sabrina* from 1971 to 1983. Salem could perform tricks of white magic (the good kind) just like Sabrina. Salem and Sabrina have also appeared in television shows, including *The Archie Comedy Hour with Sabrina* on CBS in 1969; *Sabrina, the Teenage Witch*, a series which ran on CBS in 1971, and *Superwitch* on NBC in 1977. Salem went on to be a regular character in the comic strip *The Archies.*

Salisbury Cathedral ∼ This cathedral in Salisbury, England, was home to two cats during the 1970s and 1980s—Ginge and his sister, Tid, who were born in the cathedral stoneyard of the same mother, a ginger and white stray. Of all the litters she had, Ginge and Tid were the only kittens for whom no homes were found so they remained at the cathedral. Though Tid was on the timid side, Ginge surely earned his keep, catching mice and rats. Ginge would often sit in the mason's workshop and watch as the stone was shaped and chiseled, and to make coming and going as convenient as possible for the cats, a flap door was put in the door of the workshop. On the weekends and holidays, volunteers would bring food. Ginge died in 1988 at the age of thirteen; Tid died two years later at the age of fifteen. Both have memorial stones marking their graves—stones carved in the workshop where Ginge resided for so many years.

Sarton, May ∼ (b. 1912) The American poet and essayist is a great lover of cats. In many books, such as her *Journal of Solitude* and *The Magnificent Spinster*, she mixes musings on cats with other speculations on life. In *The Fur Person*, she provides the Ten Commandments of the Gentleman Cat:

I. A Gentleman Cat has an immaculate shirt front and paws at all times.
II. A Gentleman Cat allows no constraint of his person, even loving constraint.

III. A Gentleman Cat does not mew except in extremity. He makes his wishes known and waits.

IV. When addressed, a Gentleman Cat does not move a muscle. He looks as if he hadn't heard.

V. When frightened, a Gentleman Cat looks bored.

VI. A Gentleman Cat takes no interest in other people's affairs, unless he is directly concerned.

VII. A Gentleman Cat approaches food slowly, however hungry he may be, and decides at least three feet away whether it is Good, Fair, Passable, or Unworthy. If Unworthy, he pretends to scratch earth over it.

VIII. A Gentleman Cat gives thanks for a Worthy meal, by licking the plate so clean that a person might think it had been washed.

IX. A Gentleman Cat is never hasty when choosing a housekeeper.

Scarlatti, Domenico ~ (1685?–1757)

The Italian harpsichordist, organist, and composer must have owned a cat. His piano piece "The Cat's Fugue" is said to represent a cat padding across a keyboard—a habit not uncommon to cats who have access to a piano.

See also MUSIC.

Schweitzer, Albert ~ (1875–1965)

Schweitzer, who won the Nobel Peace Prize in 1952, shared quarters with his cat Sizi while working as a missionary in Africa. Though the great French philosopher, doctor, and musicologist was left-handed, to accommodate Sizi, he would frequently write prescriptions with his right hand so as not to disturb his cat, who liked to fall asleep on his left arm. According to Schweitzer, "There are two means of refuge from the misery of life: music and cats." (A very clever man, indeed!)

Scottish fold ~

This cat breed, which arose from a spontaneous mutation, got its name from its "folded" ears, which curl tightly over its head. The first Scottish fold, a white cat named Susie, appeared in the village of Coupar Angus in east-central Scotland in 1961. Susie's parents were straight-eared farm cats. When a shepherd named William Ross and his wife, Mary, heard about the odd kitten they paid a visit and the McCraes promised them a kitten if Susie had a litter of kittens with folded ears. Two years later the Rosses received a female all-white kitten, with folded ears, whom they called Snooks. Ross bred the cat with a red tabby and the offspring included one fold-eared kitty. This cat in turn was bred with a British shorthair and the breed was born. By the 1970s three Scottish folds were in the United States at a genetics research center in Massachusetts. In 1978 they were accepted for championship competition in the United States.

The fold has a large round head, large alert round eyes, and full round cheeks. The body is short and powerful. To prevent breed irregularities, a Scottish fold with the semi-dominant "folded ear" gene may be bred with a British or American shorthair. The kittens may have either folded or straight (perk) ears. Though the perk-eared cats are recognized as pedigree folds, they cannot be shown in championship competition.

The Scottish fold longhair is descended from Susie, though it took the Scottish fold longhair a longer time to gain appreciation and recognition than its sibling—the shorthair version.

PERSONALITY: Scottish folds tend to be playful, even-tempered, and relaxed.

The Scottish fold is instantly recognized by its folded ears, a natural mutation that first appeared in Scotland in the 1960s. (PHOTOGRAPH BY ISABELLE FRANCAIS.)

Scratching ～ *See* CLAWS.

Sex ～ *See* MATING.

SH III ～ SH III is the cat in the Fancy Feast Gourmet Cat Food commercials. He is owned by Scot Hart and began his career at the age of nine weeks, when he starred in the movie *The Jerk* with Steve Martin. The Chinchilla Persian has also appeared in such movies as *Scrooged* and *National Lampoon's Christmas Vacation.* He has been called the Cary Grant of cats.

Sheba Selectacat ～ If you have doubts about getting a cat, this computer program can help you choose the type of cat you'd be most comfortable with (or the type of cat who'd be most comfortable with you!). The program analyzes your responses to ten life-style questions, such as how much company your cat will have during the day, if you already have other cats, how much time you can devote to grooming, and so forth. (The program will select the "right" breeds for you if you send a stamped, self-addressed envelope and your request for the Selectacat questionnaire to: Sheba Selectacat, 3250 East 44th Street, Vernon, CA 90058-0853.)

Shorthair ～ Cats with short hair are far more common than cats with long hair and have been around for thousands of years. It wasn't until the 1800s, that suddenly pedigree shorthairs appeared, cats who were specifically bred to be in shows and to do so had to meet specific standards. The shorthairs fall into three major categories: BRITISH SHORTHAIR, AMERICAN SHORTHAIR, and the ORIENTAL SHORTHAIRS. The British shorthair is sturdy with a strong, muscular body on short legs. Her head is broad and round and her fur is short and dense. The American shorthair, which is distantly related to the European shorthair, is generally larger and leaner with longer legs, an oblong head, and large round eyes. The Oriental, or Foreign, shorthair has long, slim legs, fine short hair, slanted eyes, and large, pointed ears. Of course, within these categories there are numerous variations including the Siamese, Manx, Abyssinian, Korat, Havana, and Burmese, to name a few of the more prominent shorthair breeds.

PERSONALITY: Just as there is a great variety of shorthairs, there is a great variety of temperaments.

Shows ～ The first cat shows took place as long ago as the end of the sixteenth century in England. The first one that was recorded in 1598 was part of an English fair. These cat shows were fairly casual events. The cat show would be at the county fair where it was an additional attraction. Cats were awarded prizes for being the biggest, the most beautiful, and the best mouser.

The first formal organization of cat fanciers was organized in England and came to be known as the National Cat Club. In 1871, the first official cat show was held at London's Crystal Palace. Artist Harrison Weir was the president of the National Cat Club and organized that show. He didn't know what to expect. In his 1889 book *Our Cats and All About Them* Weir says, "there lay the cats in their different pens, reclining on crimson cushions, making no sound save now and then a homely purring, as from time to time they lapped the nice new milk provided for them. Yes, there were big cats, very big cats, middling-sized cats, and small cats, cats of all colours and markings, and beautiful pure white Persian cats." The cat show at Crystal Palace was *very* successful and showed as well as promoted the growing enthusiasm for the cat in England.

The first notable cat show in the United States was held in 1881 at Bunnell's Museum in New York, written up in *The New York Times*. In 1895, the first official cat show in the United States took place at Madison Square Garden in New York City. It was also very successful. By 1906, eleven years later, cat shows were being held regularly all over the United States.

Cat shows are held by cat clubs and associations. In the United States the Cat Fanciers Association (CFA) in Manasquan, New Jersey, is the largest. Another large association is The International Cat Association (TICA) based in Harlingen, Texas. In 1993 there were over half a dozen breeder's clubs in the United States. (See list in Appendix.)

There are two kinds of cat shows—unofficial, which don't have the backing of a recognized club—and official, which do. In shows in the United States the classes are divided into Open, Champion, Grand Champion, and Household Pet. Many people are unaware that their cat does not have to have a pedigree to enter a cat show. The Household Pet category has its own titles and awards. In order to take part in a show, household pets must be altered. Kittens aged four to eight months can also be entered in kitten competitions. Kittens eight months and older are considered cats.

At cat shows in Great Britain, entering cats have to be "vetted in." A veterinarian will check for fleas and mouth and eye disorders to make sure the cat is healthy. This is not done in shows in North America.

Cats are judged on specific features and how well those features match the standard for that breed. Standards vary from breed to breed. For example, here are standards and points for two different breeds:

Blue Persian	points	Siamese	points
head and eyes	30	eyes	
		type	10
		color	10
coat	10	coat	
color	20	texture	10
		body color	10
		point color	10
eye color	10	head	20
balance	5	legs and paws	5
type	20	ears	5
refinement	5	tail	3
		body	22
		condition	5

Becoming a cat show judge is no easy matter. The judges must meet certain criteria. Before even applying they have to have shown their skill in breeding cats, with at least five to seven years of consecutive breeding experience. They must serve on show committees in different capacities and gain experience by clerking for judges at the shows. When they are accepted into the judging program they must pass examinations on breed standards and show-ring procedures. And they must apprentice with certified instructors at a certain number of shows. In *The Complete Cat Book*, Richard Gebhardt observes that a judge learns a lot about the cat just by carrying it from its cage in the show ring to the judging table. "Judges have already determined much about that animal," he says. "They know whether its coat feels tacky or dirty, or silky and clean. They know whether a cat is down on weight or too stout. They know whether it has the feel of an animal in peak show condition." Gebhardt, who was a president of the CFA, started judging cats early in the 1950s.

A judge spends one to two minutes evaluating each cat. In that brief time he or she is constantly comparing the cat to the standards for that breed. A judge may be required to see over two hundred cats at a show. Gebhardt says that when he judges he finds it easier to look for faults in the cat than virtues.

When I go to a cat show, every cat looks just perfect to me. I can truly appreciate what those judges do. (*See also* BREEDS.)

I shall see beauty
But none to match your living grace . . .

"To a Siamese Cat," MICHAEL JOSEPH,
twentieth century British author
and publisher

Siamese Cats

But what are their faults compared with their virtues—with their sense of humour, their fidelity, their dauntless courage . . . their conversational powers (if you have Siamese cats you must talk to them a lot), their awareness of themselves so that each one of my eleven knows its own name, their love of people rather than place; their honesty (by which I mean they'll take a lobster off the table in front of you), their continuous passionate interest in all that is going on around them, and their depth of affection, which they are able to show in so many exquisite ways?

COMPTON MACKENSIE, British novelist
(1883–1972)

Siamese ～ The Siamese is probably the most popular and well-known shorthair cat breed. She is a slender and graceful cat with a wedge-shaped face and sapphire-blue eyes. Although their exact origin is not known, it is thought that Siamese cats originated in Siam (now known as Thailand) hundreds of years ago. The *Cat-Book of Poems,* which is believed to be centuries old and was rescued from the ancient Siamese city of Ayuda, contains verses that describe white-haired cats with black tails, feet, and ears. That description could have been written today about the seal-point Siamese.

According to legend, the king of Siam owned Siamese cats who were trained to roam the palace and jump on the back of intruders. The cats played an important role in guarding the temple, and their role in the transmigration of souls was even more important. It was believed that the soul of someone who died lived on in the body of a sacred cat for a period of time before going on to total perfection in the next life. The dark mark on the back of a Siamese cat's neck has been called the temple mark, and is said to have been left by the touch of a god who reached down to pick up the cat. Siamese cats were treasured among the wealthy and titled. Owners kept them inside to protect them, and they rarely allowed an unaltered cat to leave the country. Not surprisingly, legends about the Siamese cat abound. One myth is that they developed crossed eyes after staring long and hard at the Buddha's gold goblet. Another is that the Siamese cat's tail is kinked because she knotted it to remember something.

The first Siamese cats known to be from the king of Siam's cattery were imported to England in 1884. The king gave the two seal-points, Pho and Mia, as a departure gift to the British Consul, Owen Gould. Among the more famous owners of Siamese cats were British Prime Minister Harold Wilson, whose favorite was named Nemo, and Leon Blum, the first socialist premier of France, who kept only Siamese cats.

Early in the 1900s interest in the Siamese developed in the United States. The first Siamese cat in the United States was reported to be a gift to President Rutherford B. Hayes. Here, as in England, the breed appealed to the rich and titled— the only ones who could afford them: the first Siamese to land on U.S. soil cost upward of a thousand dollars in addition to transportation costs and other fees. Siamese bred in the United States were a bit more reasonable, selling for between two hundred and a thousand dollars. Breeding the cats could be quite profitable. One Siamese cat who lived to be seventeen sired more than 1300 kittens.

During the 1950s, the great popularity of the Siamese waned. Physical problems developed with the breed, and as too many kittens were bred, supply outweighed demand. Although still widely admired, the Siamese is trying to regain the status it enjoyed in the first half of the twentieth century.

There are four major categories of Siamese:

• Seal-point (cream coat with brown markings)
• Blue-point (bluish-white coat with blue markings)
• Chocolate-point (ivory coat with milk chocolate markings)
• Lilac-point (white coat with frosty gray markings).

A beautiful blue lynx-point Elorac Siamese, Orphan Annie, owned by Carole K. Hamelman. Abandoned by her mother, Orphan Annie was hand-fed around the clock by Ms. Hamelman and became a champion. (COURTESY CAROLE K. HAMELMAN.)

This classic seal-point Siamese, Skooter, belongs to Alison Steele, owner of New York City's Complete Boutique, Just Cats. (PHOTOGRAPH COURTESY PETOGRAPHY)

Other Siamese colors include red, cream, lynx, seal tortie, blue tortie, chocolate tortie, and lilac tortie. (Tortie is a shortened version of tortoiseshell.)

The color of the Siamese is affected by a number of factors including internal body temperatures and environmental conditions. The warmer the cat, or its environment, the lighter the Siamese cat's fur will become. In a Siamese cat, a lower skin temperature causes more pigmentation to be laid down in the growing hairs.

PERSONALITY: The Siamese is the most extroverted of domestic cats. They are very playful, intelligent, trainable, and vocal, talking to their owners in a voice that is impossible to ignore. They make wonderful pets.

Siberia ∼ A relatively new breed, the Siberia cat is large, rugged, and longhair. It most resembles the MAINE COON and NORWEGIAN FOREST cat. He first appeared in the United States in 1990.

PERSONALITY: He is affectionate and devoted. He can also play rough, so might not be the ideal pet cat for a child.

The Silent Meow ∼ Subtitled *A Manual for Kittens, Strays, and Homeless Cats*, this book was written by a cat and translated, with great effort, by writer Paul Gallico who also served as editor. With chapters on takeover, property rights, attitudes, tidbits at the table, and other information of tremendous help to a cat, it may give you a little more insight into your cat's behavior but there is no guarantee.

As Mr. Gallico puts it, "The majority of cat people, deep down, have a sneaking suspicion that they have been taken over by their feline, four-footed friend and that to a considerable extent she has imposed her whims and wishes upon the household." Paul Gallico himself is also a prolific writer of books including the cat book *Thomasina*, which was made into the movie *The Three Lives of Thomasina*.

Singapura ∼ This small, brown-ticked cat resembles an ABYSSINIAN, but with a smoother coat. She is thought to be from Singapore (Singapura is the Malaysian name for the Island of Singapore), where she was known as the "drain cat" because she liked to seek shelter and a place to nap in drains. The Singapura was imported to

the United States in 1975 and shown a year later. It is still a fairly unusual breed in the United States.

In 1993, two Singapuras named Tu-Son and Misty returned to their original homes to pose as models for statues that will be placed on the Singapore River. A contest in Singapore to name the new Mascot Singapore River Cat drew more than two hundred entries. The winning name was Kucinta. Besides being on the river, Kucinta will appear in children's books, porcelain figures, and pewter souvenirs. Kucinta will serve as the official symbol of Singapore.

PERSONALITY: Singapuras are shy and somewhat reserved but like being around people. At the same time they are playful and active.

Sepia Agouti Singapura, bred and owned by Tommy Meadow. (COURTESY HAROLD M. MEADOW, SINGAPURA FANCIERS SOCIETY, PHOTO © 1991 CHANAN.)

Cats are rather delicate creatures and they are subject to a good many ailments, but I never heard of one who suffered from insomnia.

JOSEPH WOOD KRUTCH, American critic and essayist (1893–1970)

The cat pretends to sleep the better to see.

FRANÇOIS-AUGUSTE RENÉ DE CHATEAUBRIAND French writer and diplomat (1768–1848)

How neatly a cat sleeps.

PABLO NERUDA, Nobel prize-winning Chilean poet (1904–1973)

Sleeping ～ A cat actually has three types of sleep—catnaps, which are very brief periods of light sleep; a longer light sleep, which is on either end of deep sleep; and deep sleep. After about half an hour of light sleep a cat slips into a deep sleep for under ten minutes and then returns to light sleep for another half hour. Besides dreaming, which kittens do when they are little over a week old, cats may flex their paws, make scratching noises, and have rapid movement of the ears, whiskers, tail, or legs while sleeping. Altogether, when all the time outs are added up, a cat spends as many as sixteen hours or two-thirds of her day sleeping compared to us, who spend about seven and a half hours sleeping each day. When sleeping, a cat will usually stretch out when warm and curl up when it's cold.

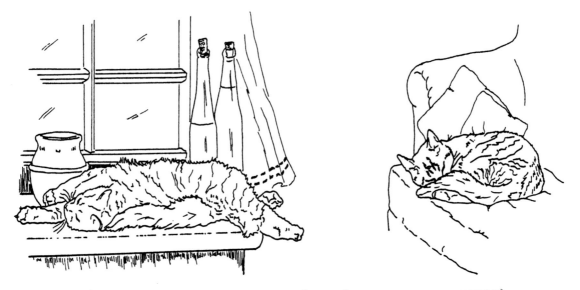

Cats can spend up to 16 hours a day sleeping, in a variety of poses. (DRAWINGS BY CHRISTINA DUNSTAN.)

In her poem *Cats*, Eleanor Farjeon uses just twenty words to sum up where you'll find cats napping:

> Cats sleep
> Anywhere,
> Any table,
> Any chair.
> Top of piano,
> Window-ledge,
> In the middle,
> On the edge.

According to newswoman Jane Pauley, "You can't look at a sleeping cat and feel tense."

Smell ∼ The cat has a very fine sense of

smell, twelve times as sensitive as our own. The cat is equipped with 67 million olfactory cells, and smell plays an important role in its social life. Scent glands are found along the tail, on each side of the forehead, on the lips and chin, and under the paws. A cat will "mark" an area with his scent by rubbing against an object with his face or by using his claws. A male cat will also leave a scent by urinating, or "spraying." Another cat arriving on the scene will sniff it and decide when the scent was left. If enough time has passed, he may stay. But if the scent was left recently, he may move quickly away, searching for a territory he can call his own. When your cat is inside he will brush along your leg to mark it with his scent, or will rub against household items to mark them as belonging in his domain. A cat can detect the faintest changes in body scent, caused by illness or emotional turmoil. You may also have noticed your cat smelling its surroundings with an open-mouthed panting gesture, known as flehming. When the cat curls back its lips, more air passes through the mouth and comes into contact with the Jacobson's organ, situated on the roof of the mouth. The organ, more highly developed in snakes and other reptiles and non-functioning in humans, is used particularly to identify sexual odors.

Watch a cat when it enters a room for the first time. It searches and smells about, it is not quiet for a moment, it trusts nothing until it has examined and made acquaintance with everything.

JEAN-JACQUES ROUSSEAU, French philosopher and writer, (1712–1778)

The official portrait of Socks, the First Cat, who took up residence in the Clinton White House in January 1993. (COURTESY THE WHITE HOUSE.)

Snowshoe ～ The Snowshoe, which combines characteristics of the Siamese with the white feet of the Birman, got its name for its white mittens. This cat was bred in the late 1960s by Dorothy Hinds-Daugherty in Philadelphia. It is believed that the breed originated with three kittens of Siamese ancestry born with white feet. The breed was then developed by crossbreeding with bicolored American shorthairs. In 1983 the snowshoe was recognized for championship competition. The snowshoe, as one would expect, has white feet and white markings on her chest and belly.

The Snowshoe has a medium lithe Oriental shape, a slightly triangular head, large pointed ears, and startingly blue eyes. The two standard varieties of the snowshoe cat are seal-point and blue-point.

PERSONALITY: The snowshoe is outgoing and unflappable.

Socks ～ When Bill Clinton took office as president of the United States and moved into the White House in January 1993, so did Socks. Socks is a domestic shorthair cat with a black and white coat. First cat Socks was given to first daughter, Chelsea Clinton, by a friend in 1990. When Clinton took office Socks became the first First Cat in

the White House in twelve years! Both Bill and First Lady Hillary are allergic to Socks.

As befitting such a public figure, Socks has already been the subject of a number of books, including *First Feline* by Mort Greenberg; *Socks: The Adventures* in comic-book format by publisher J. E. M.; and *Socks Goes to Washington, The Diary of America's First Cat* by Michael O'Donoghue. This humorous diary of America's first cat was written by Socks with a little help from the author, and illustrated by J. C. Suarès. *Socks Goes to Washington* was published in 1993, perhaps moments after Bill Clinton was sworn in as president. In his diary, Socks describes his life at the

White House, including his busy schedule on a typical morning:

Thursday
10:00 wake up
10:15 breakfast
10:30 claw rug in Oval Office
10:35 nap
11:00 eat roses in rose garden
11:10 throw up roses on rug in Oval Office
11:15 nap
11:30 nap
12:00 lunch

(After all that activity he must have been too exhausted to write his afternoon schedule!)

On one page of his diary Socks relates how he found a copy of *Millie's Book*, and comments, aptly, "A cheesy book cashing in on White House Pets. Some people will do anything for money."

Other Socks products include T-shirts, sweatshirts, key rings, buttons, magnets, jewelry, and, I'm sure, Socks socks. Socks also has a fan club, which you may join for twenty dollars. Membership benefits include a T-shirt, membership card, newsletter, and a 5 percent discount on Socks merchandise. Ten percent of the profits from Socks the Cat Fan Club is donated to charities, including the United States Humane Society. For information write PSP, 611 South Ivy Street, Arlington, Virginia 22204, or call 703/920-5193.

Somali ～ The Somali is essentially a long-haired ABYSSINIAN. Her coat is lush, silky, and easy to groom. It is believed that the Somali is a man-made breed and not the result of a spontaneous mutation.

In the 1960s, Evelyn Mague, an Abyssinian breeder in Gillette, New Jersey, who also runs a private shelter, was given a longhair Abyssinian kitten that other breeders refused to accept as a true specimen of the breed. She started breeding it and gave this longhair cat the name of Somali because Somalia forms the eastern and south-eastern borders of Ethiopia, formerly Abyssinia. The breed was recognized by 1979.

Like the Abyssinian, the Somali displays a ticked coat, but the longer hairs may be banded with ten or more colors, giving it a rich, shimmering quality.

Among the types of Somalis are the usual, or ruddy, a golden-brown ticked with black or brown; the sorrel, or chocolate-tipped copper color and the silver sorrel, which has a pale undercoat and a sorrel, or red, topcoat.

PERSONALITY: Somalis are friendly, intelligent, and athletic, and should live in a place with access to the outdoors. They are outgoing and like company.

A relatively new breed, the Somali resembles its wild ancestors. A longhaired version of the Abyssinian, the Somali displays the same banded ticking on the hairs, as seen in this lovely ruddy Somali, Your Majesty. (PHOTO COURTESY BONNY RIFKEN.)

Southey, Robert ～ (1774–1843) The English writer served as the poet laureate from 1813 until his death. His cat was named The Most Noble the Archduke Rumpelstizchen, Marquis Macbum, Earle Tomemange, Baron Raticide, Waowler, and Skaratchi. Perhaps he had a little trouble remembering the name, and nicknamed the cat Rumpel. When Rumpel died, the whole household, including the servants, went into mourning.

Sphynx ～ Deriving its name from the enigmatic creature of ancient myth, the sphynx is a

The hairless Sphynx is an extremely loving and friendly cat. (PHOTOGRAPH BY ISABELLE FRANCAIS.)

most uncat-like cat. If you have a sphynx you won't be constantly trying to get hairs off your clothing, your carpet, or your couch. He has no hair except for a small amount of down on his face, feet, ears, and tail, and is therefore an excellent cat for someone who has allergies. The skin of the sphynx is warm and soft. He is sometimes described as being like a "suede hot-water bottle."

The first "hairless" cat was reportedly bred by the Aztecs in Mexico before the sixteenth century. The New Mexican hairless was bred in the early 1900s. Today's sphynx is a natural breed that was developed by mutation in 1966 in Canada.

Because it lacks fur, the sphynx cannot cope with extreme temperatures. In addition, without hair, they can't absorb the natural oils secreted through the skin and have to be bathed or towel-washed frequently.

The sphynx comes in just about any color and pattern. It has a compact muscular body with a "barrel chest," appears slightly bow-legged, and has very large ears.

PERSONALITY: The sphynx is very friendly and affectionate and enjoys being cuddled.

Stamps ～ The United States issued its first cat stamps on February 5, 1988. The cat stamps were introduced, with much catfare, at the Winter Garden Theater on Broadway, home of the musical *Cats*. Postmaster Preston Tisch gave a little background on the origin of the cat stamps, saying that after a set of dog stamps was issued several years earlier, the Postal Service was deluged with complaints from cat lovers demanding cat stamps. (So, it appears that some persistent and dedicated caterwauling achieved the desired results.)

Each stamp in the four-stamp set features two cats: Siamese/Exotic shorthair; Abyssinian/

Himalayan; Maine coon/Burmese; and American shorthair/Persian. The stamps were designed by John D. Dawson, a commercial artist specializing in natural history. (Dawson also designed one of the Morris the Cat labels for 9-Lives cat food.)

The first cat to appear on an official government postage stamp was a little black cat named Patsy. When Spain issued a series of eight stamps honoring famous aviators in 1930, one of the stamps featured Charles Lindbergh who made the first solo nonstop flight across the Atlantic Ocean in 1927. Lindy had intended to take his cat Patsy along, but changed his mind. Patsy made it onto the stamp anyway.

The next time a cat made an appearance on a stamp was in 1952, when the Netherlands issued a stamp picturing a baby playing with a cat and some string. In 1984 Poland issued a set of ten cat stamps of different breeds. Their great popularity led to the production of cat stamps all over the world. Since the first cat stamp there have been over three hundred domestic cat stamps issued by over fifty different countries.

A popular theme for stamps is folklore. Here, for example, is a list from the newsletter *Cat Talk* of stamps honoring "Puss in Boots":

· 1960, Hungary—Puss resembles a cute kitten in full attire. A castle is in the background.

· 1968, Poland—Puss, in full regalia, takes up the whole stamp.

· 1970, Mongolia—This sheet of twenty stamps for Expo '70 includes one of the Fairy Tale Pavilion with "Puss In Boots."

· 1971, West Germany—Puss is wearing an orange jacket and black boots.

· 1971, Panama—A cartoonlike Puss in enormous boots walks toward the castle.

· 1978, Monaco—A set of nine stamps honor "Count Perrault" (the author of "Puss in Boots"). Puss is wearing a flowing red cape and displaying his riches.

With their universal popularity, it is no wonder that cats have appeared on stamps in many countries around the world.

· 1979, Paraguay—The set, issued for the International Year of the Child, features seven large stamps with cartoon-style scenes from "Puss in Boots."

· 1985, Colombia—Puss appears with a boy in a Christmas design.

· 1985, Equatorial Guinea—This souvenir sheet for UNICEF shows Puss stopping the king's carriage.

· 1985, East Germany—Eight colorful stamps show Puss as a black cat doing his good deeds.

Stats for cats ~ Here are tidbits of cat trivia with which you can impress cat lovers (and cats) at cocktail parties and the like. Did you know that . . .

· The most prolific cat was Dusty, a cat from Bonham, Texas, who gave birth to her 420th kitten on June 12, 1952.

· In March 1991, a cat in Hong Kong named Barbara survived a fifty-story fall with only minor injuries when she landed on a tin roof.

· The average weight of an adult male cat is 8.6 pounds, and an adult female cat, 7.2 pounds.

· The largest breed of cat is the ragdoll. Males weigh fifteen to twenty pounds.

· The cat has 40 more bones in its body than a human.

· The fattest cat ever may be Edward Beard, owned by Jackie Fleming of Australia. In 1988 Edward Beard had an unconfirmed weight of forty-eight pounds. Another Australian cat named Himmy, owned by Thomas Vyse, weighed 46 pounds, 15¼ ounces when he died of respiratory failure at the age of ten. In the United States, Spice, a nine-year-old tomcat residing in Ridgefield, Connecticut, weighed in at forty-three pounds.

· The smallest breed of cat is the Singapura, which weighs from four to six pounds.

· The greatest number of cats living in one home in North America in 1993 was about 640. Living with Jack and Donna Wright in Kingston, Ontario, Canada, in a two-story house, the cats consume 180 fourteen-ounce cans of moist food, 50 pounds of dry food, and nine quarts of milk a day. Food and vet bills come to about $306.00 a day. Jack says, "Sometimes you wonder what you are doing with them all . . . But I just love them."

· The greatest recorded number of toes on a cat was thirty-two. A cat named Mickey Mouse, who resided in California, had eight toes on each foot.

· The cats Hellcat and Brownie were the sole heirs to the 415,000 acre estate of Dr. William Grier of San Diego when he died in 1963.

· As of 1993 there were 63 million cats in the United States, according to the Pet Food Institute, with at last one cat in 32 percent of the households.

Steinlen, *Théophile Alexandre* ~ (1859–1923) The French graphic artist used many cats in his illustrations. Born in Switzerland, he moved to Paris in the late 1890s, where he lived in poverty as a struggling artist. Finally, he was commissioned to draw illustrations for the 'chansonniers' Bruant and Jules Jouy, a world made famous in the works of Toulouse-Lautrec. Soon his work with cats was seen frequently in advertisements and posters. He would stop along the streets of Paris, sketching cats he came across on rooftops, gutters, cemeteries, and garbage bins. His cat models were also kept by other artists, seamstresses, and concierges of the Butte de Montmartre, where he did most of his drawing. Besides drawing cats, he modeled cats in wax and cast others in bronze. He published the book *Images sans paroles*,

Cats, *a favorite subject of French artist Theophile Steinlen.* (BEQUEST OF W. G. RUSSELL ALLEN, COURTESY, MUSEUM OF FINE ARTS, BOSTON.)

which contains images of cats engaged in comical antics such as raiding a goldfish bowl, playing with a ball of wool, and so on. His own house became known as Cat's Corner.

Stroking (petting) ∼ Stroking is a sign of maternal affection for the cat. Because the owner of the cat has taken the place of the mother cat, and feeds and protects the cat as the cat mother did, the cat looks up to the owner as a mother figure. When your cat rolls over to allow you to stroke his belly, you know you've earned his trust.

> Ye shall not possess any beast, my dear sisters, except only a cat.
>
> ENGLISH NUNS' RULE, C. 1205

> It is as easy to hold quicksilver between your finger and thumb as to keep a cat who means to escape.
>
> ANDREW LANG, Scottish writer (1844–1912)

Superstitions

Cats have long been the focus of superstitions around the world regarding luck, health, farming, and other concerns. Many superstitions involve black cats and white cats, which can be lucky or unlucky depending on the country. For example, generally speaking, black cats in England are believed to be lucky, but are unlucky in the United States; whereas in the United States, Belgium, Spain, and other European countries white cats are supposed to be lucky, and unlucky in England.

Some cat superstitions are widespread. Others are found just where they originated.

Some of the following superstitions will be very familiar to you and others may evoke some surprise or a few chuckles. For many cats the superstitions, bizarre as they may sound now, were once no laughing matter, leading to torture and death for the innocent and unsuspecting cat. Undoubtedly, there are still many people who believe any number of these.

Luck ∼ In the United States, seeing a white cat on the road is lucky—seeing it at night is unlucky. In England, seeing a white cat on the way to school will bring trouble that day.

A cat on the doorstep in the morning brings bad luck. (Norway)

A strange black cat on your porch brings prosperity. (Scotland)

(continued)

Steinlen illustrated many posters and manuscripts, including those advertising the café Chat Noir, frequented by artists and intellectuals of the period.

If a black cat chooses to make its home with you, you will have good luck.

Dreaming of a white cat means good luck. (USA)

Stepping over a cat brings bad luck. (USA)

Never stroke a cat backward or your luck will turn bad. (USA)

In France, it is bad luck to cross a stream carrying a cat.

It is bad luck to put a cat out before you wind the clock. (Wales)

Killing a cat brings seventeen years of bad luck. (Ireland)

If you hear a cat sneeze, it is a good omen. (Italy)

It is lucky to have a cat in the theater, but unlucky for it to walk across the stage during a performance and unlucky, as well, for an actor to kick a cat.

If a cat sneezes near a bride on her wedding day, she will have a happy marriage.

Health, Death, and Demons ~

If a black cat lies on the bed of a sick man, he will surely die. (USA)

If a black cat crosses your path, you will die in an epidemic. (Ireland)

If you swallow a cat's hair you will never get to heaven (Korean superstition—Koreans generally consider cats to be more crafty critters than housepets.)

If a male cat jumps over food, any woman who eats it will become pregnant *with cats*, because the jumping cat could spray feline semen onto the food. (This was believed in at different times and in different places in Scotland.)

A child can get a deadly disease if a cat sucks the child's breath.

A tortoiseshell cat climbing a tree is an omen of death by accident. (France)

If a cat appears on the grave of a buried person, his or her soul is in the Devil's power. (Western Europe)

Dreaming of a black cat at Christmas foretells of a serious illness in the coming year. (Germany)

In Japan it was common practice to cut off the tails of kittens to prevent them from turning into demons. It was believed that the cat's tail was the source of the cat's supernatural powers.

If you dislike cats you will be carried to the cemetery in the rain. (Ireland and the Netherlands)

A man who mistreats his cat will die in a storm. (Germany)

Agriculture ~

In Europe it used to be customary to bury live black cats under fruit trees to stimulate the growth of the trees.

In Transylvania and Bohemia, black tomcats were killed and buried in the fields on Christmas Eve and at the sowing of the first seed in Spring to prevent evil spirits from harming the crops.

Peasants of Russia, Poland, and Bohemia buried cats alive in their cornfields because they thought that would guarantee a good crop.

Other ~

To ensure the stability of a new building, a live cat has to be put in the wall.

(continued)

Girls in Wales are told to feed cats well so that the sun will shine on their wedding day.

If you mistreat cats you will have rain at your wedding. (Ireland and the Netherlands)

If you are scared by a cat, collect hair from a cat or dog and burn it under your nose. (Lithuania)

If you see a one-eyed cat, spit on your thumb, stamp it in the palm of your hand, and make a wish. The wish will come true. (My personal favorite.) (USA)

Since cats symbolize women in dreams, if you dream of a cat beware a female friend.

Sylvester the Cat

Sylvester the Cat ~ Created by animator Fritz Freleng, Sylvester, was a cartoon star for Warner Brothers. He made his debut in 1945 in the cartoon *Live with Feathers*, in which he is tormented by a parakeet when the unhappy parakeet tries to commit suicide by jumping into Sylvester's mouth. The black-furred cat with a white belly resists, fearing that the bird may be poisoned. But the parakeet persists, heaping endless abuse and humiliation on Sylvester. Sylvester also makes what seems to be his trademark comment, "Sufferin' succotash." In his next cartoon, *Peck Up Your Troubles*, made later that year, Sylvester takes after a woodpecker—with disastrous results (and not for the woodpecker!). In 1947 Sylvester appeared in the Oscar-winning cartoon *Tweetie Pie*. The little yellow canary makes mincemeat of Sylvester, who tries numerous ways to make Tweety his dinner. In some two dozen cartoons Sylvester tries, and fails, to get the best of the canary, leading Tweety to issue his famous line, "I tawt I taw a putty tat." In *Birds Anonymous* (1957), Sylvester laments, "One little bird . . . just one! I-I-I can't stand it . . . I gotta have a bird . . . I'm weak . . . *I'm weak*. But I don't care! I can't help it! After all, I *am* a pussycat."

Tweety Pie isn't the only one Sylvester finds himself pitted against. In other cartoons Sylvester unsuccessfully meets up with Hippety Hop, a baby kangaroo whom he mistakes for a giant mouse in a dozen episodes; Wellington Bulldog; Mike the bulldog, who was his friend but was shamed into fighting him by a devious mouse; the Mexican mouse Speedy Gonzales (the 1955 cartoon *Speedy Gonzales* won an Oscar); and Sam the Cat, a neighbor who competes with Sylvester to catch and consume Tweety Pie in *Trick or Treat*. Mel Blanc provided Sylvester's voice (as well as Tweety's.)

Sylvester starred in over one hundred cartoons. and in the Dell Comics comic book *Tweety and Sylvester* from 1952 to 1962. Gold Key/Whitman published the popular comic book from 1983 to 1984.

T

If you have a tabby-cat,
If you want to please him,
Tie a ribbon round his neck,
Never, never tease him;
Tabby-cats are grave and stately,
And they like to act sedately.

A. G. HERBERTSON

Tabby ∼ The term *tabby* refers to a cat with stripes, or to a female domestic cat. According to some, the name *tabby* is derived from a section in Baghdad, Iraq, known as Attabiah, where Jewish silk weavers copied the varied designs and colors of cats' coats into the fabric called "Tabbi." Others theorize that tabby derives from the Turkish name *utabi*.

The classic tabby cat has legs that are evenly marked with rings that go up to meet the body markings, the tail is evenly ringed, and around the neck are several unbroken rings. The back of the tabby has a stripe going to the tail with a stripe on either side.

According to legend, the *M* marking on the Tabby's forehead was placed there to honor the prophet MOHAMMED, who loved cats. However, an early Christian folktale explains the *M* in another way. When the baby Jesus would not sleep, the Madonna begged the animals in the stable to help. The only one able to was a little striped gray

This champion blue mackerel Tabby American shorthair shows the nice fawn overlay, or "patina," that blue tabbies should have but rarely do. (COURTESY ANNE BURKE, SATIN SONG CATTERY, DIAMOND BAR, CALIFORNIA.)

kitten. The kitten snuggled next to the baby Jesus and purred the baby to sleep. From that day on, tabby cats had an *M* on their forehead as a reminder of the help they gave to the Madonna.

Tabby is also a term used to describe an old maid, spinster, spiteful female gossip, or tattler.

> I saw the most beautiful cat today. It was sitting by the side of the road, its two front feet neatly and graciously together. Then it gravely swished around its tail to completely and snugly encircle itself. It was so fit and beautifully neat, the gesture, and so self-satisfied—so complacent.
>
> ANNE MORROW LINDBERGH, American writer, twentieth century

> A pharoah's profile, a Krishna's grace, tail like a questionmark.
>
> LOUIS MACNEICE, Irish poet (1907–1963)

Tail ∼ In addition to its obvious aesthetic appeal, a cat's tail is also quite functional in helping her maintain her balance. The tail serves as a counterweight as she makes her way along a precarious height, assists in "cornering" when making quick turns, and acts as a rudder when she is jumping. You can tell a lot about your cat's mood by watching her tail. A tail flicked stiffly upward with a rapid motion is a greeting which may be addressed to you or another cat. When your cat walks around with his tail bent forward over his head it is a sign of dominance. He is telling female cats in the neighborhood that he is the top cat and at the same time warning other male cats to watch out. The twitching tail, rapidly moving back and forth, indicates annoyance and may be accompanied by other signs of irritation such as growling or an angry wail. When your cat's tail moves randomly, it usually means the cat is alert although resting.

According to legend, the kink in the tail of the Siamese cat occurred when a Siamese princess, bathing in a river, needed a place to put her rings. Her Siamese cat twisted his tail so that the

The position of a cat's tail is a good indication of mood. An erect tail is raised in greeting, while a tail bent forward shows dominance. A twitching tail signals annoyance. (DRAWING BY CHRISTINA DUNSTAN.)

princess could store her rings there without worry while continuing to swim. Although I prefer the legend, the real reason for a cat's kinked tail is that it is a genetic characteristic or the result of a cat's tail being caught in a door, or some other accident. Some breeds, like the MANX and the JAPANESE BOBTAIL, have a characteristically stubby tail, or no tail at all.

> He can talk but insolently says nothing. What of it?
> When One is frank, one's very presence is a compliment.
>
> MARIANNE MOORE, American poet (1887–1972)

> Cats seem to go on the principle that it never does any harm to ask for what you want.
>
> JOSEPH WOOD KRUTCH, American critic and essayist (1893–1970)

> Let cat's mew rise to a scream on a tool-shed roof.
>
> W. H. AUDEN, American poet (1907–1973)

sounds (murmur patterns), vowel sounds (variations of "meow"), and strained intensity sounds, such as the hiss or scream. (According to the study, cats use nine consonants, five vowels, two diphthongs, and one tripthong.) Scientists who have studied tape recordings of cats say that cats may very well be next in line to us, in the complexity of the sounds they can make. One blind musician claimed that he could detect some one hundred different sounds made by a cat. While English-speakers say that cats "meow," the Chinese say they "ming."

A cat makes different sounds according to whether he is angry, frightened, in pain, comfortable, or seeking attention. The most common sound is meowing, which is not usually an indication of contentment. An unhappy or frightened kitten will meow, as will a grown cat to show unhappiness, discontent, or want.

The frequency of the sounds and their loudness depend on the type of cat. Some cats, like the SIAMESE, are known to talk a lot. Some cats are known to be particularly loud, and some are generally quiet.

> A man possessed a cat on which he doted;
> So fine she was, so soft, so silky-coated—
> Her very mew had beauty.
>
> *Fables*, LAFONTAINE, 1668

Talking (vocalizing) ～ If you have a cat you are well aware that cats say more than just "meow." In fact, cats make many different sounds. When Mildred Moelk researched cat vocalizations in 1944, she concluded that cats have the ability to make seventeen different sounds, which she has broken down into three groups: purring

Television cats ～ Many illustrated cats from comic strips, books, and fairy tales, have become "animated" and made it to the small screen. The Cheshire cat appeared in the half-hour animated production of *Alice in Wonderland* in 1973.

The *Bad Cat*, a half-hour ABC Weekend Special

that first aired in 1984, is based on two children's books. (It's about a bad cat, who underneath it all, is really a good cat.) Dr. Seuss's *The Cat in the Hat* was made into a half-hour show which first aired in 1971 and has been rebroadcast at least eight times. In 1972 a half-hour version of *Puss-In-Boots* was televised.

It should come as no surprise that the mighty GARFIELD has appeared in many specials. His first prime-time feature, *Here Comes Garfield*, aired in 1982 with Lorenzo Music as the voice of Garfield. In addition to the hour-long *Garfield: His Nine Lives*, half-hour features include: *A Garfield Christmas*, *Garfield Goes to Hollywood*, *Garfield in Paradise*, *Garfield in the Rough*, *Garfield on the Town*, *Garfield's Babes and Bullets*, *Garfield's Halloween Adventure*, and *Garfield's Thanksgiving Special*.

Of course cats have been well represented in the world of Saturday-morning cartoons. The debut half-hour episode of *Courageous Cat and Minute Mouse*, which features a crime fighting cat and mouse who fight together for truth, justice, and just plain protecting themselves, took place in 1960.

The *Felix the Cat* half-hour cartoon premiered in 1960, and *Garfield and Friends*, in a production approved by Garfield's creator, Jim Davis, appeared in 1988. Besides friends from the comic strip, Nermel, the world's cutest kitten, made her first television appearance with Garfield. Heathcliff appeared in two different half-hour series: *The Heathcliff and Marmaduke Show* premiered in 1981 and ran for one year; *Heathcliff and the Catillac Cats* debuted in 1986. *The Houndcats*, and a spoof of the TV show *Mission Impossible*, starring government intelligence agents like Puttypuss, Stutz, and Rhubarb, who undertake impossible missions in the West, premiered in 1972. The still popular *Tom and Jerry Show*, a half-hour series, first aired in 1965.

> The trouble with cats is that they've got no tact.
>
> P. G. WODEHOUSE, English writer and humorist (1881–1975)

That Darn Cat ～ This 1965 Walt Disney movie stars a seal-point cat named Darn Cat and called D.C. for short. Darn Cat, or D.C., helps an FBI agent catch some criminals. Appearing with D.C. are Haley Mills and Roddy McDowall. The movie was based on the book *Undercover Cat*.

Ticked ～ This term refers to a cat's coat in which each hair is striped with bands of different colors. *See* HAIR.

Tiddles ～ This stray cat lived in the ladies' room at the London Railway station in Paddington for years and received fan mail from all over the world. Weighing in at twenty-five pounds, Tiddles was quite fat, but that's not surprising considering his diet of steak, lamb, and cod. Could the tabby Tiddles be just a bit of a peeping tom? His favorite trick was squeezing under the door of an occupied stall in the lavatories.

Tiffany ～ This new breed, the result of crossing a Burmese with a Persian, was developed in the United States. She has most of the characteristics of the Burmese, including a round head, long slim legs, and medium muscular body, as well as the long hair of the Persian. Kittens are born a creamy "cafe au lait" color and their coats darken to a brown or sable as they mature. In Britain breeders are developing other varieties. The tiffany remains relatively scarce.

PERSONALITY: The tiffany is gentle, outgoing, and inquisitive.

Tip-cat ∼ This is a game in which a short piece of wood, tapered at both ends, is struck lightly at one end with a bat, causing the wood to spring into the air so that it can be batted for a distance. Since the tapered piece of wood is called *pussy*, the game is often called *pussy*. See also CAT'S CRADLE.

To Catch a Thief ∼ In this 1955 Alfred Hitchcock movie, Cary Grant stars as a reformed "cat burglar." Grant was known as "the cat" because of his agility in stealthily climbing buildings and stealing jewels. The film also features Grace Kelly.

Tom and Jerry ∼ This well-known cartoon cat-and-mouse team features a cat named Tom and a mouse named Jerry. They debuted in 1940, in *Puss Gets the Boot*, but the cat was called "Jasper" and the mouse wasn't given a name. When the pair proved to be so popular, and even garnered an Oscar nomination, Jasper's name changed to Tom, the little brown mouse was named Jerry, and a very successful series was born.

Joe Hanna and William Barbera of MGM produced the first 113 animated cartoons, which won an unprecedented seven Oscars. Other producers took over in 1960 and produced another forty-seven cartoons, but they were never as good or as popular as the original 113, which made their way to television as *The Tom and Jerry Show*

in 1965. Subsequent TV shows featuring the cat and mouse were less successful. Tom and Jerry also danced in a movie with actor Gene Kelly.

The popular team appeared in comic books as well. They made their debut in 1942 in Dell Comics' *Our Gang Comics*. Thirty-nine issues later the subtitle *With Tom and Jerry* was added, and in 1949 the series became *Tom and Jerry Comics*. Eventually, Gold Key took over the comic book until ceasing publication in 1982, after a total 344 editions.

In 1993, Tom and Jerry starred in a full-length animated film called *Tom and Jerry: The Movie*. For the first time, Tom, Jerry, and the other characters actually spoke. They even sang! Voice tracks were supplied by Charlotte Rae, Rip Torn, and Michael Bell, among others. *Tom and Jerry: The Movie* was released by Miramax films.

It is in the nature of cats to do a certain amount of unescorted roaming.

ADLAI STEVENSON, American diplomat and statesman, twentieth century

---

Tomcat ∼ The name "tom" to generally describe a male cat originated with the publication in 1760 of the popular story "The Life and Adventures of a Cat," which featured Tom the cat. Soon people began to refer to a male cat as a tom, rather than a ram, which had been used previously. Some years before, the Jesuit priest Father Bougeant (1690–1734) had also described the life of a tom:

Such is one of those big-whiskered and well-furred tomcats, that you see quiet in a corner, digesting at his leisure, sleeping if it seems

A handsome tomcat indeed.

good to him, sometimes giving himself the pleasure of hunting, for the rest enjoying life peaceably, without being troubled by useless reflections, and little caring to communicate his thoughts to others. Truly it needs only a female cat come on the scene to derange all his philosophy; but are our philosophers wiser on such occasions?

In Old English a tomcat was referred to as gib, or a gibbe-cat. In slang, *tomcat* can refer to a man who goes roaming, looking for a sexual partner.

Tongue ～ If you've ever been awakened by a strange, dry, prickly sensation on your face, you are well aware of the texture of your cat's tongue. A cat's tongue has horny, toothlike projections on it, called 'filiform' papillae, which means filelike. But while the tongue is quite useful for GROOMING the cat, and occasionally you, the tongue's major role is in eating. Besides the filiform papillae, other papillae on the tongue contain taste buds. (They're usually on the outer edges of the tongue, while the prickly projections are in the center of the tongue.) Your cat's taste buds can discern sweet, sour, bitter, and salty. The tongue can also sense temperature and texture. A cat may reject food on the basis of smell alone, but your cat may take one bite and say, no way. This is not to say, of course, that all cats reject the same food. If you've known more than one cat you know that each cat has its own likes and dislikes. My cat Miel will eat virtually anything, from my leftover vegetables—especially corn *on the cob*—to cantaloupe. Molly, on the other hand, could care less.

When eating solid food, the rough surface of the tongue enables it to grasp and hold pieces of food as they move to the back of the mouth. The tongue can also be used to get pieces of meat off a bone. And because it is so sensitive, it can frequently discern some objects, like feathers, that should be spit out. The tongue is also used by the cat to "eat" liquids. The filiform in the middle of the tongue acts like a towel, absorbing the liquid. The cat extends the tongue into the water or milk, then cups the tongue as she withdraws it, to save as much of the liquid as possible. The cat usually laps four or five times for each swallow.

The tongue also plays a vital role in the cat's ingestion of food. It has muscles that raise the base of the tongue and pull it back so it acts like a plunger. The tongue actually contains many muscles which enables it to curl, twist, and curl. And that is very useful in nursing. When the newborn kitten locates mamma's nipple, she curls her tongue underneath. Movements of the tongue and jaw draw the milk out. When kittens themselves are about four weeks old they use their tongue to check out new surfaces and objects by licking them, and licking them, and licking them.

Tonkinese ~ The Tonkinese is the result of the breeding of a Siamese with a Burmese and is thought to combine the best characteristics of both types. While several of these "Golden Siamese" had been bred in the 1930s, it was in the 1960s that Margaret Conroy, a Canadian, renewed

The Tonkinese, developed by breeding a Siamese and a Burmese, is found in a variety of luscious mink shades. (PHOTOGRAPH BY ISABELLE FRANCAIS.)

interest in the breed and Tonkinese were recognized in the United States in 1980.

The Tonkinese is of medium build, lithe and muscular, with a longish face and almond-shaped eyes. The soft silky coat has a luxurious mink-like feel, with solid coloring and subtle points. In the United States, the varieties of the Tonkinese are the natural mink, blue mink, honey mink, champagne mink, and platinum mink, while breeders in Britain have introduced other colors, including the red-point, as well. Only about half of the kittens in a litter of Tonkinese will display all of the true breed characteristics.

PERSONALITY: The Tonkinese is one of the most affectionate and people-oriented shorthairs.

Toonces, the Driving Cat, of Saturday Night Live fame (PHOTO BY LINDA HANRAHAN, ANIMALS FOR ADVERTISING.)

> They'll take a suggestion as a cat laps milk.
>
> WILLIAM SHAKESPEARE, from
> *The Tempest* (1564–1616)

Toonces the Driving Cat ～ If you've watched the television show *Saturday Night Live*, you have probably at some time seen Toonces the Driving Cat. Toonces, whose real name is Carocats Tyrone Fletcher, calmly sits behind the wheel, usually wearing sunglasses and a leather jacket. The outcome of this ride is usually not calm, but as I said to his owner, Barbara Hanrahan, Toonces's driving is no worse than many other drivers I've encountered in New York City.

Barbara Hanrahan, who owns Animals for Advertising, says Toonces did not always look forward to his *Saturday Night Live* appearances. At first he would hide under the bed when it was time to go. But when he realized that his appear-ance also included very tasty chicken and roast beef he became eager to get behind the wheel.

Toonces is a registered silver tabby. His original home was the Carocats Cattery on Staten Island, which explains at least part of his real name. If you haven't seen him on *Saturday Night Live*, you may have seen him in one of the over 250 commercials he made, beginning with his first appearance in a commercial in Japan. He has posed for Avanti Greeting cards and appeared in Bloomingdale's catalog.

So how did Toonces prepare for his demanding role on *SNL*? Linda Hanrahan says she trained him by socializing him at an early age. She took him outside in New York City, riding in elevators, and driving in city traffic. (There are some who would dispute whether riding in New York City elevators and traffic could be called "socializing.")

Top Cat ∾

This khaki-colored animated cat made his debut on a half-hour ABC series in 1961. Top Cat and his "gang" (Choo Choo, Spook, the Brain, Fancy Fancy, Benny the Ball, Goldie and Pierre) lasted for 28 episodes—or one year. Top Cat, or TP as he was known to his buddies, wore a vest, hat (with holes for his ears), and frequently carried a cane. Standing some three feet tall, he would walk on his hind legs and sleep with a mask on his eyes. His home, with his friends, was in the trash cans in a New York City alley. Twenty-eight *Top Cat* comic books were published by Dell Comics and Gold Key Comics through 1970; Charlton Comics published twenty issues between 1970 and 1973.

These terms are used to describe cats and their relationships:

clowder—a group of older cats

kindle—a group of kittens

dam—the mother of kittens

litter—a group of kittens born together at one time

queen—a female cat in heat. Males approach with great deference, and are often punished by her in an autocratic way.

gibcat—old English name for a tomcat

tomcat—an unneutered male cat, usually a roamer

One cannot woo a cat after the fashion of the Conqueror. Courage, tact, patience are needed at every step.

AGNES REPPLIER, American essayist
(1855–1950)

Towser ∾

Towser was the mouser at the Glenturret distillery, the oldest in Scotland, for close to twenty-four years. He reigned from April 1963 to March 1987, when he died at the age of twenty-four. During that time he reportedly killed some 28,899 mice, which gave him a place in the *Guinness Book of Records*. (I'd like to know who counted all those mice.) Towser's long life is attributed to the "water of life" he imbibed by breathing in the whiskey fumes over the years. Towser's replacement was Mr. Toddy—who had a very tough act to follow.

Training ∾

It is commonly thought that cats cannot be trained to perform tricks. This is not true. In the nineteenth century Pietro Capelli gained an international reputation with his troupe of performing cats. As a boy growing up in Italy, he was too poor to have pets, but he loved cats. And when his friends were playing games in the street, Pietro was at the local dump hanging out with the cats. He watched them play and work and scrounge for food. He helped cats who were hurt and would give up his own food so that his cats would not go hungry. One day he decided to see if he could train his cats and started teaching them simple tricks. Soon he was putting on shows for kids in the neighborhood. Word spread and adults began showing up as well. Capelli ended up rich and famous, with his cats swinging from trapezes, balancing on high wires, and lying on their backs and juggling with their hind legs. He taught them to prepare rice using a mortar and pestle, play children's instruments, and draw water from a well, obtaining the number of buckets that he called for. The Englishman Leoni Clarke had a troupe of fifty trained cats who could walk across a stage on tightropes, jump through flaming hoops, and parachute down from the ceiling. He called himself The King of the Cats. And of course today, many cats have been trained to star in commercials and films.

Turkish Angora ～ This longhair cat has existed for nearly two and a half centuries, first found in the region surrounding the city of Angora, which is now called Ankara. (In the mid-1800s the Angora was known as the Ankara in the United States and England.) Turkish sultans sent Angoras to the nobles of France and England during the sixteenth century and they may have been the first longhair in Europe. Used indiscriminately in breeding programs with Persians, they eventually took on all the Persian qualities, nearly becoming extinct. In the early twentieth century, a controlled breeding program of pure Turkish Angoras was started in the Ankara Zoo in Turkey and the breed was rediscovered in 1962. (The Cat Fanciers Association only accepts registration for Turkish Angoras that were born in the Ankara Zoo.)

The Turkish Angora is lithe, with long silky hair

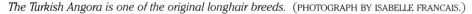

The Turkish Angora is one of the original longhair breeds. (PHOTOGRAPH BY ISABELLE FRANCAIS.)

and a plumed tail and needs regular grooming. Turkish Angoras come in a variety of colors, including pure white, black, blue-gray, red, brown, and multicolored.

PERSONALITY: Angoras are gentle, friendly, intelligent, and fun-loving.

> No one of all the women I have known
>> Has been so beautiful, or proud, or wise
>> As this Angora with her amber eyes.
> She makes her chosen cushion seem a throne,
>> And wears the same voluptuous, slow smile
>> She wore when she was worshipped by the Nile.
>
> "My Angora Cat," W. A. ROBERTS

Turkish Van ～

The Turkish Van breed is also referred to as the Turkish swimming cat because of its fondness for playing in water. She is a semi-longhair cat with a distinctive color pattern, named after Lake Van in southeastern Turkey. The cat has been known to swim out into Turkish harbors to greet incoming fishing boats, looking for a free meal.

Rare and ancient, the Turkish Van developed in Central and Southwest Asia. It was first brought into Europe by Crusaders returning from the Middle East. Over the years it has been known as the white ringtail, Russian longhair, Van cat, and Turkish cat. And though many people think that the Turkish Van is simply another version of the Turkish Angora, they developed in different areas, and when seen together, the dissimilarities in size,

type, bone structure, and coat are very apparent. An especially large and agile cat, the Turkish Van takes up to five years to reach full maturity.

Among the varieties of the Turkish van are the: odd-eyed (each eye is a different color), cream-and-white, and auburn-and-white.

PERSONALITY: The Turkish Van is highly intelligent, lively, and affectionate.

> A home without a cat, and a well-fed, well-petted and properly revered cat, may be a perfect home, *perhaps*, but how can it prove its title?
>
> MARK TWAIN

Twain, Mark ～

(1835–1910) The American writer and humorist was a lifelong cat lover and kept as many as eleven cats at his farm in Connecticut. He gave his pets some of the oddest names, including Apollinaris, Zoroaster, Blatherskite, Sour Mash, Sin, and Satan to name just a few. Twain's explanation for the exotic names was that learning the names of the cats would be good practice for his children to use and pronounce long and difficult words. His daughter Susy once said, "The difference between Mamma and Papa is that Mamma loves morals and Papa loves cats."

Twain loved to have his cats around him while he wrote, and often mentioned cats in his books. In *More Tramps Abroad*, Twain follows three big cats and a basket of kittens aboard the luxury liner *Oceana*. One of the cats goes ashore at different ports to visit his numerous families. At each stop, that cat is not seen again until the ship is ready to sail, when he climbs back on board.

In responding to a letter in 1908 asking for a photo of his cat Tammany and her kittens, Twain wrote, "One of them likes to be crammed into a corner-pocket of the billiard table—which he fits as snugly as does a finger in a glove and then he watches the game (and obstructs it) by the hour, and spoils many a shot by putting out his paw and changing the direction of the ball."

Here are a few more of Twain's observations about cats:

"One of the most striking differences between a cat and a lie is that a cat has only nine lives."

"If man could be crossed with the cat, it would improve man but deteriorate the cat."

"We should be careful to get out of an experience only the wisdom that is in it—and stop there; lest we be like the cat that sits down on a hot stove lid. She will never sit down on a hot stove lid again—and that is well; but she will never sit down on a cold one any more."

"Ignorant people think it's the noise which fighting cats make that is so aggravating, but it ain't. It's the sickening grammar they use." Amen.

Twain's well-known story "Dick Baker's Cat" follows:

Dick Baker's Cat

One of my comrades there—another of those victims of eighteen years of unrequited toil and blighted hopes—was one of the gentlest spirits that ever bore its patient cross in a weary exile; grave and simple Dick Baker, pocket miner of Dead-Horse Gulch. He was forty-six, gray as a rat, earnest, thoughtful, slenderly educated, slouchily dressed, and clay-soiled, but his heart was finer metal than any gold his shovel ever brought to light—than any, indeed, that ever was mined or minted.

Whenever he was out of luck and a little downhearted, he would fall to mourning over the loss of a wonderful cat he used to own (for where women and children are not, men of kindly impulses take up with pets, for they must love something). And he always spoke of the strange sagacity of that cat with the air of a man who believed in his secret heart that there was something human about it—maybe even supernatural.

I heard him talking about this animal once. He said: "Gentlemen, I used to have a cat here, by the name of Tom Quartz, which you'd 'a' took an interest in, I reckon—most anybody would. I had him here eight year—and he was the remarkablest cat *I* ever see. He was a large gray one of the Tom specie, an' he had more hard, natchral sense than any man in this camp—'n' a *power* of dignity—he wouldn't let the Gov'ner of Californy be familiar with him. He never ketched a rat in his life—'peared to be above it. He never cared for nothing but mining. He knowed more about mining, that cat did, than any man *I* ever, ever see. You couldn't tell *him* noth'n' 'bout placer-diggin's—'n' as for pocket mining, why he was just born for it. He would dig out after

A sketch of his cats penned by Mark Twain, a lifelong cat lover.

me an' Jim when we went over the hills prospect'n', and he would trot along behind us for as much as five mile, if we went so fur. An' he had the best judgment about mining ground—why, you never see anything like it. When we went to work, he'd scatter a glance round, 'n' if he didn't think much of the indications, he would give a look as much as to say, 'Well, I'll have to get you to excuse *me*'—'n' without another word he'd hyste his nose in the air 'n' shove for home. But if the ground suited him, he would lay low 'n' keep dark till the first pan was washed, 'n' then he would sidle up 'n' take a look, an' if there was about six or seven grains of gold *he* was satisfied—he didn't want no better prospect 'n' that—'n' then he would lay down on our coats and snore like a steamboat till we'd struck the pocket, an' then get up 'n' superintend. He was nearly lightnin' on superintending.

"Well, by an' by, up comes this yer quartz excitement. Everybody was into it—everybody was pick'n' 'n' blast'n' instead of shovelin' dirt on the hillside—everybody was putt'n' down a shaft instead of scrapin' the surface. Noth'n' would do Jim, but *we* must tackle the ledges, too, 'n' so we did. We commenced putt'n' down a shaft, 'n' Tom Quartz he begin to wonder what in the dickens it was all about. *He* hadn't ever seen any mining like that before, 'n' he was all upset, as you may say—he couldn't come to a right understanding of it no way—it was too many for *him*. He was down on it too, you bet you—he was down on it powerful—'n' always appeared to consider it the cussedest foolishness out. But that cat, you know, was *always* agin' newfangled

(*continued*)

arrangements—somehow he never could abide 'em. *You* know how it is with old habits. But by and by Tom Quartz begin to git sort of reconciled a little though he never *could* altogether understand that eternal sinkin' of a shaft an' never pannin' out anything. At last he got to comin' down in the shaft, hisself, to try to cipher it out. An' when he'd git the blues, 'n' feel kind o' scruffy, 'n' aggravated 'n' disgusted—knowin' as he did, that the bills was runnin' up all the time an' we warn't makin' a cent—he would curl up on a gunnysack in the corner an' go to sleep. Well, one day when the shaft was down about eight foot, the rock got so hard that we had to put in a blast— the first blast'n' we'd ever done since Tom Quartz was born. An' then we lit the fuse 'n' clumb out 'n' got off 'bout fifty yards—'n' forgot 'n' left Tom Quartz sound asleep on the gunnysack. In 'bout a minute we seen a puff of smoke bust up out of the hole, 'n' then everything let go with an awful crash, 'n about four million ton of rocks 'n' dirt 'n' smoke 'n' splinters shot up 'bout a mile an' a half into the air, an' by George, right in the dead center of it was old Tom Quartz a'goin' end over end, an' a-snortin' an' a-sneezin', an' a-clawin' an' a-reach'n' for things like all possessed. But it warn't no use, you know, it warn't no use. An' that was the last we see of *him* for about two minutes 'n' a half, an' then all of a sudden it begin to rain rocks and rubbage an' directly he come down ker-whoop about ten foot off f'm where we stood. Well, I reckon he was p'r'aps the orneriest-lookin' beast you ever see. One ear was sot back on his neck, 'n' his tail was stove up, 'n' his eye-winkers was singed off, 'n' he was all blacked up with powder an' smoke, an' all sloppy with mud 'n' slush f'm one end to the other. Well, sir, it warn't no use to try to apologize—we couldn't say a word. He took a sort of disgusted look at himself, 'n' then he looked at us—an' it was just exactly the same as if he had said—'Gents, maybe *you* think it's smart to take advantage of a cat that ain't had no experience of quartz minin', but *I* think different'—an' then he turned on his heel 'n' marched off home without ever saying another word.

"That was jest his style. An' maybe you won't believe it, but after that you never see a cat so prejudiced agin' quartz mining as what he was. An' by an' by when he *did* get to goin' down in the shaft agin', you'd 'a' been astonished at his sagacity. The minute we'd fetch off a blast 'n' the fuse'd begin to sizzle, he'd give a look as much as to say, 'Well, I'll have to git you to excuse *me*,' an' it was surpris'n' the way he'd shin out of that hole 'n' go f'r a tree. Sagacity? It ain't no name for it. 'Twas inspiration!"

I said, "Well, Mr. Baker, his prejudice against quartz mining *was* remarkable, considering how he came by it. Couldn't you ever cure him of it?"

"*Cure him*! No! When Tom Quartz was sot once, he was *always* sot—and you might 'a' blowed him up as much as three million times 'n' you'd never 'a' broken him of his cussed prejudice agin' quartz mining."

Vey, P. C. ～ This cartoonist has written and illustrated three cat cartoon books: *If Cats Could Talk* and *Cats Are People Too*, and *How to be a Cat's Best Friend* P. C. (the C stands for Christopher) grew up with cats, but when he and his wife discovered they were both allergic to cats, they had to give them up. Once a cat lover, always a cat lover, however, and they now enjoy the company of a part-time cat, Oho, an alley cat who manages to make his way into the Veys' apartment building in Manhattan. Oho then finds their door—where fed just once by P. C. in a weak moment—he always returns. And always gets fed.

Vocalizing ～ See TALKING

Wain, Louis ～ (1860–1939) This English artist is best known for his cat illustrations. Wain illustrated over one hundred books and his work appeared regularly in magazines, newspapers, and exhibitions. When he was starting out and newly married, he and his wife had a little kitten named Peter. Shortly after their marriage, his wife

Emily became ill with cancer and was bed-ridden for two years before dying in 1887. Peter brought comfort to Emily during her illness and Louis made sketches of the cat to amuse her. Emily encouraged Louis to submit some of his cat drawings to magazines and newspapers. In no time at all, he became the premier cat artist in England.

Although Louis Wain was a very successful artist, he was not a businessman and was taken advantage of by publishers. His interest in cats became an obsession and his behavior became stranger and stranger. In 1924 he was declared insane and admitted to the paupers' ward at the Middlesex County Mental Asylum. When H. G. Wells, a cat lover himself, heard what had happened to the artist he wrote an appeal for him which was broadcast on British radio. The prime minister stepped in and had Louis moved to a better hospital, where he received special care.

Besides creating wonderful pictures of cats riding bikes, attending teas, napping in the best chair and so on, his artwork served a different purpose for the medical profession, particularly psychiatrists. His steady descent into insanity can be seen in his pictures.

Walk on the Wild Side ～ This
1962 picture produced by Columbia stars Laurence Harvey, Capucine, Jane Fonda, Barbara Stanwyck, Joanna Moore, and, of course, a cat. It is based on the Nelson Algren story "Doll House in New Orleans" and shows the seamier side of life in that city.

Wampus cat ～ Depending on where you look, you're likely to find different definitions for this term—both favorable and unfavorable to our fine feline friends. The *Random House Dictionary of the English Language* defines wampus as "a strange or objectionable person; a lout." In the first quarter of the twentieth century during the teens and twenties the colloquial use of *wampus cat* meant "unbeatable" or "jim dandy."

In 1918 the music publisher and band leader W. C. Handy published the "Wampus Cat Rag" by Jimmie Cox. Another piece of ragtime music, "Tom-Boy" by W. F. Branford, was published in 1908. Its cover pictured a big black tomcat in front of a full moon. In the American South, *catawampus cats* were thought to be evil goblin spirits.

Weir, Harrison ～ This avid catlover organized the first cat show in 1871 in the outskirts of London at the Crystal Palace. A well-established fine painter and illustrator, he published *Our Cats and All About Them* in 1889, a significant volume which promoted cats generally, publicized cat shows, and no doubt led to the proliferation of many other cat books.

Before his descent into madness, the British artist Louis Wain created the world of "Catland," an enormously popular series of paintings of cats engaged in a wide range of activities, published from the 1800s through the 1920s. His black cats (at right) are less scary than most.

Whiskers ∼

The technical name of whiskers is *vibrissae*, which means "stiff, bristly hair." Whiskers are in fact greatly enlarged stiff, coarse hairs with nerve endings that transmit messages to the cat about air currents and nearby objects.

Generally cats have twelve whiskers on each side of their nose, lined up in four rows. The top and bottom rows can move independently; the whiskers in the second and third rows are the most sensitive. Whiskers are also found on other parts of the body, including the cheeks, over the eyes, on the chin and on the back of the forelegs.

Whiskers can move in different ways and can be an indication of different moods. Whiskers that are pointed forward and fanned out are an indication of tension and attention, and that the cat is ready to act. When whiskers are sideways and less spread out, the cat is calm and comfortable. Whiskers that are bunched together and flattened against the side of the face can be a sign of shyness.

It is not exactly known what function the cat's whiskers play. It used to be thought that whiskers enabled the cat to measure spaces; if the cat's whiskers could pass through without being bent, the theory went, so could the cat. However, a cat's whiskers don't always match its girth. Now, whiskers are thought to be used by cats as a kind of "smell radar," locating the direction of an odor from the slightest air current. The cat's whiskers can help guide it at night when it's dark, acting as antennae. The whiskers may bend downward to help guide it over obstacles in its path and may help it identify objects it can not actually see.

If an adult cat's whiskers are cut the cat may become temporarily disoriented. Kittens do not seem to be affected.

White House cats ∼

It cannot be said that the White House has been overrun with cats. However, over the years more than one first family has had one or more first cats. The first president of the United States, George Washington, was a cat lover. And so was the third, Thomas Jefferson.

The first United States president to bring felines to the White House was ABRAHAM LINCOLN. However, cats did not make a reappearance until the administration of TEDDY ROOSEVELT, the twenty-sixth president. CALVIN COOLIDGE brought his three cats, Blackie, Tiger, and Timmie. The next U.S. president to have cats at his residence was Herbert Hoover. When JOHN KENNEDY was at the

The position of the ears and whiskers can signal an attack. (DRAWING BY CHRISTINA DUNSTAN.)

White House, so was the family cat, Tom Kitten. Shan, a Siamese cat, lived in the White House when Gerald Ford was there. When Bill Clinton moved into the White House in 1993, so did Socks, a black and white cat belonging to his daughter, Chelsea.

Wilberforce ∼ Wilberforce was the official mouser for fifteen years at number Ten Downing Street, the official residence of the British prime minister, until his retirement in 1988. A large cat whose white fur was spotted haphazardly with patches of black and tabby fur, Wilberforce started in government service in 1973. He was a gift from the Royal Society for the Prevention of Cruelty to Animals to Prime Minister Edward Heath. Wilberforce was such a menace to the mice that they eventually took off for another location, but although his main occupation as mouser was over, his stay at Ten Downing Street was not. Visitors to Ten Downing Street, a popular tourist attraction, were frequently surprised to see Wilberforce basking on the front step. Although those tourists could not give Wilberforce a little pet or scratch between the ears because of security measures, they sent him bundles of Christmas cards.

Wilberforce was popular with the office staff as well as visiting politicians. When foreign dignitaries arrived he would lie in a prominent place and not move until introduced. Wilberforce was at number Ten Downing during the terms of four different prime ministers—Edward Heath, Harold Wilson, James Callaghan, and Margaret Thatcher. Wilberforce died two years after he retired.

Elizabeth Francis learned this arte of witchcraft of hyr grandmother. When shee taughte it her, she counseiled her to renounce God and to geue of her bloudde to Sathan, whyche she delyuered her in the lykenesse of a white spotted Catte.

THOMAS COOPER, from *Witches at Chelmsford*, 1617

Witchcraft

Cats, especially black cats, have long been associated with witchcraft, which dates to the thirteenth century. Witches were believed to exist all over Europe, where they met in secret covens and worshiped in strange ways. Black cats were thought to play a part in many of their rituals. Old and unattractive women, and spinsters, were often accused of being witches. It was believed that women could change into black cats and then back into women. In cat form they would take part in diabolical rites. When a "witch," or any other accused woman, was tortured, it was not uncommon for her to admit that she was indeed a witch and that she worshiped the Devil in the form of a black cat.

(continued)

The old and infirm were often thought to be witches, accompanied by their familiar, the black cat. This wood-cut of English witches dates from 1618.

The cat became known as the creature of the Devil. He was considered the source of all manner of witchcraft and sorcery, of voodoo and vampirism, of black magic and the Black Mass. *L'Evangile du Diable* (The Devil's Bible) states that, "Only imbeciles do not know that all cats have a pact with the Devil." The book tells how you can become invisible through the use of a black cat. First water is drawn into a new pot at night from a fountain; a fire is built and an agate and black cat are put in the pot which is over the fire. The lid is held down by the left hand as the water boils.

After 24 hours the cat meat is placed in a new dish and thrown over the shoulder. The person watches in a mirror as he or she disappears.

There were specific ways to tell if a cat was a witch. A cat that became alarmed when shown a cross or holy water was thought to be a witch, as was a cat who didn't die immediately when attempts were made to kill him. (That was obviously a no-win situation.) A cat in the vicinity of illness or even sour milk was deemed a witch. Poor crops were blamed on the nearest cat, who was obviously a witch. A cat loitering near a baby was a witch waiting to kill it by sucking its breath. When the Church needed a scapegoat for world problems, witch trials began. Between 1346 and 1349 the Black Death devastated Europe, and that plague and other catastrophes were blamed on witches, and the trials proliferated. In 1484 Pope Innocent VIII issued a condemnation of witchcraft. The decree demanded that whenever a witch was discovered and burned, her cats should die with her. The witch hunts escalated dramatically.

A century later, Inquisitor Nicholas Remy declared that all cats were demons. He wrote that nearly all those suspected witches whom he questioned told him that they changed into cats whenever they wanted to enter someone's home in secret.

The evil deeds of the demonic cat Sathan were recounted at the Chelmsford witch trial of 1579. Thought to be the Devil incarnate, Sathan fed on his mistress's blood and was able to speak with her.

(A little torture may have helped them "remember.") In January, 1587, Barbelline Rayel confessed that she had turned into a cat so that she could enter a house in which a two-year-old baby lived. She dusted the infant with poison powder which she carried in her paw and the baby died.

In 1608, Brother Francesco Maria Guazzo, a writer and scholar of the Roman Catholic church, wrote of a man who swore that he'd seen the transformation of a witch into a cat. He claimed that a certain witch had warned him and his wife not to shoo away any cats who approached his son. She told him his son was strongly bewitched and she would undertake the cure. About an hour later, a large cat the couple had never seen before approached their son. Frightened, they tried to drive the cat away. Finally, the man shut the door and chased the cat until finally it jumped out of a high window. After the incident, the witch stayed in bed for many days. The blows and wounds which the cat had received were found on the corresponding parts of the witch's bruised body.

Before one Isobel Gowdie was executed in 1665 as a witch she confessed that she could turn herself into a cat and back again with the following incantation.

I will goe intil ane catt,
With sorrow, and sych, and a blak shott;
And I sall goe in the Divellis nam,
Ay will I com home againe.

Catt, catt, God send thee a blak shott.
I am in a cattis liknes just now,
Bot I sall be in a womanis liknes ewin now.
Catt, catt, God send thee a blak shott.

It was believed that a witch could get to a sabbat (a midnight meeting) presided over by the Devil by turning herself into an animal, most often a cat. As late as 1718, a Scottish man thought he heard cats gossiping outside his house in human voices. He rushed out, sword and hatchet in hand, and attacked the shadows. The next day two local women were found dead and another badly wounded.

It was also believed that one witch could transform another witch into a black cat by chanting, "The Devil speed thee and go thou with me." The book *Beware of the Cat*, written in 1584, stated that a witch could be transformed into a cat just nine times. (Nine was a mystical number—a trinity of trinities—and the number of lives the cat has.)

In Scotland, the goddess of witches was called Mither o' the Mawkins. A mawkin, or malkin, was either a cat or rabbit. A greymalkin was a gray cat. The term eventually

(continued)

became *grimalkin* and was used for a witch's cat, an old female cat, or a malicious old woman.

In Germany some 100,000 people accused of witchcraft were killed in the sixteenth and seventeenth centuries. In France, 75,000 people were killed. In Europe thousands of "witches" were executed. In the American colonies some two thousand accusations of witchcraft involving cats were upheld in court. In Salem, Massachusetts, about twenty women were executed after witchcraft trials in 1692. Needless to say, black cats bore the brunt of all this. So many were tortured and killed that it is amazing that there are any left today.

Some of the superstitions surrounding witches and black cats persist. During a witch alarm in York County, Pennsylvania, in 1929, a newspaper instructed its readers to keep the Devil from the door by plunging a black cat into boiling water. Once cooked, the last bone of the cat's tail would serve as a protective amulet.

A Scottish scholar, poet, and folklorist who died in 1912 made this observation:

Everyone is aware that a perfectly comfortable, well-fed cat will occasionally come to his house and settle there, deserting a family by whom it is lamented, and to whom it could, if it chose, find its way back with ease. This conduct is a mystery which may lead us to infer that cats form a great secret society, and that they come and go in pursuance of some policy connected with education, or perhaps with witchcraft.

See also BLACK CATS.

The cat in gloves catches no mice.

—BENJAMIN FRANKLIN, 18th century American statesman, author, inventor

Working cats ∼ Many cats live their lives as pampered pets—their work consists of a snooze on a sunny windowsill (hard work), eating food prepared and provided by someone else (harder work), and being a loving, caring companion (not hard at all). But there are some cats who earn their keep. Many cats have served as mousers, ridding granaries and other places of rodents. According to legend, cats were created when Noah's ark became rampant with rats. Noah caused the lion to sneeze and out came the cat—and the mouse problem was solved.

While mousing remains the primary occupation of most "employed" cats, many can be found in quite diverse surroundings performing other jobs as well. It would be impossible to list them all—and some particularly well-known cats have their own entry in this book—but here are just a few of the other working cats that you may chance upon in traveling around the United States.

The Night Watchman on Pine Island, New York, started off in the traditional role of mouser but went on to bigger and better (?) things. A stray cat, the Night Watchman showed up one day, uninvited, at Webster's Feed Store. Nobody asked him to leave, since he started working as soon as he showed up—catching mouse after mouse after mouse. When he rid the store of mice he became the office manager. (It was rumored that when he was at the helm no one passed a bad check.) He could be found most often lounging on the desk in the office. The Night Watchman worked at Webster's for eighteen years until dying, quietly, in his sleep.

As one might expect from his name, Feedback has worked at radio station WJCO in Jackson, Michigan, since 1988, when he was six months old. Surrounded by cornfields, WJCO was home for a lot of mice who dined on wires and left droppings inside equipment and on the studio floor. The droppings were bad enough, but the station was off the air for a full day when a mouse dined on some wires. Enough was enough.

Feedback was adopted from the Cascade Humane Society and proved to be the perfect mouser, feeding himself on every mouse in sight. Fame and fortune have not gone to his head, though; he appreciates all the gifts and cards he receives, from as far away as Arizona, California, Minnesota, and New Jersey. When not in the lobby greeting visitors Feedback may be hanging out in the air studio. He will go in when the mike is turned on and say hello to listeners in his own inimitable way.

A working cat in a shop window in Lille, France, taken by the great French photographer Henri Cartier-Bresson. (COURTESY MAGNUM PHOTOS.)

Fang is a twenty-pound, white, longhair cat who has his own picture ID card, signed by his boss, the police chief in Grand Prairie, Texas. Fang was found at the local pound by two officers on the force who asked for the "biggest, baddest" cat there. According to the Grand Prairie *Daily News*, the need for a big, bad cat arose when rats were feasting on evidence in the property room. Fang went on to be the official welcomer.

Another cat with his own ID is Donut. Donut's ID is a special cat-sized security badge, number 52½. This black and white cat, along with other security guards, patrols Lockheed's Shipyard in Harbor Island, Seattle. Donut, who has never missed a day of work, resides in the company's payroll booth, where he has his own bed. His cupboard, which has his name on it, has his cat food, chicken treats, luster bath, and flea powder.

On staff at a library in Spencer, Ohio, since January 1988, is Dewey Readmore Books. Workers arrived to find a twelve-week-old kitten who'd been put through the bookdrop. The staff adopted the little kitten and made him the official and permanent library cat. They temporarily named him Dewey (for the Dewey Decimal System) and then asked patrons to help name the cat. From close to four hundred entries, the more formal Dewey Readmore Books was chosen. Dewey's paycheck, which covers expenses for his food and vet visits, is funded by contributions.

Riley serves as the mascot, desk paperweight (as does my cat), and paw printer of clean log sheets (as does my cat on manuscript pages) at an electronics company. Riley has his own company ID, of course, with a full color picture—as does every employee. One day an employee switched badges with Riley, wore Riley's badge all day, and no one noticed. Snoozing on a chair in an office one day, a salesman brought in another chair for his customer—so that Riley would not be disturbed.

Tanna resides at the Crystal Clear Sound re-cording studio in Dallas, Texas. A calico cat, Tanna just showed up one day and was about to partake of some of the food offered by the owners when she spotted a mouse. To the delight of her hosts, she chose the mouse instead, endearing herself to them forever. (Resident mice at the studio were not as happy.) When she's not greeting customers, Tanna frequently naps on the warm, cozy recording panel—which must be totally disassembled regularly to remove cat hairs! But Tanna does earn her keep. Some clients choose to do business with Crystal Clear because they are so fond of Tanna. Of course, many cats have also earned their keep by working in show business. See ADVERTISING for more details.

If I let her in and go on writing without taking notice of her, there is a real demonstration of affection for five minutes. She purrs, she walks round and round me, she jumps on my lap, she rubs her head and nose against my chin.

MATTHEW ARNOLD, English writer and literary critic (1822–1888)

The cat, if you but singe her tabby skin,
The chimney keeps, and sits content within:
But once grown sleek, will from her corner run,
Sport with her tail and wonton in the sun:
She licks her fair round face, and frisks abroad
To show her fun, and to be catterwaw'd.

from "The Prologue of the Wyves' Tale of Bathe," *Canterbury Tales*, c. 1380s, GEOFFREY CHAUCER, British poet (c. 1340–1400)

Writers ～ Many celebrated writers have kept cats, and most of them have included their favorite cat or cats somewhere in their work. And some writers have made their cat the focal point of their stories, plays, poems, music, and films. Who knows how literature would have been affected if writers did not have their loyal, loving, and very occasionally critical cats by their sides?

Folklore and fables involving cats are found all over the world. They date back centuries and were passed on from generation to generation, from parent to child, parent to child. Consequently, many have more than one version. The English folktale DICK WHITTINGTON AND HIS CAT for example, survives in several different versions.

One of the best known writers (or recorders) of fables was AESOP, who lived in the mid-sixth century B.C. A traditional writer of Greek fables, he used cats and other animals to make moral points. For example, in his tale "Belling the Cat," the moral of the story is spoken by a mouse at the end: "It is easy to propose impossible remedies," he says.

Another classic fairy tale is "PUSS IN BOOTS" by the seventeenth-century French writer Charles Perrault, who wrote other tales such as well, such as "Little Red Riding Hood," "Cinderella," and "Sleeping Beauty."

Cats are frequently the subject of CHILDREN'S CAT BOOKS. One of the most popular is *The Cat in the Hat* by Dr. Seuss, whose real name is Theodore Seuss Geisel. (Plenty of adults, myself included, enjoy *The Cat in the Hat*; whether you are twelve or one hundred twelve, this book belongs in the collection of every ailurophile.)

In addition to appearing in fairy tales and NURSERY RHYMES, which have been passed down from generation to generation, cats have played prominent roles in "serious" novels, stories and poems. One of the earliest known poets to sing the praises of cats is the sixteenth-century poet JOACHIM DU BELLAY. He wrote a two hundred–verse

---

My Small Grey Cat

He was my very dear
Companion everywhere,
My room, my bed, my table,
Even more companionable
Than a little dog; for he
Was never one of those
Monsters that hideously
Fill night with their miaows;
And now he can't become,
Poor little puss, a tom—
Sad loss, by which his splendid
Line is abruptly ended.

JOACHIM DU BELLAY (1525–1560)

---

memorial poem to his cat Gri Argentin Petit Belaud. The nineteenth century French poet, novelist, and critic THÉOPHILE GAUTIER, wrote a libretto for the composer Frédéric Massenet. However, Massenet's opera *Le Preneur de Rats* (The Ratcatcher) was never performed.

Some cat tales are among the treasures of literature. One of the best known is "THE BLACK CAT" by Edgar Allan Poe. Edouard Charles Antoine Zola, better known as ZOLA, wrote the lovely moral tale *The Paradise of Cats*, while RUDYARD KIPLING penned the instructive *The Cat That Walked by Himself*. And who could resist a story by American writer and humorist MARK TWAIN? His *Dick Baker's Cat* is also included. LILLIAN JACKSON BRAUN has featured a cat detective in a series of mysteries that have promptly become bestsellers, as have CLEVELAND AMORY's accounts of his cat, Polar Bear. Other authors who wrote frequently about cats include COLETTE, ERNEST HEMINGWAY, VICTOR HUGO, DR. SAMUEL JOHNSON, EDWARD LEAR, and ROBERT SOUTHEY.

Numerous anthologies of cat stories and

poems have been published, including works by such writers as Wordsworth, Kipling, Saki, Chekhov, Balzac, Baudelaire, Verlaine, Rilke, Ambrose Bierce, Paul Gallico, Dorothy L. Sayers, Stephen Vincent Benet, Henry James, P. G. Wodehouse, Damon Runyon, and Doris Lessing. (See the Author Index for a complete list of authors who works are included or quoted in this volume.)

> Sages austere and fervent lovers both,
> In their ripe season, cherish cats, the pride
> Of hearths, strong, mild, and to themselves allied
> In chilly stealth and sedentary sloth.
>
> "Cats," Charles Baudelaire,
> French poet (1821–1867)

You Only Live Twice ～ In this 1967 James Bond thriller, Sean Connery plays Agent 007. His evil enemy, Ernst Stavro Blofield, is played by Donald Pleasence. Having a cameo role in the film is Blofield's white chinchilla cat named Solomon. Solomon and Sean Connery appeared together again four years later, in 1971, in the Bond film *Diamonds Are Forever*.

> Cats, like men, are flatterers.
>
> WALTER SAVAGE LANDOR, English poet, critic prose writer (1775–1864)
>
> The cat is never vulgar.
>
> CARL VAN VECHTEN, American writer (1880–1964)

> She walks her chosen path by our side; but our ways are not her ways, our influence does not remotely reach her.
>
> AGNES REPPLIER, American essayist (1855–1950)

Z

Zola, *Emile Edouard Charles Antoine* ∼
(1840–1902) This French writer and cat lover,
born in Paris, began his career as a journalist and
clerk, later becoming a well-known novelist

and social critic. The story that follows reveals
that even when he wrote about cats, his work
maintained a moral tone, conveying a mes-
sage.

The Paradise of Cats

An aunt bequeathed me an Angora cat, which is certainly the most stupid animal I
know of. This is what my cat related to me, one winter night, before the warm
embers.

I

I was then two years old, and I was certainly the fattest and most simple cat anyone
could have seen. Even at that tender age I displayed all the presumption of an animal
that scorns the attractions of the fireside. And yet what gratitude I owed to Providence
for having placed me with your aunt! The worthy woman idolized me. I had a regular
bedroom at the bottom of a cupboard, with a feather pillow and a triple-folded rug.
The food was as good as the bed; no bread or soup, nothing but meat, good
underdone meat.

Well! amidst all these comforts, I had but one wish, but one dream, to slip out by the
half-open window, and run away on to the tiles. Caresses appeared to me insipid, the

softness of my bed disgusted me, I was so fat that I felt sick, and from morn till eve I experienced the weariness of being happy.

I must tell you that by straining my neck I had perceived the opposite roof from the window. That day four cats were fighting there. With bristling coats and tails in the air, they were rolling on the blue slates, in the full sun, amidst oaths of joy. I had never witnessed such an extraordinary sight. From that moment my convictions were settled. Real happiness was upon that roof, in front of that window which the people of the house so carefully closed. I found the proof of this in the way in which they shut the doors of the cupboards where the meat was hidden.

I made up my mind to fly. I felt sure there were other things in life than underdone meat. There was the unknown, the ideal. One day they forgot to close the kitchen window. I sprang on to a small roof beneath it.

II

How beautiful the roofs were! They were bordered by broad gutters exhaling delicious odors. I followed those gutters in raptures of delight, my feet sinking into fine mud, which was deliciously warm and soft. I fancied I was walking on velvet. And the generous heat of the sun melted my fat.

I will not conceal from you the fact that I was trembling in every limb. My delight was mingled with terror. I remember, particularly, experiencing a terrible shock that almost made me tumble down into the street. Three cats came rolling over from the top of a house towards me, mewing most frightfully, and as I was on the point of fainting away, they called me a silly thing, and said they were mewing for fun. I began mewing with them. It was charming. The jolly fellows had none of my stupid fat. When I slipped on the sheets of zinc heated by the burning sun, they laughed at me. An old tom, who was one of the band, showed me particular friendship. He offered to teach me a thing or two, and I gratefully accepted. Ah! your aunt's cat's meat was far from my thoughts! I drank in the gutters, and never had sugared milk seemed so sweet to me. Everything appeared nice and beautiful. A she-cat passed by, a charming she-cat, the sight of her gave me a feeling I had never experienced before. Hitherto, I had only seen these exquisite creatures, with such delightfully supple backbones, in my dreams. I and my three companions rushed forward to meet the newcomer. I was in front of the others, and was about to pay my respects to the bewitching thing, when one of my comrades cruelly bit my neck. I cried out with pain.

"Bah!" said the old tom, leading me away; "you will meet with stranger adventures than that."

III

After an hour's walk I felt as hungry as a wolf.

"What do you eat on the roofs?" I inquired of my friend the tom.

"What you can find," he answered shrewdly.

This reply caused me some embarrassment, for though I carefully searched I found nothing. At last I perceived a young work-girl in a garret preparing her lunch. A beautiful chop of a tasty red color was lying on a table under the window.

"There's the very thing I want," I thought, in all simplicity.

And I sprang on to the table and took the chop. But the work girl, having seen me, struck me a fearful blow with a broom on the spine, and I fled, uttering a dreadful oath.

"You are fresh from your village then?" said the tom. "Meat that is on tables is there for the purpose of being longed for at a distance. You must search in the gutters."

I could never understand that kitchen meat did not belong to cats. My stomach was beginning to get seriously angry. The tom put me completely to despair by telling me it would be necessary to wait until night. Then we would go down into the street and turn over the heaps of muck. Wait until night! He said it quietly, like a hardened philosopher. I felt myself fainting at the mere thought of this prolonged fast.

IV

Night came slowly, a foggy night that chilled me to the bones. It soon began to rain, a fine, penetrating rain, driven by sudden gusts of wind. We went down along the glazed roof of a staircase. How ugly the street appeared to me! It was no longer that nice heat, that beautiful sun, those roofs white with light where one rolled about so deliciously. My paws slipped on the greasy stones. I sorrowfully recalled to memory my triple blanket and feather pillow.

We were hardly in the street when my friend the tom began to tremble. He made himself small, very small, and ran stealthily along beside the houses, telling me to follow as rapidly as possible. He rushed in at the first street door he came to, and purred with satisfaction as he sought refuge there. When I questioned him as to the motive of his flight, he answered:

"Did you see that man with a basket on his back and a stick with an iron hook at the end?"

"Yes."

"Well! if he had seen us he would have knocked us on the heads and roasted us!"

"Roasted us!" I exclaimed. "Then the street is not ours? One can't eat, but one's eaten!"

V

However, the boxes of kitchen refuse had been emptied before the street doors. I rummaged in the heaps in despair. I came across two or three bare bones that had been lying among the cinders, and I then understood what a succulent dish fresh cat's meat made. My friend the tom scratched artistically among the muck. He made me run about until morning, inspecting each heap, and without showing the least hurry. I was out in the rain for more than ten hours, shivering in every limb. Cursed street, cursed liberty, and how I regretted my prison!

At dawn the tom, seeing I was staggering said to me with a strange air:

"Have you had enough of it?"

"Oh yes," I answered.

"Do you want to go home?"

"I do, indeed; but how shall I find the house?"

"Come along. This morning, when I saw you come out, I understood that a fat cat like you was not made for the lively delights of liberty. I know your place of abode and will take you to the door."

The worthy tom said this very quietly. When we had arrived, he bid me "Good-bye," without betraying the least emotion.

"No," I exclaimed, "we will not leave each other so. You must accompany me. We will share the same bed and the same food. My mistress is a good woman—"

He would not allow me to finish my sentence.

"Hold your tongue," he said sharply, "you are a simpleton. Your effeminate existence would kill me. Your life of plenty is good for bastard cats. Free cats would never purchase your cat's meat and feather pillow at the price of a prison. Good-bye."

And he returned up on to the roofs, where I saw his long outline quiver with joy in the rays of the rising sun.

When I got in, your aunt took the whip and gave me a thrashing which I received with profound delight. I tasted in full measure the pleasure of being beaten and being warm. Whilst she was striking me, I thought with rapture of the meat she would give me afterwards.

You see—concluded my cat, stretching itself out in front of the embers—real happiness, paradise, my dear master, consists in being shut up and beaten in a room where there is meat.

I am speaking from the point of view of cats.

Miel, now a city cat. (DRAWING BY CHRISTINA DUNSTAN.)

My cat, Miel, is from a farm in upstate New York, where he was found meowing pitifully in the grass by someone passing by. He was just four weeks old and had lost his mother. I took him home with me, and though he usually seems content, I sometime wonder if there's a part of him that longs to return to the life of a farm cat.

The Road Not Taken or The Cat Speaketh

Sitting on the table, he eyes me once or twice
Then turns away and licks his paws, he's ready for some mice.
Sadly though, they're hard to find, in so pristine a home,
For decent mice, or birds or fish, so far he'd have to roam.
You see, Miel's a city cat, whose food comes from some cans
Via the local A & P and not from wild lands
Veal with gravy, chicken and cheese . . . just to name a few,
He eats them all, or most of them, and then gives one long mew.
But content he's not, I do fear—it's not a mew of pleasure,

Alas, he would prefer to have, just one mouse . . . at his leisure
He lives in a prewar apartment, on the plush Upper East Side,
But if I said it's his first choice, I surely would have lied.
For Miel comes from a farm upstate, with grass, a barn and mice
If Miel were asked by any cat he'd furnish this advice:
"It's an easy life in a city apartment; food and water each day,
But I'd trade it in a minute—to wander and to stray,
To different places, far and wide, I'd explore it all,
'Tis not as easy as city life—but I would walk so tall,
And run and play and catch my prey for dinner or a snack,
A nearby stream, a sunny spot, for nothing would I lack.
So you can take the easy life, choose the easy way,
I would choose the freedom route, and live from day to day.
For even with nine lives, life's short, I do not want regret.
I'd rather live a life that's free, than be a pampered pet.
To be free in the wilderness is not an easy life,
But living free is the only way, and that is my advice.

Roberta Altman

I am the cat of cats. I am
    The everlasting cat!
Cunning, and old, and sleek as jam,
    The everlasting cat!

"The Cat of Cats," WILLIAM BRIGHTY
RANDS, British poet (1823–1882)

Resources

Humane, Education, and Advocacy Groups

*Actors and Others for Animals—nonprofit,
   celebrity-supported education/advocacy group*
5510 Cahuenga Blvd.
North Hollywood, CA 91601
818/985-6263

*American Society for the Prevention of Cruelty to
   Animals (ASPCA)*
424 E 92 St.
New York, NY 10128
212/246-2096

Cat Socializers Program
San Francisco SPCA
2500 16th St.
San Francisco, CA 94103
415/554-3087

Delta Society
sponsors the Pet Partners program and
   promotes beneficial relationships between
   animals and people.
321 Burnett Avenue South, Third Floor
Renton, WA 98055-2569
206/226-7357

Friends of Cats
15587 Old Highway 80
El Cahor, CA 92021
619/561-0361

The Fund for Animals
200 W 57 St.
New York, NY 10021
212/246-2096

Humane Society of the United States
2100 L St. NW
Washington, D.C. 20037
202/452-1100

The Last Post—a retirement community
for cats
95 Belden St.
Falls Village, CT 06031
203/824-0831

Morris Animal Foundation
45 Inverness Drive
East Englewood, CO 80112-5480
800/243-2345

Pets for Patient Progress
P.O. Box 143
Crystal Lake, IL 60039-0143
815/455-0990

Pets for People
call the Animal Shelter in your area,
or 314/982-3028 for information

POWARS (Pet Owners with AIDS/ARC Resource
Service, Inc.)
P.O. Box 1116, Madison Square Garden
New York, NY 10159
212/744-0842

Sheba Selectacat—Computerized selection
process to determine which cat breeds are
right for your personality and life-style.
3250 E. 44th St.
Vernon CA 90058-0853

Tree House Animal Foundation, Inc.
1212 West Carmen Avenue
Chicago, IL 60640-2999
312/784-5605

State-by-State Listing
of Humane Societies

Following is a list of humane societies, by state, that do not euthanize animals unless it is medically necessary. If this is important to you, check with the organization before bringing a cat there or making a donation to find out if that policy is still in effect.

ALASKA

Alaska Humane Society
P.O. Box 103567
Anchorage, AK 00510

ARIZONA

Animals Benefit Club of Arizona
P.O. Box 26627
Phoenix, AZ 85608

Pet Pride of America
P.O. Box 44915
Phoenix, AZ 85064

Arizona Animal Anticruelty Society
P.O. Box 78359
Tucson, AZ 85703

CALIFORNIA

Berkeley East Bay Humane Society
P.O. Box 2222
Berkeley, CA 94702-0222

Love and Care for God's Animalife
68-769 First Street, Apt. 289
Cathedral City, CA 92234

D.E.L.T.A. Rescue
P.O. Box 9
Glendale, CA 91209-0009

Friends of Cats, Inc.
P.O. Box 1613
Lakeside, CA 92040

Animal Helpline
P.O. Box 944
Morongo Valley, CA 92256

Living Free Animal Sanctuary
P.O. Box 5
54250 Keen Camp Road
Mountain Center, CA 92361

Pet Pride
P.O. Box 1055
Pacific Palisades, CA 90272

Lend-A-Paw Operation Shelter, Inc.
226 Airlane Drive
Palm Springs, CA 92262

Helen Woodward Animal Center
6461 El Apajo
P.O. Box 64
Rancho Santa Fe, CA 92067

San Francisco SPCA
2500 16th Street
San FRancisco, CA 94103

N.A.R.F.
P.O. Box 26587
San jose, CA 95159

Animal Lovers Unlimited
P.O. Box 274
Yuba City, CA 95992

COLORADO

Animal Rescue & Adoption Society
2390 South Delaware
Denver, CO 80223

Cat Care Society
5985 W. 11th Avenue
Lakewood, CO 80214

Fur Purries
111 W. Abriendo
Pueblo, CO 81004

CONNECTICUT

Aid to Helpless Animals, Inc.
P.O. Box 434
Bloomfield, CT 06002

Last Post
Belden Street, Rt. 126
Falls Village, CT 06031

Abandoned Animals
215 Highland Avenue
Hamden, CT 06581

MEOW, Inc.
P.O. Box 999, 10 Naser Road
Litchfield, CT 06759

Meriden Humane Society
546 South Curtis Street
Meriden, CT 06450

Animal Friends of Connecticut
P.O. Box 370306
West Hartford, CT 06137-0306

FLORIDA

K & C Pet Rescue and Adoption Society
9160 Commonwealth Avenue
Jacksonville, FL 32220

Leesburg Humane Society
P.O. Box 895334
Leesburg, FL 34789-5334

Adopt-A-Pet Inc.
11900 232nd Street S.W.
Miami, FL 33170

Animal Aid Society
2309 Boone Boulevard
Tallahassee, FL 32303

GEORGIA

Good News Animal Foundation
788 Sandtown Road
Marietta, GA 30060

All C.A.T.S. Inc.
9880 Robinwood Lane
Roswell, GA 30075-4128

IDAHO

Just Strays
P.O. Box 8812
Boise, ID 83707

ILLINOIS

Tree House Animal Foundation
1212 West Carmen Avenue
Chicago, IL 60640

Animal Protective Association
P.O. Box 18098
Chicago, IL 60618

Felines, Inc.
P.O. Box 268020
Chicago, IL 60626

The Assissi Foundation
P.O. Box 143
Crystal Lake
Crystal, IL 60014

Kindness Inc.
P.O. Box 7071
Elgin, IL 60120

West Suburban Humane Society
P.O. Box 757
Lombard, IL 60148

Humane Society of Rock Island County
724 West 2nd Avenue
Milan, IL 61264

Save-A-Pet
2019 North Rand
Palatine, IL 60074

INDIANA

Independent Cat Society
P.O. Box 841
Michigan City, IN 46360

Pet Refuge
800 E. Jefferson Boulevard
South Bend, IN 46617

MAINE

Protectors of Animal Life (P.A.L.S.)
Case Road
Winthrop, ME 04343

MARYLAND

Animal Rescue Inc.
P.O. Box 35
Maryland Line, MD 21105

MASSACHUSETTS

Bosler Humane Society
P.O. Box 520
Barre, MA 01005

The Alliance for Animals
P.O. Box 909
Boston, MA 02103

Just Cats
P.O. Box 531
Mansfield, MA 02048

Last Resort
1126 Broadway
Hanover, MA 02339

Northeast Animal Shelter
204 Highland Avenue
Salem, MA 01970

MINNESOTA

Animal Relief Fund
P.O. Box 234
Hopkins, MN 55411

MISSOURI

Open Door Animal Sanctuary
6065 Duda Road
House Springs, MO 63041

*Society for Treatment of Abandoned and
   Fractured Friends*
P.O. Box 1061
Laurie, MO 65038

NEW JERSEY

American Society for the Welfare of Cats
P.O. Box 487
Bellmawr, NJ 08099

Animal Haven Farm
124 Evergreen Avenue
Newark, NJ 07114

NEW YORK

Kent Animal Shelter
River Road
Calverton, NY 11933

North Shore Animal League
25 Davis Avenue
Port Washington, NY 11050

League for Animal Protection of Huntington, Inc.
P.O. Box 390
Huntington, NY 11743

Bide-A-Wee Home Association
410 East 38th Street
New York City, NY 10016

Bide-A-Wee Home Association
3300 Beltaugh Avenue
Wantaugh, NY 11793

Bide-A-Wee Home Association
118 Old Century Road
Westhampton, NY 11977

The Humane Society of New York
306 East 59th Street
New York City, NY 10022

Pet Pride of New York Inc.
P.O. Box Mendonlonia Road
Mendon, NY 14506

Mid-Hudson Animal Aid Inc.
40 Echo Lane
Newburgh, NY 12550

Animal Haven, Inc.
35-22 Prince Street
P.O. Box 390
Flushing, NY 11354

NORTH CAROLINA

Humane Society of Charlotte
P.O. Box 221028
Charlotte, NC 28222

OHIO

Bide-A-Wee Cat Shelter
8800 Akins Road
North Royalton, OH 44133

OKLAHOMA

Free to Live
P.O. Box 130072
Edmond, OK 73013-0072

Petfinders Animal Welfare Society, Inc.
P.O. Box 7083
Moore, OK 73153

Second Chance Animal Sanctuary, Inc.
P.O. Box 1266
Norman, OK 73070

OREGON

Spay and Neuter Humane Association
333 W. Maine Drive
Astoria, OR 97103-6205

Evergreen-Doe Humane Society
10605 S.E. Loop Road
Dayton, OR 97114

PENNSYLVANIA

Animal Care Fund, Inc.
Animal Care Sanctuary
P.O. Box A
East Smithfield, PA 18817

Kitty and K-9 Connection
P.O. Box 312
Drexel Hill, PA 19026

Animal Friends, Inc.
2643 Pennsylvania Avenue
Pittsburgh, PA 15222

TEXAS

Operation Kindness
1029 Trend
Carrollton, TX 75006

Animal Adoption Center
117 North Garland Avenue
Garland, TX 75040

Special Pets
4211 Bellaire Blvd.
Houston, TX 77025

Pals of Katy
P.O. Box 6575
Katy, TX 77492

Animal Defense League
11300 Nacogdoches Road
San Antonio, TX 782009

UTAH

Wasatch Humane Society
P.O. Box 61
Hooper, UT 84025-0059

Best Friends Animal Sanctuary
P.O. Box G
Kanab, UT 84741-5020

VIRGINIA

Animal Allies
P.O. Box 353
Fairfax Station, VA 22039

Homeless Animal Rescue Team
P.O. Box 7261
Fairfax Station, VA 22039-7261

Lend-A-Paw Relief Organization
P.O. Box 4864
Falls Church, VA 22044

Caring for Creatures
Route 2, P.O. Box 1009
Palmyra, VA 22963

Peace Plantation
15-B Catoctin Circle S.E. #207
Leesburg, VA 22075

WASHINGTON

Spokanimal Care
North 710 Napa, P.O. Box 3151
Spokane, WA 99220

Pend Oreille Humane Society
HCR 1, P.O. Box 27
Springdale, WA 99173

CANADA
Animal Rescue Missions
773 Warden Avenue
Scarborough, Ontario M1L4C2

Medical Organizations

Animal Blood Bank—This medical service for cats in need (and other animals) was founded in 1989 by Stan Carlin, D.V.M. So far, three blood types have been identified for cats: A,B, and AB.
P.O. Box 6211
Vacaville, CA 95696

Animal Medical Center—One of the best medical facilities in the country, founded in 1911.
510 E. 62nd Street
New York, NY 10021
(212) 838-8100

Robert H. Winn foundation—Nonprofit organization supporting health-related research benefitting cats; founded by the CFA.
P.O. Box 1005
Manasquan, NJ 08736-1005
(908) 528-9797

Breeders Associations

American Cat Association (ACA)
8101 Katherine
Panorama City, CA 91402
(818) 782-6080

American Cat Fanciers' Association, Inc. (ACFA)
P.O. Box 203
Point Lookout, MO 65726
(417) 334-5430

Canadian Cat Association
52 Dean Street
Brampton, Ontario
Canada L6W 1M6
(416) 459-1481

Cat Fanciers Association (CFA)
P.O. Box 1005
Manasquan, NJ 08736-1005
(908) 528-9797

Cat Fanciers' Federation, Inc. (CFF)
9509 Montgomery Road
Cincinnati, OH 45242
(513) 984-1841

The International Cat Association (TICA)
P.O. Box 2684
Harlingen, TX 78551
(210) 428-8046

United Cat Federation
5510 Ptolemy Way
Mira Loma, CA 91752
(714) 685-7896

Breed and Household Pet Clubs

Following, in alphabetical order by cat breed, are clubs catering to owners of particular breeds. As you can see, there are clubs for non-pedigree, or household cats, as well as established breeds.

Abyssinian Cat Club of America
Mary Janes
4060 Croaker Lane
Woodbridge, VA 22193

American Curl Cat Club
Patricia Speciale
100 Westmont Road
Syracuse, NY 13219

National American Shorthair Club
Rosemary Kendrick
1331 No. Wingra Drive
Madison, WI 53715

National Birman Fanciers
Jan Walker Rogers
P.O. Box 1830
Stephenville, TX 76401

Sacred Cat of Burma Fanciers (Birman)
Ed Rindfleisch
5542 Cleveland Road
Wooster, OH 44691

International Bombay Society
Suzanne Swecker
5782 Dalton Drive
Farmington, NY 14425

United Burmese Cat Fanciers
Marianne Bolling
2395 N.E. 185th Street
North Miami Beach, FL 33180

Calico Cat Registry International
Judith Lindley
P.O. Box 944
Morongo Valley, CA 92256

Cameo Cat Club of America
Jean Nordlund
1800 W. Ardel
Kuna, ID 83634

Chartreux East
Jill Rasmussen
305 Aylee Avenue, N.W.
Leesburg, VA 22075

Cornish Rex Society
Carol Barbee
720 Fisherville Road
Fisherville, KY 40023

Cymric Cat Club
Cynthia Whitney
1307 W. 134th Street, #25
Gardena, CA 90247

National Egyptian Mau Club
Tobe Goldman
52 Gregory Road
Framingham, MA 01701

Havana Brown Fanciers
Donna Kovach
893 Lincoln Court
San Jose, CA 95125

International Havana Brown Society
Norma Placchi
101 Vagabond Way
Danville, CA 94256

The Havana (Brown) Preservation Society
Lisa Quat
40 Clinton Street
Brooklyn Heights, NY 11201

The Himalayan Society
Jean Jahoda
P.O. Box 17343
Anaheim, CA 92817-7343

Happy Household Pet Cat Club
Lois Evers
P.O. Box 334
Rome, NY 13440

Japanese Bobtail Breeders' Society
Janet Bassetti
1272 Hillwood Lane
Vineland, NJ 08360

*The Longhair Clan—Longhaired (Scottish Fold)
   Breed Club*
Jean Viel III
49 Hancock Street
Salem, MA 01920

Maine Coon Club
Jacqueline Luke-Hayes
7452 N. Port Washington Road
Fox Point, WI 53217

The International Manx and Cymric Society
Susan Stude
70 Nottingham Road
Elkton, MD 21921

The International Mitten Cat Association
J. Hamel
P.O. Box 472, West Hill Station
Scarborough, Ontario
Canada M1E 4Y9

National Norwegian Forest Cat Club
Jane Barletta
17 Ashwood Road
Trenton, NJ 08610-1328

Norwegian Forest Cat Fanciers' Association
Patti Gavin
2507 Ocean Drive South
Jacksonville Beach, FL 32250

Ocicats International
Toni Kaser
8 Turnberry
Arden, NC 28704

Orientals West
Cherylee DeYoung
1464 N. Mulberry
Rialto, CA 92376

Persian Bicolor and Calico Society
Evelyn Locke
187 N. Madison Drive
South Plainfield, NJ 07080

United Silver (Persian) Fanciers
Wilma Van Scoyk
663 N. Dayton Lakeview Road
New Carlisle, OH 45344

Ragdoll Fanciers Club
Rosemary Howarth
7041 67th Street N.W.
Gig Harbor, WA 98335

Ragdoll Lovers Club
Georgann Chambers
5510 Ptolemy Way
Mira Loma, CA 91752

Rex Breeders United
Diane Straka
446 Itasca Court, N.W.
Rochester, MN 55901

Russian Blue Society
Patt Knudtson
1602 Southbrook Drive
Wadena, MN 56482

Siamese Cat Society of America
Henri Pelletier
304 S.W. 13th Street
Fort Lauderdale, FL 33315

Traditional (Apple-headed) Siamese Breeder and
    Fanciers Association
Diana Fineran
1000 Pegasus Farms Lane
Alpharetta, GA 30201

International Singapura Alliance
Donna Lowe
P.O. Box 32218
Oakland, CA 94604

Singapura Fanciers' Society
Hal Meadow
82 W. Catalina Drive
Oakview, CA 93022

United Singapura Society
Cathie McHenry
2135 Edison
Santa Ynez, CA 93460

Snowshoe Cat Fanciers of America
Daline Toft
P.O. Box 121
Watkins, CO 80143

The Great Somali Society
Phil Mariner
238 Church Street
Poughkeepsie, NY 12601

Somali Cat Club
Evelyn Mague
10 Western Boulevard
Gillette, NJ 79633

Somali Cat Club of America
Margot Sweet
5027 Armstrong
Wichita, KS 67204

International Sphynx Breeders and Fanciers
    Association
Kathy Speed
Route 1, Box 190
Benton, MS 39039

Tonkinese Breed Club
Jane Barletta
17 Ashwood Road
Trenton, NJ 08610-1328

Turkish Van Cat Club of North America
Carol Van Orden
1302 Exchange
Emporia, KS 66801

Cultural Organizations, Magazines, Newsletters, Catalogs

The Animal Connection and College Fur Cats—
    training school for careers in show business.
5323 Colodny Drive
Old Agoura Hills, CA 91301
818/597-8760

Animal Watch
(published by the ASPCA)
424 E. 92 St.
New York, NY 10128
212/876-7700

Cat Claws, Inc.
1004 W. Broadway
P.O. Box 1001
Morrilton, AR 72110
800/738-0977

Cat Collectors—Newsletters/catalog to members.
33161 Wendy Drive
Sterling Heights, MI 48310
313/264-0285

Cat Fanciers' Newsletter
304 Hastings
Redlands, CA 92373

Cat Fancy
P.O. Box 6050
Mission Viejo, CA 92690

Catnip
Newsletter of Tufts University Medical Center
P.O. Box 420014
Palm Coast, FL 32142-0014
800/829-0926

Cats
P.O. Box 290037
Port Orange, FL 32129-0037
904/788-2770

Cats, Cats & More Cats—The complete catalog for catlovers.
Route 17M, P.O. Box 270
Monroe, NY 10950

Cats "R" Us
P.O. Box 112
Jonesville, IN 47247

Cat World International
P.O. Box 35635
Phoenix, AZ 85069

Drs. Foster & Smith, Inc.
2253 Air Park Road
P.O. Box 100
Rhinelander, WI 54501-0100
800/826-7206

The Felix Company
3623 Freemont Avenue North
Seattle, WA 98103
800/24-FELIX

Friends of Heart
322 Commercial St.
Provincetown, MA 02657
508/487-1136

Here Kitty Kitty
7491-C5N Federal Highway
Suite 259
Boca Raton, FL 33487

"I Love Cats"
950 Third Avenue, 16th Floor
New York, NY 10022

Just Cats
Box 1831
New Fairfield, CT 06812
203/746-6760

Library Cat Society
Box 274
Morehead, MN 56560

Pawprints
P.O. Box 833
North Hollywood, CA 91603

The Persian Quarterly
4401 Zephyr Street
Wheat Ridge, CO 80033-3299

Pethouse
386 Park Avenue South
Suite 1108
New York, NY 10016
212/679-1850

Popular Cats
1115 Broadway
New York, NY 10010
212/679-1850

Cat Stores

Following is a list, by state, of stores for cats. Cat stores are opening at such a rapid clip that there may very well be a new one where you live by the time this book comes out. But if there is, I'm sure you'll know about it! Note, please, the variety of store names and even some imaginative phone numbers. It's a good idea to call and check the days and hours the store is open.

ARIZONA

Cactus Cats
3519 West Thunderbird
Phoenix, AZ 85023
602/938-3269

Cactus Cats
7233 E. First Avenue
Scottsdale, AZ 85251
602/938-3269

Classic Cat
34505 N. Scottsdale Road
Suite 10
El Pedregal Shopping Center
Scottsdale, AZ 85262
602/488-0105

Kat Krazy
Smith's Shopping Center
6990 E. 22nd Street
Suite 100
Tucson, AZ 85712
602/754-5545

Maude's House of Cats
Box 365
154 Main Street
Jerome, AZ 86331
602/634-7903

Pur-suasion
7036 Fifth Avenue
Scottsdale, AZ 85251
602/281-7775

ARKANSAS

Kitty, Kitty, Kitty
2 Spring Street
Eureka Springs, AR 72632
501/253-5287

Kitty, Kitty, Kitty
5611 Kavanaugh
Little Rock, AR 72207
501/664-MEOW

CALIFORNIA

Cats by Stonomals
1557 Polk Street
San Francisco, CA 94109
415/563-PURR

Cat's Corner
101 Donner Pass Road
Truckee, CA 96160
916/587-5489

The Cat's Meow
9 City Boulevard W.
The City Mall
Orange, CA 92668
714/978-3836

The Cat's Meow
3965 Twiggs Street (Old Town)
San Diego, CA 92110
619/295-9898

The Cat's Meow
31762 Camino Capistrano
San Juan Capistrano, CA 92675
714/661-6115

The Cat's Meow
Ports O' Call
San Pedro, CA 90731
213/831-2927

The Cat's Meow
Westminster Mall
Westminster, CA 92683
714/373-1104

The Cat Store
111 Front Street
Old Sacramento, CA 95814
916/446-2334

The Catterfly
1566A Lincoln Way
Auburn, CA 95603
916/885-PURR

Cindy Kitty Castle
The Mall
San Carlos (between 5th and 6th)
P.O. Box 4568
Carmel, CA 93921
408/624-6469

Feline Connection
8300 Sierra College Boulevard
Roseville, CA 95661
916/791-CATS

Kitty City
Pier 39
San Francisco, CA 94133
415/986-7684

Magic Cat
2414 E. Third Street
Los Angeles, CA 90033

Owl & Pussycat
728 Village Court
Montgomery Village
Santa Rosa, CA 95405
707/523-4815

Purrsnickety
9 University Avenue
Los Gatos, CA 95030
408/395-CATS

The Sleeping Kitten
Butterfield Square
28690 Front Street, #410
Temecula, CA 92590
714/694-5506

FLORIDA

Cat-a-Copia
6557 Superior Avenue
Sarasota, FL 34231
813/923-KATS

The Cat House
411 Greene Street
Key West, FL 33040
305/294-4779

Cats Unlimited
3323 N.E. 33rd Street
Fort Lauderdale, FL 33308
305/565-1827

The Purrfect Cat
7400 Gulf Boulevard
St. Petersburg, FL 33706
813/367-6969

Pussyfoot
605 S. Olive Avenue
West Palm Beach, FL 33401
407/655-3109

ILLINOIS

Catique
6388 W. Gunnison
Chicago, IL 60630
312/632-9090

The Catnip Shoppe
319 Old McHenry Road
Long Grove, IL 60047
312/634-2370

Cats
1525 Chicago Avenue
Evanston, IL 60201
708/492-9442

Cats 'n' Dogs
210 W. Wesley Street
Wheaton, IL 60187
708/682-0636

Cats Only
9234 Broadway
Brookfield, IL 60513
708/485-4723

Feline Inn
1445 N. Wells
Chicago, IL 60610
312/943-2230

Jazze'e Junque
3831 N. Lincoln Avenue
Chicago, IL 60613
312/472-1500

INDIANA

The Mitchell House
P.O. Box 191
Rosedale, IN 47874
317/548-2163
(seasonal)

KANSAS

D.J.'s C.A.T. House
Highway 50
Offerle, KS 67563
316/659-2374

KENTUCKY

Cat's Corner
3340 Holwyn Road
Lexington, KY 40503
606/224-3776

LOUISIANA

Animal Art Antiques
1139 Arabella Street
New Orleans, LA 70114
504/895-9576

The Local Cathouse
Riverwalk, Space #99
1 Poydras Street
New Orleans, LA 70116
504/488-5377

New Orleans Cat House
840 Royal Street
New Orleans, LA 70116
504/524-5939

MARYLAND

Calico Cats
Woodlawn Village
2137 Gwynn Oak Avenue
Baltimore, MD 21207
301/944-2450

The Cat's Meow
23 Goldsborough Street
Easton, MD 21601
301/820-4220

For Cat's Sake
10513 Metropolitan Avenue
Kensington, MD 20895
301/933-KITY

MAINE

Haddeleigh House
RD 2
Box 482
North Berwick, ME 03906
207/676-3309

Suzy's Seasport Boutique
U.S. Route 1
Searsport, ME 04974
207/548-6522

MASSACHUSETTS

Friends of Heart
322 Commercial St.
Provincetown, MA 02657
508/487-1136

MICHIGAN

The Gifted Kitty
7 Squires Lane
Rockford, MI 49341
616/866-1126

Happicats
133 E. Grand River
Williamston, MI 48895
517/655-1251

MINNESOTA

Anything Cats
9428 36th Avenue N.
New Hope, MN 55427
612/546-7373

The Cat House
1621 Plymouth Road
Bonaventure Shopping Center
Minnetonka, MN 55343
612/544-4143

MISSOURI

The Cat's Meow
Crown Center
Kansas City, MO 64108
816/471-4713

Whiskers & Wags
12328 Olive Boulevard
St. Louis, MO 63141
314/453-9393

NEBRASKA

All About Cats
1627 S. 17th Street
Lincoln, NE 68502
402/477-7877

NEVADA

Catlynns Crafts
270 Flicker Circle
Carson City, NV 89704
702/849-2374

Cat's Meow
2234 Paradise Road
Las Vegas, NV 89104
702/734-7337

NEW HAMPSHIRE

The Cat House
2 Ceres Street
Portsmouth, NH 03801
603/436-4344

NEW JERSEY

Just Cats
U.S. Route 9
Smithville, NJ 08201
609/748-9449

Whiskers
103 Ocean Street
Cape May, NJ 08204
609/898-1232

The Pet Set
22 Gentry Drive
Englewood, NJ 07631
201/568-0673

NEW MEXICO

Log Cabin Cats
Route 15
Box 2570
110 El Otro Lado
Mimbres, NM 88049
505/536-3165

Mabel's
201 Canyon Road
Santa Fe, NM 87501
505/986-9105

NEW YORK

Cat in the Bag
148 E. Main Street
Port Jefferson, NY 11777
516/331-9287

Cat's in the Kitchen
367 West Avenue
Canandaigua, NY 14424
716/394-3994

The Cat Store
562 Amsterdam Avenue
New York, NY 10024
212/595-8728

Cattails
24 S. Village
Rockville Centre, NY 11570
516/766-4940

Just Cats
244 E. 60th Street
New York, NY 10022
212/888-CATS

Mabel's
849 Madison Avenue
New York, NY 10021
212/734-3263

Pat's Cats
2080 Western Avenue
Guilderland, NY 10284
518/456-5672

Reigning Cats and Dogs
43 Main Street
Cold Spring Harbor, NY 11724
516/367-3482

NORTH CAROLINA

Jeanine's Cat House
Sea Holly Square
Kill Devil Hills, NC 27948
919/430-3008

Sassy Cats
5 Henderson Road
Asheville, NC 28803
919/274-1701

OHIO

Coventry Cats
1812 Coventry Road
Cleveland Heights, OH 44118

OKLAHOMA

The Cat's Whiskers
1104 N.W. 30
Oklahoma City, OK 73118
405/524-5610

Kitty, Kitty, Kitty
8230 S. 71st
Tulsa, OK 74133
800/783-0528

OREGON

Raining Cats and Dogs
814 N.W. 23rd
Portland, OR 97201
503/295-4024

PENNSYLVANIA

The Black Cat
University City
3424 Sansom Street
Philadelphia, PA 19104
215/386-6664

Cat's Paw Gallery
31 Race Street
Jim Thorpe, PA 18229
717/325-4041

The Lamb on Wheels
806 W. Baltimore Pike
Kennett Square, PA 19348
215/444-3876

Meow Meow
8 S. Main Street
New Hope, PA 18938
215/862-0404

*The Pleasant Valley Animal
   Hospital and Lucky Chance*
Quakerstown, PA 18951
215/346-7300

The Yankee Cat
1106 Castle Shannon Boulevard
Pittsburgh, PA 15234
412/563-0777

SOUTH CAROLINA

Wild Cats
Rainbow Market
40 N. Market Street
Charleston, SC 29401
803/577-4420

TENNESSEE

Smoky Mountain Cat House
Old Mill Craft Village
110 Marshall Street
Pidgeon Forge, TN 37863
615/428-6133

TEXAS

The Alley Cat
555 Bitters Road
San Antonio, TX 78216
512/494-8443

A-Mews
12215 Coit Road, #222
Dallas, TX 75251
214/387-7941

Cat Connection, Inc.
14233 Inwood Road
Dallas, TX 75234
214/382-MEOW

Cats Cats Cats
Allendale Village
5720 Burnet Road
Austin, TX 78756
512/494-8443

Cats Cats Cats
Rivercenter Mall
849 E. Commerce Street, #200 E
San Antonio, TX 78205
512/227-0301

Cats First
1701 N. Market Street, #125
Dallas, TX 75202
214/748-2070

The Cat's Meow
705 S. Vine
Tyler, TX 75701-1434
903/595-1265

The Cat's Retreat
Park Plaza II
Highway 3
Webster, TX 75234

San Jacinto Cat House
2807 W. 6th Street
Amarillo, TX 79106
806/372-4427

VIRGINIA

The Cat's Closet
815 Caroline Street
Fredericksburg, VA 22401
703/371-0404

Classy Cat Gifts
102 Loudoun Street, S.W.
Leesburg, VA 22075
703/777-7373

Our Little Friends
118 King Street
Alexandria, VA 22314
703/684-1620

WASHINGTON

The Collectible Cat
20528 108th Avenue S.E.
Kent, WA 98031
206/854-PURR

WISCONSIN

The Mad Catter
1505 W. Mequon Road
East Towne Square
Mequon, WI 53092
414/241-4006

CANADA

The Cat House
110 Crowchild Trail N.W.
Calgary T29 4R9
Alberta
403/CAT-CATS

Heavenly Cats
College Park Mall
444 Yonge Street
Market Level 147
Toronto M5B 2H4
Ontario
416/591-6833

Whittington's Cat Store
79 Prince Edward Drive
Toronto M8Y 3V5
Ontario
416/236-3239

AUSTRALIA

Cat's Alley
121 / 18 Argyle Street
The Rocks
Sydney 20000
02/27-7709

ENGLAND

The Cat Gallery
34 High Street
Ealing, London W5 5DB
081/567-6580

The Cat Shop
12 King George V Place
Thames Avenue
Windsor, Berkshire

Felix Gallery
2 Sun Street
Lewes, Sussex BN7 2QB
0273/472-6680

FRANCE

Au Chat Dormant
31 rue de Bourgogne
75007 Paris
45/50-38-06

Le Chat en Majesté
1 rue des Prouvaires
75001 Paris
40/26-56-12

La Compagnie des Chats
4 rue Beaugrenelle
75015 Paris
45/77-60-30

Galerie Européenne du Chat
73 rue du Cherche-Midi
75006 Paris
45/48-61-53

GERMANY

*Engel, Geschenke für
    Katzenfreunde*
Papenhunderstre. 33
2000 Hamburg

ITALY

Evelyn Nicod Gallery
Vicolo Volta 14
37010 Torri Del Benaco (VR)

SWITZERLAND

*Chat Botte—This is a restaurant
    with a cat theme and many
    cat items for sale*
Hotel Beau Rivage
13 Quai du Mont Blanc
Geneva CH-1201
022/731-02-21

Katzen-Galerie
St. Alban-Vorstadt 88
4006 Basel

Travel Destinations/Services for Cat Lovers

UNITED STATES

Air Transport Association of America—This organization has a free pamphlet called "Air Travel for Your Dog or Cat." Send a SASE to:
Air Transport Association of America
1709 New York Avenue
Washington, DC 20006-5206

American Automobile Association—The triple A has a 20-page pamphlet on traveling with your pet by car. Request "Pets on the Go" by sending a SASE to:
American Automobile Association
Public Relations Department
1000 AAA Drive
Heathrow, FL 32746-5206

ASPCA—The noted humane society publishes the booklet "Traveling With Your Pet," which includes general travel information as well as state and international regulations. The booklet may be ordered for $5.00 from:
The ASPCA Education Department
441 East 92nd St.
New York, NY 10128

Take Your Pet USA. A Guide of Accommodations for Pets and Their Owners, by Arthur Frank—lists more than 4,000 hotels across the country that accept pets. The book may be ordered for $9.95 plus $1.50 shipping and handling from:
Artco
12 Channel St.
Boston, MA 02210

Jane Russell Webster Mansion Inn—full of cat memorabila, and cats
115 E. Main Street
Waterloo, NY 13165
315/539-3032

Anderson House—historical hotel with cats in residence, which may be "borrowed" for the night
333 West Main St.
Wabasha, MN 55981-1218
612/565-4524

Cypress Inn—owned by cat lover Doris Day
Lincoln St. and 7th Ave., PO Box Y 93921
Carmel, CA 93921
408/624-3871

Glendale Central Library—the world's largest collection of cat publications
222 East Harvard Street
Glendale, CA 91205
818/548-2021

Gotham Book Mart
41 West 47th St.
New York, NY 10036
212/719-4448

Cat House in Key West
411 Green Street,
Key West, FL 33040
305/294-4779

Hemingway Museum—the great writer was also a great cat lover
907 Whitehead Street
Key West, FL 33040
305/294-1575

Cathouse Restaurant
213 South Circle
Sebring, FL 33870
813/385-6653

ENGLAND, EUROPE, AUSTRALIA,
NEW ZEALAND

Cat House in Henfield—of historical interest
Sussex, England

The Felix Gallery—
2 Sun Street
Lewes, Sussex BN7 2QB
England

Katten Kabinet—cat museum
Amsterdam, Holland
31/20-626-53-78

Katzen Museum—with more than 10,000 items
Baselstrasse 101
4125 Rihen
Basel, Switzerland
41/61-672694

Cozy Cat Cottage—a bed-and-breakfast with many cats in residence
41 South Highway
Whitianga, New Zealand
0843/64-488

Musée du Chat—more than 2000 cat related objets d'art
Rue de l'Eglise
70880 Ainvelle, France
84/49-89-19

OTHER SERVICES

Bereavement Counseling—Bide-A-Wee Home Association
410 E. 38 St.
New York, NY 10016
212/532-6395 or
516/785-4199 (Wantaugh, NY)

Petography—unique sepia photos of your pet or you with your pet by professional photographers. Their work appears in leading magazines and books. The author photo of me and Miel, (flattering to both) was taken by award-winning photographer Paul Coughlin, for The Quintessential Cat.
212/245-0914

Bibliography

Amory, Cleveland. *The Cat Who Came for Christmas*. New York: Little, Brown and Company, 1987.

————. *The Cat and the Curmudgeon*. New York: Little, Brown and Company, 1990.

Becker, Suzy. *All I Need to Know I Learned From My Cat*. New York: Workman Publishing Company, 1990.

Briggs, Catharine M. *Cats in Folklore*. London, Eng.: Routledge & Kegan Paul Ltd., 1980.

Canemaker, John. *Felix: The Twisted Tale of the World's Most Famous Cat*. New York: Pantheon Books, 1991

Caras, Rober A. *A Cat Is Watching: A Look at the Way Cats See Us*. New York: Simon & Schuster, 1989.

Chandoha, Walter. *The Literary Cat*. Philadelphia: J. B. Lippincott, Company, 1977.

Crimmins, C. E. (ed.). *The Quotable Cat: A Collection of Quotes, Facts, and Lore for Feline Fanciers*. Philadelphia: Running Press Book Publishers, 1992.

Corey, Paul. *Do Cats Think?* Secaucus, NJ: Castle, 1977.

Daniels, Mary. *Morris: An Intimate Biography*. New York: Dell Publishing Company, 1974.

Darnton, Robert. *The Great Cat Massacre and Other Episodes in French Cultural History*. New York: Basic Books, Inc. Publishing, 1984.

Euclaire, Sally. *The Cat in Photography*. New York: Bullfinch Press, 1990.

Eliot, T. S. *Old Possum's Book of Practical Cats*. Orlando, FL: Harcourt Brace Jovanovich, 1992 (originally published in 1939).

Fireman, Judy (ed.). *Cat Catalog: The Ultimate Cat Book*. New York: Workman Publishing Company, Inc., 1976.

Fox, Dr. Michael W. *Understanding Your Cat*. New York: St. Martin's Press, 1974.

Gallico, Paul. *The Silent Meow: A Manual for Kittens, Strays, and Homeless Cats*. New York: Crown Publishers, Inc., 1964.

Gebhardt, Richard H. *The Complete Cat Book*. New York: Howell Book House, 1991.

Gettings, Fred. *The Secret Lore of the Cat*. New York: Carol Publishing Company, 1989.

Greene, David. *Your Incredible Cat*. New York: Ivy Books, 1984.

Holland, Barbara. *Secrets of the Cat: Its Lore, Legend, and Lives*. New York: Ballantine Books, 1989.

Lamb, G. F. *Animal Quotations . . . Straight from the Horse's Mouth*. Eng.: Longman Group Ltd., 1985.

Lawson, Tony, and Paté Lawson. *The Cat-Lovers Cookbook*. Pownal, VT: Storey Communications, 1986.

Leman, Jill and Martin. *Cat's Companion*. London, Eng.: Pelham Books, Ltd., 1986

Leman, Martin, *Martin Leman's Painted Cats*. London, Eng.: Pelham Books, Ltd., 1988.

Lorie, Peter. *Superstitions*. New York: Simon & Schuster, 1992.

Mallone, John. *The 125 Most Asked Questions About Cats (And the Answers)*. New York: William Morrow and Company, Inc. 1992.

McHattie, Grace. *The Cat Lover's Dictionary*. London, Eng.: H.R.& G. Witherby Ltd., 1989.

Mery, Fernand (translated by Emma Street). *The Life, History and Magic of the Cat*. New York: Grosset & Dunlop, 1968.

Morris, Desmond. *Catlore*. New York: Crown Publishers, 1987.

————. *Catwatching*. New York: Crown Publishers, 1986.

Muncaster, Alice L., and Ellen Yanow Sawyer. *The Cat Sold It*. New York: Crown Publishers, 1986.

Nickles, Liz, and Tamara Asseyer. *Always Kiss with Your Whiskers: Love Advice from My Cat*. New York: Pocket Books, 1991.

Oates, Joyce Carol, and Daniel Halpern. *The Sophisticated Cat*. New York: Dutton, 1992.

O'Neill, John P. *Metropolitan Cats*. New York: Harry N. Abrams, Inc., 1981.

Pippin, Wilbur, and Marian Winters. *Catwise*. New York: Random House, 1979.

Rutledge, Leigh W. *A Cats' Little Instruction Book*. New York: Dutton, 1993.

Shojai, Amy. *The Cat Companion: The History, Culture, and Everyday Life of the Cat*. New York: Mallard Press, 1992.

Siller, Frederick Cameron, and Ruth Mary Meyler. *Cats Ancient and Modern*. New York: The Viking Press, Inc. 1966.

Silvester, John, and Anne Mobbs. *A Catland Companion: Classic Cats by Louis Wain and Many Others*. New York: Simon & Schuster, 1991.

Stephens, John Richard. *The Enchanted Cat*. Rocklin, CA: Prima Publishing & Communications, 1990.

Sturgis, Matthew. *The English Cat at Home*. Topsfield, MA: Salem House Publishers, 1989.

Suarés, Jean-Claude, and Seymour Chwast. *The Illustrated Cat*. New York: Pushpin Press/Harmony Book, 1976.

————. *The Literary Cat*. New York: Pushpin Press/ Berkley Windhover, 1977.

Taylor, David. *The Little Calico & Tortoiseshell Cat Book*. New York: Simon & Schuster, 1990.

————. *The Little Tabby Cat Book*. New York: Simon & Schuster, 1990.

————. *The Little Marmalade Cat Book*. New York: Simon & Schuster, 1990.

————. *The Ultimate Cat Book*. New York: Simon & Schuster, 1989.

Whittier, Sara L. (ed.). *101 Favorite Cat Poems*. Chicago: Contemporary Books, Inc. 1991.

Wilson, Michael (ed.). *V & A Cats*. London: Victoria and Albert Museum, 1989.

Wright, Michael, and Sally Walders (eds.). *The Book of the Cat*. New York: Summit Books, 1980.

Index of Authors

Poems, excerpts, stories and information about these authors can be found on the following pages. See also the entry *Writers* on pages 255–256.